KIDS LOVE OHIO

A PARENT'S GUIDE TO EXPLORING FUN PLACES IN OHIO WITH CHILDREN. . .YEAR ROUND!

Kids Love Publications
1985 Dina Court
Powell, OH 43065

Dedicated to the Families of Ohio

For the latest major updates corresponding to the pages in this book visit our website:

www.kidslovepublications.com

Although the authors have exhaustively researched all sources to ensure accuracy and completeness of the information contained in this book, we assume no responsibility for errors, inaccuracies, omissions or any other inconsistency herein. Any slights against any entries or organizations are unintentional.

- ***REMEMBER:*** *Museum exhibits change frequently. Check the site's website before you visit to note any changes. Also, HOURS and ADMISSIONS are subject to change at the owner's discretion. If you are tight on time or money, check the attraction's website or call before you visit.*
- ***INTERNET PRECAUTION:*** *All websites mentioned in KIDS LOVE OHIO have been checked for appropriate content. However, due to the fast-changing nature of the Internet, we strongly urge parents to preview any recommended sites and to always supervise their children when on-line.*

ISBN# 09663457-9-7

KIDS ♥ OHIO ™ Kids Love Publications

TABLE OF CONTENTS

State Map

With Major Routes & Cities Marked

Chapter Area Map

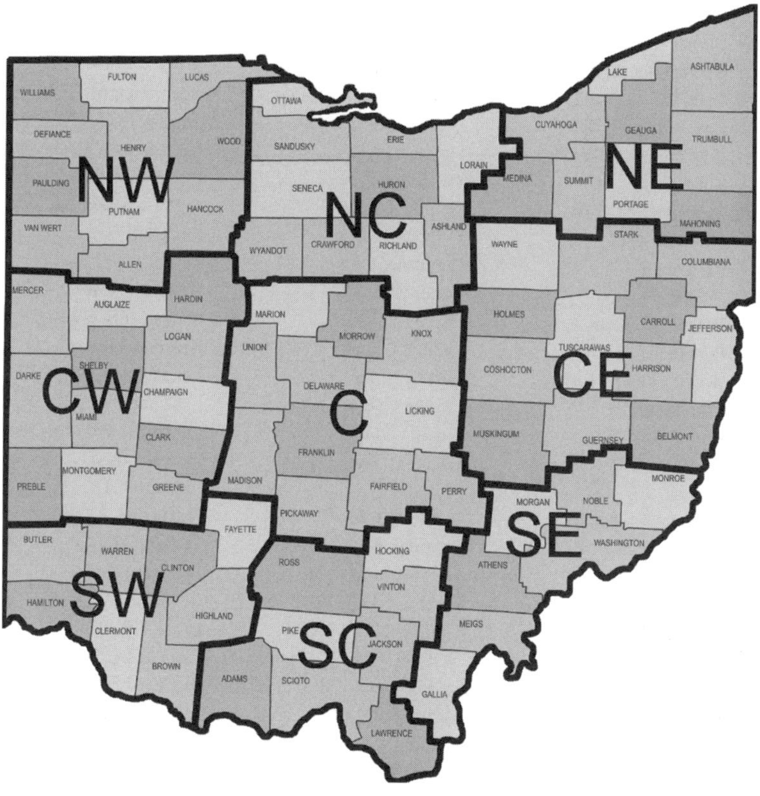

CITY INDEX (Listed by City & Area)

CITY INDEX (Listed by City & Area)

*Acknowledgements*

We are most thankful to be blessed with our parents, Barbara (Darrall) Callahan & George and Catherine Zavatsky who help us every way they can – researching, proofing and babysitting. More importantly, they are great sounding boards and offer unconditional support. Also, thanks to our departed Dad, Edwin Darrall, who started this flame of historical tourism in his kids. So many places around Ohio remind us of family vacations years ago…

Our own kids, Jenny and Daniel, were delightful and fun children during our trips (even numerous historical sites) across the state. What a joy it is to be their parents…we couldn't do it without them as our "kid-testers"!

We both sincerely thank each other – our partnership has created an even greater business/personal "marriage" with lots of exciting moments, laughs, and new adventures in life woven throughout. Above all, we praise the Lord for His so many blessings through the last few years. God does answer prayer…all prayer, *eventually*!

We couldn't wait to write this Bicentennial Edition celebrating the creative, gutsy ways folks made history here. Even more so, to see the efforts of so many today who work hard to preserve Ohio's history and make it real to kids. As Tecumseh *(the actor, in costume)* said to our daughter after the drama *(as she approached him sobbing)*, "I can tell from your emotion that you understand…".

Our sincere wish is that this book will help everyone "fall in love" with Ohio and its interesting past.

In a Hundred Years…

It will not matter, The size of my bank account…
The kind of house that I lived in, the kind of car that I drove…
But what will matter is…
That the world may be different
Because I was important in the life of a child.

\- *author unknown*

HOW TO USE THIS BOOK

If you are excited about discovering BICENTENNIAL Ohio, this is the book for you and your family! Look for Ohio History Listings in this special historical type. We've spent over a thousand hours doing all the scouting, collecting and compiling (*and most often visiting!*) so that you could spend less time searching and more time having fun.

Here are a few hints to make your adventures run smoothly:

- ❑ Consider the **child's age** before deciding to take a visit.
- ❑ Know **directions** and parking. Call ahead (or visit the company's website) if you have questions *and* bring this book. Also, don't forget your camera! *(please honor rules regarding use).*
- ❑ **Estimate the duration** of the trip. Bring small surprises (favorite juice boxes) travel books, and toys.
- ❑ Call ahead for **reservations** or details, if necessary.
- ❑ Most listings are **closed major holidays** unless noted.
- ❑ Make a **family "treasure chest"**. Decorate a big box or use an old popcorn tin. Store memorabilia from a fun outing, journals, pictures, brochures and souvenirs. Once a year, look through the "treasure chest" and reminisce. "Kids Love Travel Memories!" is an excellent travel journal & scrapbook that your family can create. *(See the order form in back of this book).*
- ❑ Plan **picnics** along the way. Many Historical Society sites and state parks are scattered throughout Ohio. Allow time for a rural/scenic route to take advantage of these free picnic facilities.
- ❑ Some activities, especially tours, require **groups** of 10 or more. To participate, you may either ask to be part of another tour group or get a group together yourself (neighbors, friends, organizations). If you arrange a group outing, most places offer discounts.
- ❑ For the latest **updates** corresponding to the pages in this book, visit our website: **www.kidslovepublications.com.**
- ❑ Each chapter represents an area of the state. Each listing is further identified by city, zip code, and place/event name. Our popular **Activity Index** in the back of the book **lists places by Activity Heading** (i.e. State History, Tours, Outdoors, Museums, etc.).

MISSION STATEMENT

At first glance, you may think that this is a book that just lists hundreds of places to travel. While it is true that we've invested thousands of hours of exhaustive research (*and drove nearly 3000 miles in Ohio*) to prepare this travel resource…just listing places to travel is not the mission statement of these projects.

As children, Michele and I were able to travel extensively throughout the United States. We consider these family times some of the greatest memories we cherish today. We, quite frankly, felt that most children had this opportunity to travel with their family as we did. However, as we became adults and started our own family, we found that this wasn't necessarily the case. We continually heard friends express several concerns when deciding how to spend "quality" and "quantity" family time. 1) What to do? 2) Where to do it? 3) How much will it cost? 4) How do I know that my kids will enjoy it?

Interestingly enough, as we compare our experiences with our families when we were kids, many of our fondest memories were not made at an expensive attraction, but rather when it was least expected.

It is our belief and mission statement that if you as a family will study and use the contained information to create family memories, these memories will grow a stronger, tighter family. Our ultimate mission statement is, that your children will develop a love and a passion for quality family experiences that they can pass to another generation of family travelers.

We thank you for purchasing this book, and we hope to see you on the road (*and hearing your travel stories!*) God bless your journeys and happy exploring!

George, Michele, Jenny and Daniel

GENERAL INFORMATION

In addition to the historical listings contained in this special Bicentennial Edition of "Kids Love Ohio", you will find other memorial marker sites of historical signifance by visiting, **www.ohiohistory.org**.

Call *(or visit the websites)* for the services of interest. Request to be added to their mailing lists.

- ❑ **www.ArtsinOhio.com**
- ❑ Ohio Division of Travel & Tourism (800) BUCKEYE or **www.ohiotourism.com**
- ❑ **C** - Columbus Metro Parks (614) 508-8000
- ❑ **C** - Columbus Recreation & Parks (614) 645-3300
- ❑ **C** - Greater Columbus CVB (800) 345-4FUN or **www.visitcolumbus.org**
- ❑ **C** - Licking County Parks (740) 587-2535 or **www.msmisp.com/lpd**
- ❑ **CE** - Canton Park District (330) 489-3015
- ❑ **CE** - Carroll County CVB (877) 727-0103 or **www.carrollcountyohio.com**
- ❑ **CE** - Tuscarawas County CVB (800) 527-3387 or **www.neohiotravel.com**
- ❑ **CW** - Dayton Metroparks (937) 275-PARK
- ❑ **CW** - Greene County CVB (800) 733-9109 or **www.greenecountyohio.org**
- ❑ **CW** - Greene County Parks (937) 562-7440 or **www.co.greene.oh.us/parks.htm**
- ❑ **NC** - Lorain County Metroparks (440) 45805121 or **www.loraincountymetroparks.com**
- ❑ **NC** – Mansfield/Richland County CVB – (800) 642-8282 or **www.mansfieldtourism.org**

General Information (cont.)

- ❑ **NC** - Ottawa County Visitors Bureau (800) 441-1271 or **www.lake-erie.com**
- ❑ **NC** - Port Clinton Park & Rec (419) 732-2206
- ❑ **NC** - Sandusky County Parks (419) 334-4495
- ❑ **NC** - Sandusky/Erie County VCB (800) 255-ERIE or **www.buckeyenorth.com**
- ❑ **NE** - Akron Rec Bureau (330) 375-2804 or **www.ci.akron.oh.us/rec.html**
- ❑ **NE** - Ashtabula County Metroparks (800) 3 DROP IN
- ❑ **NE** - Convention & Visitors Bureau of Greater Cleveland (800) 321-1001 or **www.travelcleveland.com**
- ❑ **NE** - Cleveland Metroparks (216) 351-6300
- ❑ **NE** - Lake Metroparks (800) 669-9226
- ❑ **NE** - Medina County Parks (330) 722-9364
- ❑ **NE** - Summit County Metroparks (330) 867-5511
- ❑ **NW** - Lima City Parks & Rec (419) 221-5195
- ❑ **NW** - Lima/Johnny Appleseed Metroparks (419) 221-1232
- ❑ **NW** - Toledo Area Metroparks (419) 535-3050
- ❑ **SC** - Ross County-Chillicothe CVB (800) 413-4118
- ❑ **SW** - Butler County Metroparks (513) 867-5835
- ❑ **SW** - Cincinnati Parks Department (513) 352-4080
- ❑ **SW** - Cincinnati Recreation Department (513) 352-4001
- ❑ **SW** - Cincinnati CVB (800) CINCYUSA or **www.cincyusa.com**
- ❑ **SW** - Hamilton County Park District (513) 521-PARK

SKIING / TOBOGGANING

Usually December – early March. Ski Conditions, (800) BUCKEYE. Or contact local MetroParks or Ohio Department of Natural Resources for cross-country skiing.

- **C** - CLEARFORK – (800) 237-5673, Butler. **www.skiclearfork.com**.
- **CE** - BEAR CREEK RESORT RANCH KOA, 3232 Downing St. S.W., East Sparta. (330) 484-3901. Ohio's longest, fastest, and safest way to toboggan. Newly rebuilt twin half-mile-long refrigerated toboggan chutes operate 40 degrees or colder, snow or no snow. A bus takes riders and toboggans back to the top so there's no walking and hauling the toboggan back up the hill.
- **CW** - MAD RIVER MOUNTAIN – (937) 599-1015 or (800) 231-7669, Bellefontaine. **www.skimadriver.com**
- **NC** - SNOW TRAILS – (800) DEC-SNOW or (800) OHIO-SKI, Mansfield. **www.snowtrails.com**.
- **NE** - ALPINE VALLEY - (440) 729-9775, Chesterland. **www.alpinevalleyohio.com**.
- **NE** - BOSTON MILLS / BRANDYWINE – (800) USKI241, Peninsula or Northfield. **www.bmbw.com**. (snowboarding capital of Ohio)
- **NE** – Cleveland Metroparks Chalet in Mill Stream Run Reservation, Strongsville. (440) 572-9990. Toboggan chutes 1000 feet long and 42 feet tall.
- **SC** - SPICY RUN - (740) 493-2599, Latham. **www.skispicy.com**

COLLEGE ATHLETICS

- **C** - OHIO STATE UNIVERSITY BUCKEYES - (614) 292-2524 or **www.ohiostatebuckeyes.com**. Big 10 College sports: Football, Basketball (Men's & Women's), Hockey, OSU Ice Skating, Golf, Swimming, Tennis & Volleyball.

- **SW** - UNIVERSITY OF CINCINNATI - (513) 556-CATS or **www.ucbearcats.com**. 18 sports. Fall, Winter, Spring.
- **SW** - XAVIER UNIVERSITY, Cintas Center - (513) 745-3900 or **www.xu.edu**. Volleyball, basketball.

OUTDOORS

- Ohio Department of Natural Resources, (877) 4BOATER OR (800) WILDLIFE or **www.dnr.state.oh.us/odnr**
- Ohio Campground Owner's Association (614) 764-0279
- Ohio State Parks (614) 466-0652 or **www.dnr.state.oh.us/parks**
- Ohio Camping (800) 376-4847
- National Camping Info, **www.gocampingamerica.com**
- Muskingum Watershed Conservancy District (877) 363-8500 or **www.mwcdlakes.com**. Well-maintained boating, swimming and fishing lakes in CE Ohio.
- State Park Lodges & Resorts (800) 282-7275
- Rent-A-Camp State Park Programs

The State Parks offer camping, horseback riding, boating, fishing, golfing, hiking, winter sports, and vacation planning assistance. The camping facilities can be lodges, cabins, or tents. The ODNR offers Rent-A-Camp. It is a unique program for beginning or infrequent campers to enjoy the experience of camping without purchasing the equipment. The cost begins at $20 per night. You will arrive at your campsite to find a 10 x 12-foot sleeping tent already set up complete with a dining canopy. Inside are two cots, sleeping pads, cooler, propane stove, lantern, broom, dustpan and welcome mat. Outside, you will find a fire ring and picnic table. This way of camping allows you to pick up and go without packing up a lot of gear. The campsites are limited, so make your plans early and call to make your reservation.

Check out these businesses / services in your area for tour ideas:

AIRPORTS

All children love to visit the airport! Why not take a tour and understand all the jobs it takes to run an airport? Tour the terminal, baggage claim, gates and security / currency exchange. Maybe you'll even get to board a plane.

ANIMAL SHELTERS

Great for the would-be pet owner. Not only will you see many cats and dogs available for adoption, but a guide will show you the clinic and explain the needs of a pet. Be prepared to have the children "fall in love" with one of the animals while they are there!

BANKS

Take a "behind the scenes" look at automated teller machines, bank vaults and drive-thru window chutes. You may want to take this tour and then open a savings account for your child.

CITY HALLS

Halls of Fame, City Council Chambers & Meeting Room, Mayor's Office and famous statues.

ELECTRIC COMPANY / POWER PLANTS

Modern science has created many ways to generate electricity today, but what really goes on with the "flip of a switch". Because coal can be dirty, wear old, comfortable clothes. Coal furnaces heat water, which produces steam, that propels turbines, that drives generators, that make electricity.

FIRE STATIONS

Many Open Houses in October, Fire Prevention Month. Take a look into the life of the firefighters servicing your area and try on their gear. See where they hang out, sleep and eat. Hop aboard a real-life fire engine truck and learn fire safety too.

HOSPITALS

Some Children's Hospitals offer pre-surgery and general tours.

NEWSPAPERS

You'll be amazed at all the new technology. See monster printers and robotics. See samples in the layout department and maybe try to put together your own page. After seeing a newspaper made, most companies give you a free copy (dated that day) as your souvenir. National Newspaper Week is in October.

RESTAURANTS

PIZZA HUT & PAPA JOHN'S

- ❑ Participating locations

Telephone the store manager. Best days are Monday, Tuesday and Wednesday mid-afternoon. Minimum of 10 people. Small charge per person. All children love pizza – especially when they can create their own! As the children tour the kitchen, they learn how to make a pizza, bake it, and then eat it. The admission charge generally includes lots of creatively made pizzas, beverage and coloring book.

KRISPY KREME DONUTS

- ❑ Participating locations

Get an "inside look" and learn the techniques that make these donuts some of our favorites! Watch the dough being made in "giant" mixers, being formed into donuts and taking a "trip" through the fryer. Seeing them being iced and topped with colorful sprinkles is always a favorite of the kids. Contact your local store manager. They prefer Monday or Tuesday. Free.

SUPERMARKETS

Kids are fascinated to go behind the scenes of the same store where Mom and Dad shop. Usually you will see them grind meat, walk into large freezer rooms, watch cakes and bread bake and receive free samples along the way. Maybe you'll even get to pet a live lobster!

TV / RADIO STATIONS

Studios, newsrooms, Fox kids clubs. Why do weathermen never wear blue clothes on TV? What makes a "DJ's" voice sound so deep and smooth?

WATER TREATMENT PLANTS

A giant science experiment! You can watch seven stages of water treatment. The favorite is usually the wall of bright buttons flashing as workers monitor the different processes.

U.S. MAIN POST OFFICES

Did you know Ben Franklin was the first Postmaster General (over 200 years ago)? Most interesting is the high-speed automated mail processing equipment. Learn how to address envelopes so they will be sent quicker (there are secrets). To make your tour more interesting, have your children write a letter to themselves and address it with colorful markers. Mail it earlier that day and they will stay interested trying to locate their letter in all the high-speed machinery.

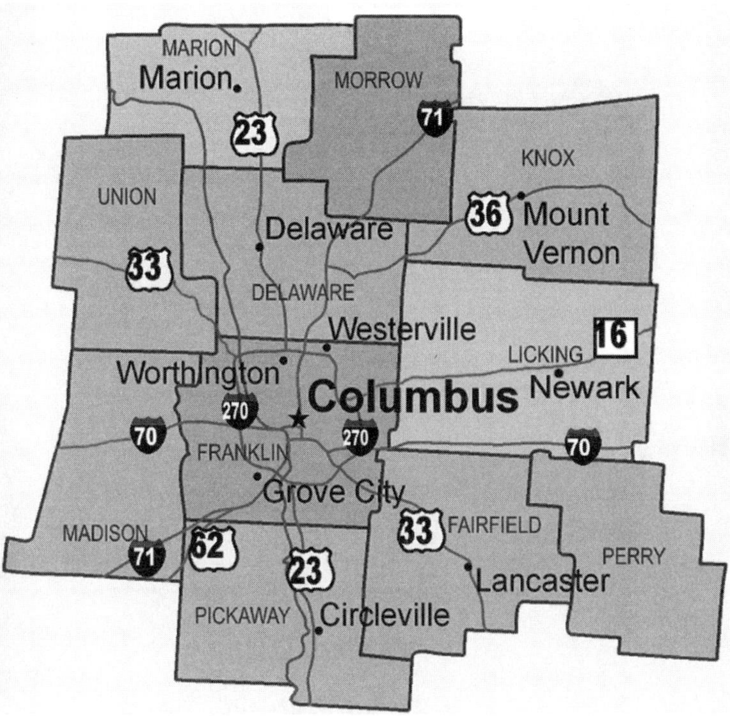

Chapter 1
Central Area

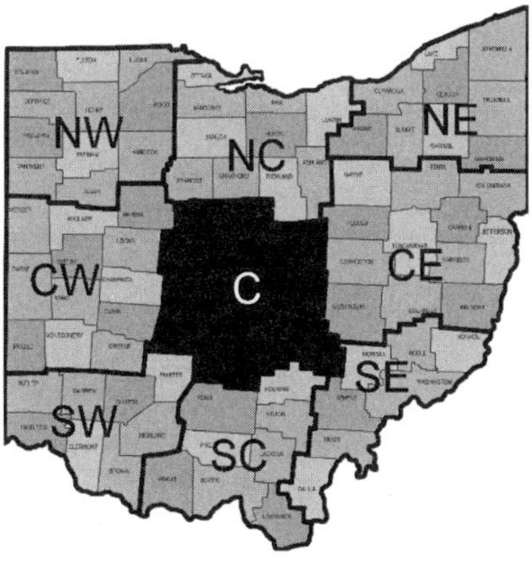

Our Favorites...

American Whistle

COSI

Great Circle Earthworks

Ohio Village & Historical Center

Popcorn Outlet

Santa Maria

The Ohio State University Campus

Velvet Ice Cream & Olde Mill

HOMESTEAD PARK

Amlin - *4675 Cosgray Road (I-270 to SR 33 to Plain City exit, head south towards Hilliard), 43002. Hours: Dawn to Dusk. Admission: FREE.* Homestead Park is a fabulous adventure for everyone. The country setting, pond, trails, shelter houses, picnic area and grill provide a great place for an all day picnic. The special feature for the children is the elaborate playground with everything from a sandpit to concrete tunnels, swings and bridges, towers and cranes. Separate from this play area is "Fort Washington", a fully equipped fort featuring seasonal wet activities. The attached squirt guns have a continuous supply of water!

OHIO'S SMALL TOWN MUSEUM

Ashville - *34 Long Street, 43103. Phone: (740) 983-9864. Hours: Daily 1:00-3:00pm. Closed holidays.* The village of Ashville is home to a national, award winning collection of incredible local history. The displays tell about the silver nuggets unearthed at the Snake Den Mounds and gives information about famous writers, inventors, politicians, entertainers, and the not-so-famous who once lived in this railroad boom town.

SLATE RUN HISTORICAL FARM

1375 SR 674 North (in Slate Run Park on SR 674)

Ashville 43103

- Phone: (614) 508-8000 or (614) 833-1880
- Hours: Tuesday, Wednesday, Thursday 9:00am– 4:00pm, Friday and Saturday 9:00am – 6:00pm, Sunday 11:00am – 6:00 pm (June – August) Wednesday – Saturday 9:00 am – 4:00 pm, Sunday 11:00 am – 4:00 pm (September – May) Memorial and Labor Day, Noon – 6:00 pm
- Admission: FREE to browse around. Small admission for special programs.
- Tours: Available by appointment (special prices). Metro Park open 6:30am-dusk.

This historic farm depicts life on a working family farm of the 1880's. Visitors may join in with the barnyard and household chores. All the work is done using equipment and methods of the time (some horse-powered machinery). Some of the specially scheduled programs may be: maple syrup demonstrations and production, toy making, fishing, ice cream socials, making root beer, rope making and pretend old-fashioned school. Kids love getting involved and doing chores at Slate Run. They offer nature trails, picnic grounds, and children's play facilities at the adjoining Slate Run Metro Park.

MID-OHIO HISTORICAL DOLL AND TOY MUSEUM

Canal Winchester - *700 Winchester Pike (off US 33 at Gender Road, east side of Columbus), 43110. Phone: (614) 837-5573. Hours: Wednesday - Saturday 11:00am - 5:00pm, (Spring - Mid December). Miscellaneous: Gift Shop, Old and New Collectibles.* As you step in the door, you will see a train display in the lobby. To your left, you will go through a door into the magical world of dolls. The collection includes rare antique dolls and toys dating from the 1700's to contemporary. Barbie fans of all ages will love the extensive Barbie collection. Admission $3.00 (6 and over).

A.W. MARION STATE PARK

Circleville - *(5 miles East of Circleville off SR 23 to SR 22), 43113.* ***Web: www.dnr.state.oh.us/parks/parks/awmarion.htm****. Phone: (740) 869-3124.* 454 acres of camping, hiking trails, boating and rentals, fishing, and winter sports. The nearby floodplains of the Scioto River are adorned with a variety of wildflowers. Wildlife indigenous to the area includes fox squirrel, ring-necked pheasant, a variety of songbirds, red fox and white-tailed deer.

PICKAWAY COUNTY HISTORICAL SOCIETY CLARKE MAY MUSEUM

Circleville - *162 West Union Street, 43113. Phone: (740) 474-1495. Hours: Tuesday – Friday 1:00 – 4:00pm (April – October). Wednesday-Thursday only (November-March).* Ohio bird's eggs and nests, Indian artifacts, and early dental office.

OHIO STATE UNIVERSITY GROUP TOURS

Woody Hayes Dr. & High Street (most facilities between High St. & Olentangy River - off SR 315), **Columbus** 43201

- Phone: (614) 292-3030
  http://campusvisit.osu.edu/grouptour/grouptourinfo.html
- Miscellaneous: The Buckeye Hall of Fame Café (casual restaurant & gameroom) is down the road 1412 Olentangy River Rd. Call (614) 291-2233.

Start with the OSU Scavenger Hunt – younger elementary and junior high students in a group of any size are provided with an OSU fact sheet, clues for the scavenger hunt, and a map of campus. Get your Scavenger Hunt packet at the Student Visitor Center. Now, learn more about the history and traditions of Ohio State in this self-guided, adult supervised tour.

Many other "add-on" Tour Options are available:

- Athletic Facility Tours – Value City Arena, Monday-Friday on non-event days between. 9:00am-3:30pm. 60 minutes. (614) 292-3231. Ohio Stadium, Monday-Friday between 8:00am-5:00pm. (614) 292-9748.
- Jack Nicklaus Museum - 2355 Olentangy River Road. Monday-Saturday 9:00am-5:00pm, Sunday 1:00-5:00pm. Admission: $6-$9.00. Shows the long history of the game, Mr. Nicklaus' place in that history, famous OSU golfers and a prototype of the Nicklaus family's den with personal stories narrated by his wife.
- Wexner Center for the Arts – Family days and guided tours. **www.wexarts.org/ctr/gen/overview.shtml** or (614) 292-3535.
- Astronomy – (614) 292-1773 or **www.astronomy.mps.ohio-state.edu/events/star.html**. Perkins Observatory Lectures or monthly Star Talks.
- Biological Sciences Greenhouse Facility – Insectary, a quarantine facility, two research labs, a growth chamber area and prep room. Monday-Friday 8:30am-4:30pm, except holidays.
  www.biosci.ohio-state.edu/~plantbio/greenhouse/index.html
- Engineering Hands-on programs – (614) 292-2651
- Chadwick Arboretum – **http://chadwickarboretum.osu.edu/** or (614) 688-3479

- ❑ Food Science Bldg. – tours of miniature pilot plant, OSU Dairy Store (ice cream treats, breakfast, lunch items), Parker Building, 2015 Fyffe Road (off Woody Hayes Dr) (614) 292-6281.
- ❑ Horse Center – (614) 459-4208
- ❑ Orton Geological Museum – skeleton of a giant sloth, fossils, fluorescent minerals, and rocks. 9:00am-5:00pm. On the oval, open free to the public.
- ❑ Historic Costume & Textiles Collection – Historic textiles from the 15th century to 20th century in costume pieces including men's, women's, and children's garments and accessories. **www.hec.ohio-state.edu/cts/collect/bucket/geninfo.htm** or (614) 292-3090.

OHIO STATEHOUSE

Columbus - *Broad and High Streets (10 acre square in downtown) 43201. **Web: www.statehouse.state.oh.us/welcome.** Phone: (614) 728-2695 or (888) OHIO-123, Admission: FREE. Tours: Walk-in tours begin at 10:00am, 11:30am, 1:00pm and 3:00pm on weekdays. Weekends: 11:15am, 12:30pm, 2:00pm and 3:00pm. Miscellaneous: Museum shop.* Learn about Ohio's Statehouse history, its architecture and the legislative process. Visit the place where Abraham Lincoln made speeches in 1859 and 1861. Inside you'll see the rotunda with the state seal and historic paintings and documents. If the Ohio House or Senate is in session, you'll be able to listen to the debates. Outside is home to several war memorials and statues including the new Veterans Plaza where visitors read the letters sent home from enlisted men and women. Educational displays and touch-screen kiosks (ex. Pass through all 88 counties in the Map Room) along with a great Museum shop are found in the basement. The basement is all white painted brick and stone. Why are the formal walls painted light shades of pink or peach? The Atrium used to be called Pigeon Alley - why?

CENTRAL OHIO FIRE MUSEUM

Columbus – *240 N. 4th Street, 43215. Phone: (614) 464-4099.* **www.fire.ci.columbus.oh.us/** *Hours: Tuesday - Saturday, 10:00am-4:00pm Admission: $4.00 adult, $2.00 student, Under 6 FREE. Group tours by appointment only.* Hand-drawn, horse-drawn, & motorized fire apparatus. Day-to-day lives in an engine house. Hands-on lifesaving exhibits.

FRANKLIN PARK CONSERVATORY AND BOTANICAL GARDENS

Columbus - *1777 East Broad Street (off I-71), 43203.* ***Web: www.fpconservatory.org****. Phone: (614) 645-TREE or (800) 214-PARK, Hours: Tuesday – Sunday & Holiday Mondays, 10:00am-5:00pm. 1st Wednesday 10:00am-8:00 pm. Admission: $6.50 adult, $5.00 senior/student, $3.50 child (2-12).* A place where you can learn where coffee comes from or watch the careful pruning of Bonsai trees. The kid-friendly ants, iguanas, and lories are becoming permanent enhancements to the conservatory. The large 1895 glass structure resembles the style of London's Crystal Palace. Walk through a simulated tropical rain forest, a desert, a tree fern forest, a Pacific Island water garden and then on to the Himalayan Mountains. Outside is a sculpture garden.

COLUMBUS MOTOR SPEEDWAY

Columbus - *1845 Williams Road, 43207. Phone: (614) 491-1047,* ***Web: www.columbusspeedway.com****.* Stock car racing. Kids Day (late August or September). Climb into a real race car! 7:00 pm race starts Saturdays.

COLUMBUS CREW

Columbus - *Crew Stadium (near Ohio State Fairgrounds), 43211. Phone: (614) 221-CREW,* ***Web: www.thecrew.com****.* Major League Soccer (Mid April – Late September).

OHIO HISTORICAL CENTER

1982 Velma Avenue (I-71 to 17th Avenue Exit), **Columbus** 43211

- Phone: (614) 297-2300 or (800) 646-5184
  Web: www.ohiohistory.org/places/ohc
- Hours: Tuesday - Saturday 9:00am - 5:00pm, Sunday and Holidays Noon - 5:00pm. Closed Christmastime, Thanksgiving & New Years.
- Admission: $6.00 adult, $2.00 student. Parking fee $3.00 per vehicle. Includes Ohio Village entrance.
- Miscellaneous: Gift Shop, food and picnic tables. Summer Kids Kamps and Discovery Days bring out the hands-on fun. Pick up Educational Resource scavenger hunt game flyers near many area entrances.

This is a museum and a whole lot more. There are exhibits and artifacts covering the history of Ohio from archaeology to natural history and the history of Ohio. There are many historical collections from early fossils and Indian tribes (large dioramas and artifact study of prehistoric Indians), original accounts from early explorers, and papers from political leaders such as General Meigs and Thomas Worthington. The building is recognized as an architectural landmark. The Center's permanent natural history exhibit features Ohio's plants, animals, geology, geography, and climate and weather. "The Nature of Ohio" exhibit is guarded by a huge mastodon found in a swamp in Clark County. See the quirky 2-headed calf and Egyptian mummy, too. Continuous 1920s (or semi-permanent exhibits like "Kilroy was here - 1940's) newsreels, an operating 1880s carriage shop, and vintage automobiles, Adena Pipe and Hopewell mica cutouts. Discovery Park and Theater provide modern audiovisual technology, and hands-on or computer game stations in each area help make learning interesting.

OHIO VILLAGE

1982 Velma Avenue (I-71 and 17th Avenue Exit)

Columbus 43211

- ❑ Phone: (614) 297-2300
  Web: www.ohiohistory.org/places/ohvillag
- ❑ Hours: Saturday 9:00am-5:00pm, Sunday & Holidays (except Mondays) Noon-5:00pm (Memorial Day-October). Open Wednesday-Friday for scheduled group tours.
- ❑ Admission: $6.00 adult, $2.00 student. Includes Historical Center. Parking fee $3.00 per vehicle. Buggy rides with character descriptions for additional small fee per person.
- ❑ Miscellaneous: Baseball fans can catch the Ohio Village Muffins or the Lady Diamonds in a real game played according to 19th Century rules (614) 297-2606. Pick up the Village Kids Map & Games.

See an 1800's village that is a must for all ages. Sixteen buildings, connected by a wooden boardwalk, house twenty-two businesses, residences, and public buildings. "Residents" of the Ohio Village engage visitors with the routines of daily life as well as with the issues and events that concerned members of a Civil War era community. Ask some folks why they are here? Your children will see how doctors, printers and many others practiced their trades in the America of the 1860's. Other village buildings include the Town Hall, Church (ring the church bell), Pharmacy, Female Seminary (the headmistress is particularly interested in young ladies who can draw – try to qualify on the spot!), Dressmaker's Shop and Millinery, German Immigrant's Residence, Bank (sign a promissory note), Livery, Undertaker's and Furniture Store, Ladies' Aid Society, Attorney's Office, Rooming House, Freight Office (send a package with instructions)and Stagecoach Stop, American House Hotel, and Schoolhouse (adorable interaction and photo ops here!). Livestock in the village includes horses, goats, ducks, peacocks, and guinea hens. The Ohio Historical Center is next door, so plan your day for both of these.

BALLETMET

Columbus - *322 Mt. Vernon Avenue, 43215. Phone: (614) 229-4860,* ***Web: www.balletmet.org****.* Classic to contemporary ballet including the famous Nutcracker. Step-by-Step program - spend time with dancers or Morning at the Ballet (mini programs like Cinderella) seem to engage the younger kids the most.

COLUMBUS ASSOCIATION FOR THE PERFORMING ARTS

Columbus - *55 East State Street, 43215. Phone: (614) 469-1045,* ***Web: www.capa.com****.* CAPA operates theatres and presents touring arts and entertainment including children's concerts.

COLUMBUS BLUE JACKETS HOCKEY

Columbus - *(Nationwide Arena), 43215. Phone: (614) 246-PUCK or (800) NHL-COLS,* ***Web: www.bluejackets.com****.* NHL Hockey in Ohio. Look for their mascot, Stinger here and at special events. Season runs October-early April.

COLUMBUS CHILDREN'S THEATRE

Columbus - *512 North Park Street, 43215. Phone: (614) 224-6672,* ***Web: http://colschildrenstheatre.org****.* Theatre activities for youth of all ages, backgrounds and cultures. Many lessons to be learned watching plays like Oliver, Emperors New Clothes or the seasonal the Best Christmas Pageant Ever. (July-May)

COLUMBUS MUSEUM OF ART

Columbus - *480 East Broad Street (four blocks east of the Capitol), 43215.* ***Web: www.columbusmuseum.org****. Phone: (614) 221-4848 info line. Hours: Tuesday-Sunday 10:00am-5:30pm. Thursday until 8:30pm. Admission: $6.00 adult, $4.00 senior and student (age 6+). FREE on Thursday. Parking $3.00.* American and European art from 1850-1950. See the life-size horse of welded steel or the works of Columbus realist George Bellows and folk artist Elijah Pierce. Family Fun Workshops, Its My Museum Gallery/Sculpture Guide, Art Speaks audio tour $3.00- where art talks, EYE SPY adventure in art-interactive- docent-led creative, colorful weekday mornings in groups area. Café and gift shop.

COLUMBUS SYMPHONY ORCHESTRA

Columbus - *55 East State Street (most performances at Ohio Theatre). 43215.* ***Web: www.columbussymphony.org****. Phone: (614) 228-8600.* Lollipop Concerts, Sunday Funday concerts and Youth Orchestra performances usually have pre-concert activities for families. Average $10.00 tickets.

COSI

333 West Broad Street (I-71 exit Broad or Front St. or I-70 exit Broad or Fourth St. to downtown riverfront), **Columbus** 43215

- Phone: (614) 228-COSI or (888) 819-COSI
  Web: www.cosi.org
- Hours: Monday-Saturday 10:00am-5:00pm. Sunday Noon-6:00pm. Closed most major holidays.
- Admission: $12.00 adult, $10.00 senior, (60+), $7.00 child (2-12)
- Miscellaneous: Science 2 Go Store, AtomiCafé. Extreme Screen, Planetarium and Motion Simulators $3-$6.00 additional fee (reserve spot at admissions desk).

The newer structure is divided into learning worlds. Explore hands-on exhibits focusing on science, technology, health and history. Take your preschool-aged children to Kid-Space. They pretend they are a doctor or nurse, paint their faces, do a puppet show, water play, ride in a boat, and just have a good active time there. Other favorite areas are Big Science Park (outdoor), where older kids conquer their fears and ride the high wire cycle. Ocean Learning World features a simulated shipwreck with dive tanks and a yellow submarine you can climb inside. Adventure World takes you on an archeological dig and the area is full of climbing and balancing areas (tilted room).Gadgets is a giant "erector set". The Life area has an Echo Free room, Hot/Cold Coils and Rat Basketball. In Space, you get dizzy in a tunnel and see a great space 3D movie. The idea of learning worlds really makes visitors feel like they are someplace else!

DAVIS DISCOVERY CENTER

Columbus - *549 Franklin Avenue, 43215. Phone: (614) 645-SHOW.* The Children's Drama Company for 9 to 12-year-olds are held at the center. At the Davis Youth Complex, classes for children ages 4 through 19 include magic, piano, ballet, acting, puppetry and more. Children who are home-schooled may take advantage of theater and dance classes offered in the daytime at both locations.

SANTA MARIA

Battelle Riverfront Park Scioto River (Downtown – Northeast of Broad Street Bridge at Marconi), **Columbus** 43215

- Phone: (614) 645-8760, **Web: www.santamaria.org**
- Hours: Wednesday-Friday 10:00am – 3:00pm. Weekends & Holidays Noon-5:00pm. (April, May, September, October). Open until 5:00pm (summer).
- Admission: $3.00 adult, $2.50 senior (60+), $1.50 student (5-17).

The Columbus Santa Maria is the world's most authentic, museum quality representation of Christopher Columbus' flagship. Climb aboard and return to 1492 as costumed guides share facts about the ship and the famous voyage. Feel the challenges and hardships faced by Columbus and his crew. Hear the wood structure creek as you hear stories about what they ate (no wonder they got sick a lot!) or how they managed through rough waters. Most everything is touchable - something we like in historical tours. You better be on your best behavior or you'll have to "walk the gang plank"! Sleeping quarters available for campouts.

THURBER HOUSE

Columbus - *77 Jefferson Avenue (Downtown), 43215. Phone: (614) 464-1032,* ***Web: www.thurberhouse.org.*** *Hours: Daily Noon – 4:00pm. Tours: Guided tours by appointment (for special events and groups). A small fee is charged.* James Thurber, the well-known humorist and cartoonist, grew up in Columbus. The restored home is where James lived during his college years. The house is featured in several of Thurber's stories. Be sure to read some of Thurber's works before you visit or purchase some of his books at the bookstore in Thurber House.

TOPIARY GARDEN

Columbus - *480 East Town Street (Old Deaf School Park,NW corner of E. Town & Washington, downtown, east of the Main Library), 43215.* ***Web: www.topiarygarden.org****. Phone: (614) 645-0197.* The topiary (greenery shaped like people, boats, animals, etc.) garden and pond depicts the theme "A Sunday Afternoon on the Island of La Grande Jaffe". FREE (open daily dawn to dusk).

GRAETER'S ICE CREAM FACTORY

Columbus - *2555 Bethel Road (near intersection of Sawmill Road), 43220. Phone: (614) 442-0622,* ***Web: www.graeters.com*** *Tours: Group tours by appointment.* Gourmet ice cream is made in small batches in French Pots (old-fashioned, no air whipped in as in modern, commercial brands). Tour the factory and then stay for a treat and soft play area.

POPCORN OUTLET

1500 Bethel Road (SR 315 to Bethel Road exit west)

Columbus 43220

- Phone: (614) 451-7677 or (800) 396-7010
  Web: www.thepopcornoutlet.com
- Hours: Monday-Friday 11:00am-9:00pm, Saturday 10:00am-8:00pm.
- Admission: FREE
- Tours: By Appointment, Approximately 20-30 minutes. No minimum or maximum number of people.

What a treat to meet Al, The Popcorn Man! This wonderfully enthusiastic owner will answer every question you've ever had about popcorn. Kids love watching the 2-minute video tour of the large poppers and closely watch the popped corn flow out. They have a tremendous assortment of 70 spicy and sweet flavors to coat the popcorn. They have a challenge presented with the Bubble Gum flavor: If you can blow a bubble from it (it tastes that real!), you get loads of free popcorn. You won't leave without trying lots of favorite flavors like Pizza, Columbus Mix or Jelly Bean. Kids and parents will want to bring their allowance to spend on these treats!

SHRUM MOUND

Columbus - Campbell Park, McKinley Avenue (5 miles northwest of downtown), 43222. **Web: www.ohiohistory.org/places/shrum**. Phone: (614) 297-2630. Conical 2000 year old Adena Indian burial mound - 2 feet high and 100 feet in diameter. Grass covered, it has steps leading to the summit. Open daylight hours.

COLUMBUS CLIPPERS

Columbus - *Cooper Stadium, 43223. Phone: (614) 462-5250,* ***Web: www.clippersbaseball.com***. Semi-professional farm team for the New York Yankees. Kids Club and Mascot "LouSeals". Many postgame concerts and occasional fireworks. Tickets: $3.00-$9.00. (April – Labor Day)

ANTHONY THOMAS CANDY COMPANY

1777 Arlingate Lane (I-270W to Roberts Road Exit)

Columbus 43228

- Phone: (614) 274-8405 or (877) Candy-21
  Web: www.anthony-thomas.com
- Admission: FREE
- Tours: Reservations Required for group tours (Minimum 10 people, 60 minutes). Monday-Friday 10:00a.m. to 3:00p.m. Call 614-272-9221.Annual open house is usually just before Easter. Summer tours on Tuesdays and Thursdays from 9:30am to 2:30pm. You don't need to make an appointment and there is no size limit on the group. Free sample at end of tours.

- Miscellaneous: Gift shop open during tour times. You finish your tour in the retail store. Factory Candy Shop.

Have you seen "Willy Wonka's Chocolate Factory?" This tour will remind you of that movie, especially when you first see the clean bright white equipment, near spotless flours and dozens of silver insulated pipes running to several production lines. View chocolate and fillings being prepared and molded in rooms remaining at a constant 90 degrees F. with 0% humidity (so workers and chocolate don't sweat!) Walk along the comfortable, glass-enclosed suspended "Cat-Walk" and observe eight lines producing 25,000 pounds of chocolates per shift. A couple of wrapping machines are exclusively for fundraisers and airline chocolates, but most of the production line packers can be seen hand packing chocolates for stores. All employees are taste testers – they can pop a morsel anytime to be sure it meets high standards...What a job!

AMERICAN WHISTLE CORPORATION

6540 Huntley Road (I-71 to Route 161 west, turn right on Huntley- look for small sign), **Columbus** 43229

- Phone: (877)876-2380, **Web: www.americanwhistle.com**
- Admission: $3.00 per person. Minimum $45.00 per group. Everyone on the tour goes home with a shiny new "American Classic" chrome finish whistle.
- Tours: Monday-Friday 9:00am-4:00pm. One hour long, 15-40 people, appointment necessary.
- Miscellaneous: Gift shop where you'll want to buy a lanyard to go with your new whistle or a gold plated whistle!

Do you know what a lanyard is? Do you know what makes a whistle louder? See and hear the only metal whistle manufactured in the United States (used by police, referees, coaches, etc.). These "American Classics" are the loudest whistles in the world - 4 decibels higher pitch than the competitors! You'll learn everything you ever wanted to know about whistles and really get to see a small manufacturing operation up close. See mechanical engineering at work - in one-of-a-kind machines designed to perform specific tasks. Learn how a whistle works - and how sciences like aerodynamics and chemistry contribute. Learn how a whistle can be an effective safety tool for people of all ages. These people know how to give great tours! Each person gets to take home a whistle they just watched being made!

GLASS AXIS

Columbus (Grandview) - *1341B Norton Avenue (near SR 315, between Third and Fifth Sts.), 43212. Phone: (614) 291-4250,* ***Web: www.glassaxis.org***. Glass Axis is a non-profit glass art facility. It was founded by twelve 1987 OSU Glass program graduates, who shared a common goal: to enhance the vision of contemporary art by enabling people to experience glass art and glass making. Visit a working glassblowing studio with a step-by-step explanation of the process. Tour lasts about 1 hour and must be scheduled in advance. Nominal admission fee. (September –June)

MOTORCYCLE HERITAGE MUSEUM

Columbus (Pickerington) - *13515 Yarmouth Drive (I-70 east exit 112A, left on SR 204), 43147. Phone: (614) 856-2222,* ***www.motorcyclemuseum.org***. *Hours: Daily 9:00am-5:00pm. Closed winter holidays. Open summer holidays Noon-4:00pm. Admission: $5.00 adult, $1.00 discount for Motorcycle Association members and seniors. FREE child (under 18).* The Museum is more than just a wide range of motorcycles on display. Its goal is to tell the stories and history of motorcycling. A self-guided tour features a wall mural, the history of motorcycles, and the Glory Days. Kids are most attracted to the 50 motorcycles on display.

COLUMBUS ZOO AND AQUARIUM

9990 Riverside Drive (Route 257, I-270 to Sawmill Road exit, follow signs), **Columbus (Powell)** 43065

- ❑ Phone: (614) 645-3550 or (800) MONKEYS
  Web: www.columbuszoo.org
- ❑ Hours: Daily 9:00am – 5:00pm (Year-round – extended hours in the summer). Open 365 days a year.

- Admission: $8.00 adult, $7.00 senior (60+), $6.00 child (2-11). Family Membership available. Parking fee $3.00.
- Miscellaneous: Gift Shops and Concessions. Food Court similar to a mall. Pony, train and carousel rides (small additional fee). Play gym. Picnic facilities.

The famous Director Emeritus of the zoo, Jack Hanna, is a regular on national talk shows. Highlights of the naturally landscaped zoo include cheetahs, black rhinos, lowland gorillas, Habitat Hollow (what makes human/animal habitats home- play & pet area), and North American Bald Eagles (named George and Barbara). A 100,000-gallon coral reef exhibit and one of the largest reptile collections in the United States are also featured. The habitat "Manatee Coast" is modeled after the famous Island Refuge in Florida with a 190,000 gallon pool and floor to ceiling glass viewing walls! The expanded African Forest exhibit offers a walk-through rainforest-themed area with incredible interaction with all kinds of monkeys. Newer exhibits include the Islands of Southeast Asia (primitive ruins, Indonesian buildings and music, komodo dragons, orangutans and otters) and Australia. A waterway will allow narrated boat rides through the exhibit to give visitors a different view while still providing more room for the animals to roam freely. It just keeps getting better!

WYANDOT LAKE ADVENTURE PARK

10101 Riverside Drive (I-270 to Sawmill Road Exit)

Columbus (Powell) 43065

- Phone: (614) 889-9283 or (800) 328-9283
  Web: www.sixflags.com/wyandotlake
- Hours: Daily 10:00am-7:00pm, 8:00pm or 9:00pm (Memorial Day– Labor Day). Weekends only (mid-May to Memorial Day).
- Admission: $19.00-$25.00. $12.50 senior (55+). After 4:00pm, $14.50. FREE child (age 2 and under). Season Pass and Combo Packs with Columbus Zoo available.
- Miscellaneous: Concessions, Kiddie rides, and Gift Shops.

This is great fun for a summer day. Wyandot offers a huge wave pool, numerous thrilling water slides and a Tadpool water fun area for the little ones. Then, put on your shoes and get on the roller coaster or one of the amusement rides available. All this for one admission charge. Life vests and rafts are available, free, first come.

- Christopher Island Water Play Area – Tree house, lagoons, abandoned ships, heated water guns and sprayers, jet steams, and dark speed tunnels.

HANBY HOUSE

Columbus (Westerville) – *160 West Main Street, (Westerville) (across from Otterbein College), 43081. Phone: (614) 891-6289.* ***Web: www.ohiohistory.org/places/hanby****. Hours: Saturday and Sunday 1:00-4:00pm (May-September). Small admission. Groups by appointment.* Benjamin Hanby was the composer of over 80 folk songs and hymns including "Sweet Nelly Gray" and "Up On the Rooftop". Children will enjoy seeing Ben's original instruments and musical scores. This home was part of the Underground Railroad. Be sure to notice and ask about the roses in a vase by the front window. The tour also includes viewing a short introduction movie.

JORGENSEN FARMS

5851 East Walnut Street (I-270 to SR 161 east to New Albany Rd exit, turns into New Albany Condit, continue east to Walnut St., turn left), **Westerville** 43081

- Phone: (614) 855-1647, **Web: www.jorgensen-farms.com**
- Hours:Wednesday-Friday 10:00am-6:00pm, Saturday 8:00am-2:00pm (April-December).
- Admission: Farm Market Area is FREE. Group Programs (min. 15 students-preschool to 6th grade): $5.00-$10.00 per student, adults admitted FREE.
- Tours: 2 hours per session, morning and/or afternoons.

A special treat right in the middle of a growing suburb! "Got Organic?". Know what it is? The fresh taste and unique variety of the products grown here (without chemicals) is what attracts many to the market, but the Education Center programs are what engage the kids. Many living in the city will get a chance to "hang out" on a friendly, safe farm run by the nicest people you'll find anywhere. Where does food come from? Students are encouraged to explore the barns, meadows, creeks, wetlands, pastures and woods. Many will want to learn about busy bees (they have easy-to-read storyboards and a demo tent showing how bees work); or, see sheep shearing, then card the wool, then make a "sheepish" craft; or, try to guess the scents of different herbs. Maybe tend the veggie garden; collect brown eggs in the hen house (a big treat!); pet some lambs or ducks; or, giggle at the antics of the turkey and pheasant. In the fall, you'll want to go out in the field to pick your own pumpkin.

OHIO RAILWAY MUSEUM

Columbus (Worthington) - *990 Proprietors Road (Off State Route 161), 43085.* ***Web: www.ohiorailwaymuseum.org.*** *Phone: (614) 268-4075. Hours: Sunday 1:00 – 5:00 pm (Memorial Day-Labor Day).* They have displayed approximately 30 pieces of Ohio Railway History dating from 1897 – 1950. The guide explains that steam engines have their own personality. Get close to one under steam and hear it talk! Special seasonal train excursions take you on a steam train day-trip. See website for details. Small admission for museum.

ORANGE JOHNSON HOUSE

Columbus (Worthington) - *956 North High Street, (Worthington) (just north of State Route 161), 43085. Phone: (614) 885-1247,* ***Web: www.worthington.org.*** *Hours: (Open House) Sunday 2:00 - 5:00pm (mid-February to mid-December). Admission: $2.00-$3.00.* The Orange Johnson House is a restored early 1800's home. Part of it is Federal style, the back part is pioneer. There are many authentic objects and toys that children can pick up and pretend to use. The guide will describe chores children were given in those days (your own children will think they have it made!). A good time to visit is when they have cooking demonstrations. The smell in the air engages everyone to explore early settler's kitchen tools and techniques. The Old Rectory in downtown Worthington has a doll museum with changing exhibits.

ALUM CREEK STATE PARK

Delaware - *3615 South Old State Road (7 miles Southeast of Delaware off State Route 36/37, 1 mile West of I-71), 43015.* ***Web: www.dnr.state.oh.us/parks/parks/alum.htm.*** *Phone: (740) 548-4631.* 8,600 acres with a great beach with life guarded swimming and food service available. Camping, hiking trails, lots of good boating and rentals, fishing and winter sports. Large-flowered trillium, wild geranium, bloodroot, and spring beauties carpet the forest floor. The forest is home to the fox squirrel, woodchuck, rabbit, white-tail deer and many other species of wildlife.

DELAWARE STATE PARK

Delaware - *(6 miles North of Delaware on US 23), 43015.* ***Web: www.dnr.state.oh.us/parks/parks/delaware.htm.*** *Phone: (740) 369-2761.* Dense woodlands, expansive meadows and a reservoir blend to create Delaware State Park. Once home to the Delaware Indians, this recreational area offers 3,145 acres of camping, hiking trails, boating and rentals, fishing, swimming, and winter sports. Eat at the nearby Hamburger Inn downtown (740) 369-3850, 16 North Sandusky Street, 50's theme.

OLENTANGY INDIAN CAVERNS

1779 Home Road (US 23 North to Home Road, follow signs, 6 miles north of I-270), **Delaware** 43015

- ❑ Phone: (740) 548-7917, **Web: www.olentangyindiancaverns.com**
- ❑ Hours: Daily 9:30am - 5:00pm (April - October).
- ❑ Admission: $8.00 adult, $5.00 child (7-15).
- ❑ Miscellaneous: Large picnic facilities. Frontierland (cute western village) with gem mining and mini-golf $3.50. Climbing wall (2 climbs for $5.00) Gift shop, playground.

Wyandot Indians used these underground caves until 1810 for protection from the weather and their enemies. The caves were formed by an underground river that flows to the Olentangy River hundreds of feet below the surface. The caves were originally discovered during a search for oxen that broke loose from a wagon train. Their owner, J. M. Adam's name and date can be seen on the entrance wall. The tour lasts 30 minutes and takes you through winding passages and coves underground. Then, you visit the museum where Indian artifacts found in the caves are displayed. If you're still in an adventurous mood, play a game of miniature golf, climb a rock wall, mine for gems or go on a nature hike past teepees and longhouses. Something for every size adventurer here.

PERKINS OBSERVATORY

Delaware - *State Route 23 (2 miles south of Delaware, 1 miles south of US 23/SR 315), 43015. Phone: (740) 363-1257,* ***Web: www.perkins-observatory.org/perkins.html.*** *Hours: Friday or Saturday nights (except for 2nd Saturday & holidays. Call for schedule. Admission: $5.00 adult, $3.00 senior/child. $1.00 more if purchased day of program. To order in advance, send self-addressed stamped envelope to: Perkins Observatory, P.O. Box 449, Delaware OH 43015.* Children who have studied astronomy will especially enjoy this. The stars naturally fascinate them at night so this is a real treat to see them this close. The program includes a tour of the observatory, an amusing talk on astronomy (ex. "Space Crud" or "Lifestyles of the Huge & Stellar"), and then telescope observation if it is a clear night (otherwise, planetarium show). Occasional lawn telescope observation and rocket launches.

FLINT RIDGE STATE MEMORIAL MUSEUM

7091 Brownsville Road SE (SR 16 east to SR 668 south)

Glenford 43739

- Phone: (740) 787-2476 or (800) 283-8707
  Web: www.ohiohistory.org/places/flint
- Hours: Wednesday - Saturday 9:30am - 5:00pm, Sunday Noon - 5:00pm (Memorial Day - Labor Day). Weekends Only (September and October).
- Admission: $3.00 adult, $2.00 child (6-12).
- Miscellaneous: Flint Preserve open April - October, 9:30am to Dusk.

Indians came to see this stretch of hills for flint stone (official gemstone of the State of Ohio) to use for tools and weapons. Displays show how flint is formed from silica and what objects can be made today with flint (like sparks that start flames when flint is rubbed against steel). Outdoors you can explore the trails past ancient quarry pits. How else can we use flint?

GRANVILLE LIFE STYLE MUSEUM

Granville - *121 South Main Street, 43023. Phone: (740) 587-0373 Hours: 1st Saturday each month from 1:00 – 4:00 pm (May – September).* A grandmother's style Victorian home with handed-down and saved possessions for more than 100 years. Adults (and even children) are invited to play the 1911 Steinway piano or learn about the lifestyle of Robinson families through the 1900s. The kitchen is a 1949 design. Tours, by appointment, include "learn & laugh" programs or Victorian Undergarments & Flirts. Great "girls day out" Victorian era fun. FREE, except for special tours.

MOTTS MILITARY MUSEUM

Groveport - *5075 South Hamilton Road, 43125. Phone: (614) 836-1500.* ***Web: www.mottsmilitarymuseum.org****. Hours: Tuesday-Saturday 9:00am-5:00pm, Sunday 1:00-5:00pm. Admission: $5.00 adult, $4.00 senior, $3.00 student.* Its purpose is to bring military history into perspective by collecting and preserving memorabilia. Secondly, it educates the public on the importance of past, present and new military events that impact our lives (good way to "tie-in" current events).

JURASSIC JOURNEY

Heath - *4600 Ridgely Tract Road (Burning Tree Golf Course, off SR 79 south of Heath), 43056. Phone: (740) 522-3464 or (888) 37-DINOS,* ***www.jurassicjourney.com****. Hours: Daily 7:00am-9:00pm (when course is open). Closed when golf course is closed due to weather. Admission: $2.00-$3.00.* 50 individual, full-size cast replicas of dinosaurs. Also an Ice Age exhibit featuring the Burning Tree Mastodon, which was discovered on the golf course in 1989 while forming the back 9 holes.

BUCKEYE CENTRAL SCENIC RAILROAD

US 40 (3 miles East of Hebron – I-70 to Route 79 North Exit to US 40), **Hebron** 43025

- ❑ Phone: (740) 928-3827 or (800) 579-7521
  Web: www.buckeyecentralrailroad.org

- Hours: Weekends and Holidays, 1:00 and 3:00 pm Departures (Memorial Day – October). Seasonal rides also available. Call or visit website for details.
- Admission: $7.00 Adult, $5.00 Children (2-11). Extra $2.00 to ride in caboose.

Take a trip through Ohio farmland for a 90 minute ride on the same route the train traveled in the mid-1800's on the Shawnee line (important line for pioneers heading west). School-aged kids will want to check out the Wild West/Great Train Robbery. Be part of the action as the train is boarded and held up by outlaws. Will the sheriff save the day?

NATIONAL TRAIL RACEWAY

Hebron - *2650 National Road SW (I-70 to SR 37north to US 40) 43025.* ***Web: www.nationaltrailraceway.com****. Phone: (740) 928-5706.* Drag racing. Super Gas Races & Night Under Fire (jet cars & trucks with fire exhaust, drag racing, fireworks, funny car acts). Weekends & Wednesdays. Day & Evening. (late April - October)

GEORGIAN / SHERMAN HOUSE MUSEUM

Lancaster - *105 East Wheeling and Broad Street and 137 East Main Street, 43130.* ***Web: www.fairfieldheritage.org****. Phone: (740) 654-9923. Hours: Tuesday – Sunday 1:00-4:00pm (April thru mid-December). Admission $4.00 per person. Guided tours last 45 minutes for each home.* 19th Century homes with period furnishings. War mementos of Civil War General William Tecumseh Sherman (his birthplace). Imagine how life must have been in the "Little Brown House on the Hill," the Sherman House, with eleven children and four adults as you visit the wooden structure in which one of the most famous/infamous Civil War Generals was born.

WAHKEENA NATURE PRESERVE

Lancaster - *2200 Pump Station Road (US 33 to County Road 86 west, follow signs), 43155. Phone: (740) 746-8695 or (800) 297-1883,* ***Web: www.ohiohistory.org/places/wahkeena****. Hours: Wednesday-Sunday 8:00am-4:30pm (April-October). Admission: $2.00 per vehicle.* Wahkeena, named with an Indian word meaning "most beautiful" is a located on the edge of the Hocking Hills.

Trees, ferns, mountain laurels, wildflowers and orchids. Wahkeena's sandstone cliffs, part of the famous Black Hand sandstone, are forested primarily with tulip trees and oak. All that beauty plus 70 species of birds and 15 species of mammals including woodpeckers and white-tailed deer. Museum and nature trails.

MARION COUNTY INTERNATIONAL RACEWAY

LaRue - *2303 Richwood – LaRue Road (Route 37), 43332. Phone: (740) 499-3666 or (800) 422-MCIR,* ***Web: www.mcir.net****. Admission: $5.00-$10.00 (age 12+).* Quarter mile drag racing includes 7up Pro Am and Sunoco IHRA Finals. Concessions. (Saturdays, April – October.)

LITHOPOLIS FINE ARTS/ WAGNALLS MEMORIAL LIBRARY

Lithopolis - *150 East Columbus Street, 43136. Phone: (614) 837-7003.* ***Web: http://cwda.net/LAFAA****.* Series of musical concerts and dramatic events in Wagnalls Memorial (Adam Wagnall was the co-founder of the Funk and Wagnalls Publishing Co.). The series programs and workshops have included light and serious drama, dance groups, mime, a puppeteer and a wide variety of musical events ranging from the classical to bluegrass. Tickets $8.00-$12.00. Tours of the library are available by appointment and include a description of the unusual architectural features and history of the Memorial and Wagnalls family.

MADISON LAKE STATE PARK

London - *(3 miles East of London off State Route 665), 43140.* ***Web: www.dnr.state.oh.us/parks/parks/madison.htm****. Phone: (740) 869-3124.* 186 acres of boating, fishing, swimming and winter sports. One of the best examples of existing prairie in Ohio is within the Darby Plains of Madison County. Bigelow Cemetery State Nature Preserve near Chuckery contains prairie plants including big bluestem, Indian grass and purple coneflower. Smith Cemetery Prairie contains stiff goldenrod, gray willow and wild petunia.

HARDING MEMORIAL AND HOME

380 Mount Vernon Avenue (2 miles west of State Route 23 on State Route 95), **Marion** 43302

- Phone: (740) 387-9630 or (800) 600-6894
  Web: www.ohiohistory.org/places/harding
- Hours: Wednesday - Saturday 9:30am - 5:00pm, Sunday and Holidays Noon - 5:00pm (Summer). Weekends Only (September and October) By appointment in Spring.
- Admission: $3.00 adult, $2.00 child (6-12).
- Miscellaneous: Memorial is a circular monument (with columns of white marble) containing the tombs of Mr. and Mrs. Harding. Delaware Avenue.

A great way to learn Presidential history without a fuss from the kids. Do you know what the fancy pot is in the guestroom - the one lying on the floor? They have displayed a podium used at Harding's inauguration in 1920 as our 29th President. See the porch where Harding campaigned what was later called the "Front Porch Campaign", speaking to over 600,000 people overall. The original porch collapsed and a new one had to be built during the campaign. A special small house was built behind the main house for the press associates visiting the area to cover the campaign. Look for the ornate collar worn by their dog "Laddie Boy".

MYSTERIOUS REVOLVING BALL

Marion - *Marion Cemetery, 43302. Hours: Dawn – Dusk.* Can you scientifically solve the "Marion Unsolved Mystery"? Here's the scoop! The ball is a grave monument for the Merchant family (located in the northeast corner of the cemetery) erected in 1896. The 5200-pound granite ball turns mysteriously with continuous movement. There has been no scientific explanation for this revolution and the phenomenon is featured in many newspapers including "Ripley's Believe It or Not"!

WYANDOT POPCORN MUSEUM

Marion - *169 East Church Street (Heritage Hall – Marion County Museum of History), 43302. Phone: (740) 387-HALL or (800) WYANDOT,* ***Web: www.wyandotpopcornmus.com****. Hours: Wednesday – Sunday 1:00 – 4:00pm (May – October). Weekends Only (November –*

April). Closed most holidays. Before you enter the Popcorn Museum, see the hand-made miniature, working carousel and Prince Imperial (a stuffed 25 year old horse from France). You won't believe how they braided his mane! As you enter the large, colorful tent, you'll be enchanted by the antique popcorn poppers and concession wagons. See the first automated popper and the first all electric popper – all in pristine condition. It's the only museum like it in the world and is popular with stars like Paul Newman, who borrowed a Wyandot Concession Wagon to promote his popcorn, "Old Time Style", in Central Park.

BUCKEYE LAKE STATE PARK

Millersport - *(9 miles South of Newark off State Route 13), 43046.* ***Web: www.dnr.state.oh.us/parks/parks/buckeye.htm****. Phone: (740) 467-2690.* 3,557 acres of boating, fishing, swimming and winter sports. Permanent & rental properties are available around the lake.

KNOX COUNTY HISTORICAL SOCIETY MUSEUM

Mount Vernon - *875 Harcourt Road (routes 3 and 36), 43050. Phone: (740) 393-KCHS. Hours: Thursday-Sunday 2:00-4:00pm, Wednesday 6:00-8:00pm (February-mid December).* Exhibits portray the life and travels of Johnny Appleseed, the story of educational institutions, the postal service and radio stations history, toys and dolls, business and industry collections (Cooper Heritage Collection 19th century steam farm engines- became Rolls Royce), Bridge Company exhibit and the musical heritage of the county (Dan Emmett-composer, musician "Turkey in the Straw" and "Old Dan Tucker").

MOUNT GILEAD STATE PARK

Mt. Gilead - *(1 mile East of Mt. Gilead on State Route 95), 43338.* ***Web: www.dnr.state.oh.us/parks/parks/mtgilead.htm****. Phone: (419) 946-1961.* 172 acres of camping, hiking trails, boating, fishing and some winter sports. The mature woodlands (second-growth beech-maple) provide a glimpse of what Ohio was to the early settlers. Wildflowers such as wild geranium, hepatica, trillium and bloodroot, carpet the spring forest floor. The leafy canopy is occupied by the woodthrush, white-breasted nuthatch, Carolina wren and other songbirds. Skunks, raccoons, white-tailed deer and a variety of other mammals make this park their home.

DEER CREEK STATE PARK

22300 State Park Road (I-71 to SR 56 to SR 207, 7 miles south of town), **Mt. Sterling** 43143

- Phone: (740) 869-3124 Park or (740) 869-2020 Lodge or (877) 678-3337 Reservations. **Web: www.visitdeercreek.com**
- Admission: FREE

Nature Programs, bike rentals, camping, hiking trails, boating and rentals, fishing, golf, and winter sports available throughout park. Resort has over 100 guest rooms (some with bunk beds, some with lofts), 25 fully furnished two-bedroom cottages (screened porch, many with gas fireplaces, fire ring and grills), indoor/outdoor pools, whirlpool/sauna, gamerooms, sport courts, fitness center, full service restaurant and plenty of activities. Great to plan a group/family get-together here as there are things to do and places everywhere to gather for games (cards, board games) or crafts (Shrinky Dink, buttons, sand art, etc) or evening family videos or hayrides or campfires. They have short hiking trails that are "kid-friendly" (we loved "tracking" the paw prints on the trails early morning) and their Holiday or Theme Weekends are well-planned with entertainment and special guests (ie. astronauts). Be careful, this place could be habit forming!

PERRY STATE FOREST

New Lexington - *(off of SR-345, 4 miles north of New Lexington) 43764. Phone: (740) 674-4035 (Blue Rock office),* ***Web: www.dnr.state.oh.us/forestry/Forests/stateforests/perry.htm***. 4,567 acres in Perry County. Area was formerly strip mined for coal. All purpose vehicle trails (16 miles), bridle trails (8 miles). Open daily 6:00am - 11:00pm.

GREAT CIRCLE EARTHWORKS

99 Cooper Avenue (I-70 to SR 79 north, between Parkview Drive and Cooper), **Newark** 43055

- Phone: (740) 344-1920 or (800) 600-7174 **www.ohiohistory.org/places/newarkearthworks/greatcircle.cfm**
- Hours: Museum, Wednesday – Saturday 9:30am - 5:00pm, Sunday and Holidays Noon - 5:00pm (Summer). Weekends Only (September and October).

- ❑ Admission: $3.00 Adult, $2.00 Children (6-12).
- ❑ Miscellaneous: Octagon State Memorial - Small mounds, Wright Earthworks State Memorial. Park open daylight hours.

The Moundbuilders is a circular mound 1200 feet in diameter with walls 8 to 14 feet high. In the museum, we found the primitive stamps most interesting. The engraved tablets were probably used for clothing decorations or tattoos. They feel the tablets were used as stamps because they found colored pigment on them. As you walk outside the museum, you walk right into the mouth opening of a circular mound. Once inside, just imagine the Hopewell Indian ceremonies that occurred many years ago. Research has concluded that the central Eagle shaped mound was the site of a grand ceremonial site.

DAWES ARBORETUM

Newark - *7770 Jacksontown Road (SR 13, I-70 exit 132), 43056.* ***Web: www.dawesarb.org****. Phone: (740) 323-2355 or (800) 44-DAWES, Hours: Grounds open daily dawn to dusk. Closed Thanksgiving, Christmas and New Years.* The Dawes Arboretum features plants tolerant of central Ohio's climate. Azaleas, crab apples, hollies, oaks and conifers are a few of the collections accessible from the 4.5 mile Auto Tour and more than 8 miles of hiking trails. There's also meadows, woods, gardens, cypress swamp, holly and a special Japanese Bonsai garden. Free admission.

THE WORKS - OHIO CENTER OF HISTORY, ART & TECHNOLOGY

Newark - *55 South First Street (I-70 to SR 13 north to between 1st & 2nd streets), 43058. Phone: (740) 349-9277,* ***Web: www.attheworks.org****. Hours: Monday-Friday 9:00am-4:00pm, Saturday Noon – 4:00pm. Admission: $5.00 adult, $2.00 child (4-16).* "The Works" is a reoccurring theme. The art gallery and studio have the name, "Art Works."(Pottery and ceramics are the central theme of the studio; you decide how you want to experience them, whether creating your own Bisque Studio (once fired pottery), or throwing on the wheel in the mud room.) The newly refurbished glass studio has become "Glass Works" (watch or workshop glass blowers demonstrate their craft as they create artistic pieces of glassware, including intricate vases, bowls, paperweights and seasonal items). Also found in the complex is the

Digital Works (web design and TV studio). The original 1880s machine shop complex houses The Works (traces the development of industry in central Ohio from prehistoric Indians to the 21st century). Learn something about Licking County history and its future. Learn methods of transportation thru the years or which products were made here (Mason jars and engines for farm machines). See where local raw materials are used in manufacturing, farming and fuel production. Interactive touch displays educate kids on what, where, and how materials are extracted (raw and finished forms).

GREEN'S HERITAGE MUSEUM

Orient - *10530 Thrailkill Road (State Route 762), 43146. Phone: (740) 877-4254.* Historical village with Blacksmith Shop, Antique Farm, 1929 Gas Station, Ice House, Depot, Sawmill, 1871 Church, Country Store with original counters and benches, and original White Castle Gift Shop. Carriage House with 50 antique horse drawn carriages. Call for hours/tours.

VELVET ICE CREAM: YE OLDE MILL ICE CREAM MUSEUM

Velvet Ice Cream (State Route 13), **Utica** 43080

- Phone: (740) 892-3921or (800) 589-5000
  Web: www.velvet-icecream.com
- Hours: Daily 11:00am – 9:00pm (May-October).
- Admission: FREE

Did you know that the ice cream cone originated by mistake at the St. Louis World's Fair when a waffle vendor rolled waffles into cones for an ice cream vendor who ran out of serving cups? Learn all sorts of ice cream trivia at the Ice Cream Museum located in the restored 1817 mill and water wheel which is surrounded by 20 acres of wooded parklands with ducks and picnic areas. While you are at the mill, stop by the viewing gallery to watch ice cream being made and packaged. Then, catch a light meal and ice cream or yogurt dessert at the 1800's Ice Cream Parlor and gift shop.

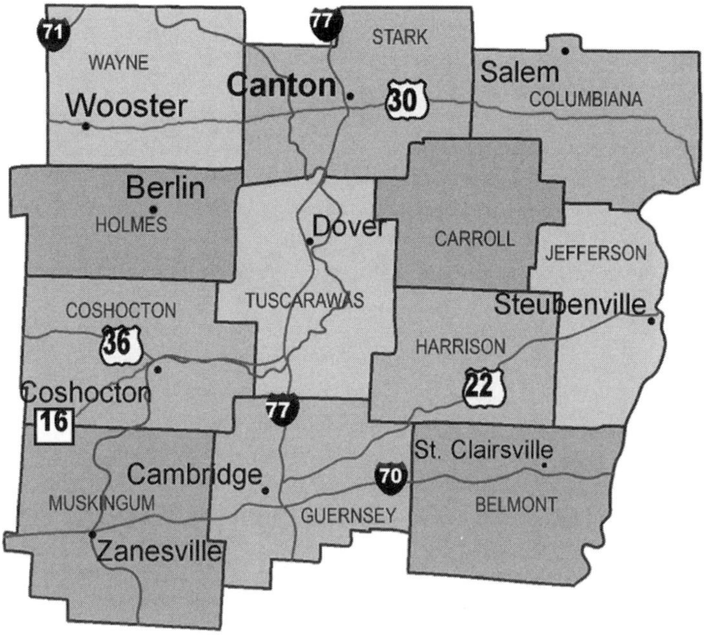

Chapter 2
Central East Area

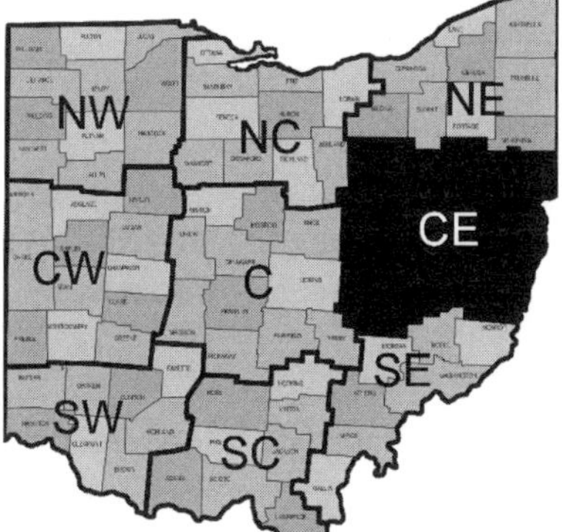

Our Favorites...

Amish Farms & Cheese Factories

Bluebird Farm

Creegan Company Animation Factory

Glass & Pottery Factory Tours

Harry London Chocolate Factory

Longaberger Factory & Homestead

Roscoe Village

Schoenbrunn / Gnadenhutten Village

Warther Carving Museum

Wendall August Forge

First Settlement Church - Schoenbrunn

GLAMORGAN CASTLE

Alliance - *200 Glamorgan Street, 44601. Phone: (330) 821-2100,* ***Web: www.aviators.stark.k12.oh.us/History.html****. Tours: By Appointment. Generally weekdays at 2:00 pm. Small admission fee.* Home of the City School District's Administration office and once the early 1900's home of the late Col. William Henry Morgan (inventor/businessman). The building measures 185 feet in overall front elevation, with 13 inch thick walls, and truly looks like a giant castle.

BELMONT COUNTY VICTORIAN MANSION MUSEUM

Barnesville - *532 North Chestnut Street, 43713. Phone: (740) 425-2926. Thursday – Sunday, 1:00 – 4:30 pm (May – October).* 26 rooms furnished in Gay 90's style home. Admission.

DICKSON LONGHORN CATTLE COMPANY

Barnesville - *35000 Muskrat Road (I-70 exit 202 south, then west) 43713. Phone: (740) 758-5050,* ***Web: www.texaslonghorn.com****. Hours: Monday-Saturday 10:00am-5:00pm, Sunday 1:00-6:00pm (June-Labor Day). Tours: One hour. Tours for adults are $10.00 with special rates for youth. Gift shop.* Large, family-owned ranch offers narrated tours on an adorable purple with white polka-dotted cow bus. See up to 1000 Texas Longhorns grazing the fields, hand-feed the cattle and clear water fish. Gizmo is an International Champion Sire that is on the tour route. What shape do they use for branding?

BARKCAMP STATE PARK

Belmont - *65330 Barkcamp Park Road (I-70 exit 208, off SR 149) 43718.* ***web:www.dnr.state.oh.us/odnr/parks/parks/barkcamp.htm****. Phone: (740) 484-4064.* Nature Programs. 1,232 acres of camping, hiking trails through rolling hills and woodlands, boating, fishing, swimming and winter sports.

BEHALT

5798 County Road 77 (north of State Route 39)

Berlin 44610

- Phone: (330) 893-3192, **Web: http://pages.sssnet.com/behalt**
- Hours: Monday – Thursday 9:00am – 5:00pm, Friday-Saturday 9:00am-8:00pm. Only open till 5:00pm November-May.
- Tours: 30 minute guided or video (15 minute background to Amish area).

Behalt means "to keep or remember". This 10' x 265' cyclorama mural by artist Heinz Gaugel clearly explains the heritage of Amish and Mennonite people from the beginnings of their faith to the present day. The circular mural took four years to paint using an old technique called "sgraffito" which means scratched. Mr. Gaugel applied five layers of plaster to the wall (green, dark red, dark yellow, white and black). The artist starts scratching through the layers to expose the colors he wants. This makes the mural almost 3D when viewing. The tour is narrated with stories so vivid that you feel as if you are a part of the scene. We were fortunate to meet Heinz Gaugel in the gift shop and it was amazing to meet such a humble man with such apparent, unique artistic talent.

SCHROCK'S AMISH FARM AND HOME

4363 State Route 39 (1 mile East of Downtown)

Berlin 44610

- Phone: (330) 893-3232, **Web: www.amish-r-us.com**
- Hours: Monday – Friday 10:00am - 5:00pm, Saturday 10:00am-6:00pm (April - October).
- Tours and Admission: Buggy Ride - $2.00-$3.00 (age 3+). Home Tour and Slides - $2.00-$3.00 (age 3+). Farm Only - $1.50 (age 3+). Discount combo prices.
- Miscellaneous: Gifts shops (many)

We started with a buggy ride driven by an Amish man and his horse named "Leroy". After our ride, we were given a sticker to wear that says, "I rode my first Amish buggy ride with Leroy". We then stopped at the farm to pet animals and then watched a slide show about Amish lifestyles. The guide then shows you through the home. Kids, even adults, were surprised to see that all appliances were gas fueled including the lamps (the gas generated light source was hidden in the table under the lamp). We learned why there are no faces on Amish dolls and why only pins and occasional buttons are used in clothing.

WENDALL AUGUST FORGED GIFT TOUR

7007 Dutch Country Lane (3 miles West of Berlin - Route 62)

Berlin 44610

- Phone: (330) 893-3713 or (800) 923-4438
  Web: www.wendell.com
- Tours: Tuesday-Saturday 9:00am-4:00pm.

Free tour of the production workshop as metal giftware is taken through a fascinating eleven step process. The gift metal is hammered over a pre-designed template with random hand, or machine operated hammer motions. It was interesting to think someone close to the craft had to design the machine operated hammer for this specific purpose – probably a craftsman who's hands got tired! The impression is now set in one side and the signature hammer marks will stay on the other side. The artist stamps his seal and then the item is forged (put in a log fire) to get smoke marks that bring out the detail of the design. After the item cools, it is cleaned to remove most of the dark smoke color and the metal object is then thinned by hand hammering. The facility also features a video highlighting the company's history and the showroom has the World's Largest Amish Buggy – over 1200 pounds, and each wheel is over 5 feet tall!

BLUE ROCK STATE FOREST

Blue Rock - *6665 Cutler Lake Road (located 12 miles southeast of Zanesville off SR 60), 43720. Phone: (740) 674-4035,* ***Web: www.dnr.state.oh.us/forestry/Forests/stateforests/bluerock.htm***

Hours: Daily 6:00am - 11:00pm. 4,579 acres in Muskingum County. 26 miles of bridle trails and fishing are offered. Former fire lookout tower. Blue Rock State Park is adjacent.

FORT LAURENS STATE MEMORIAL AND MUSEUM

Bolivar - *11067 Fort Laurens Rd. NW (I-77 and State Route 212 - Follow Signs), 44612. Phone: (800) 283-8914 or (330) 874-2059,* ***Web: www.ohiohistory.org/places/ftlauren****. Hours: Wednesday - Saturday 9:30am - 5:00pm, Sunday and Holidays Noon - 5:00 pm (Summer). Weekends Only (September and October) Grounds open daily April-October. Admission: $3.00 adult, $2.00 child (6-12).* Visit the site of the only U.S. Military fort in Ohio during the American Revolution. Built in 1778 in an ill-fated campaign to attack the British at Detroit. Supplying this wilderness outpost was its downfall, as its starving garrison survived on boiled moccasins and withstood a month-long siege by British-led Indians. The fort was abandoned in 1779. Also included is a museum (with visual and action packed audiovisual displays), that sits on what was once the fort's west gate. Re-enactment weekends are the best time to visit to help visualize the horrible conditions of the now, non-existent fort.

HARRISON STATE FOREST

Cadiz - *(3 miles north of Cadiz, east of SR-9), 43907.* ***Web: www.dnr.state.oh.us/forestry/Forests/stateforests/harrison.htm*** *Phone: (330) 339-2205 (New Philadelphia office).* 1,345 acres in Harrison County. Area formerly strip mined for coal. Bridle and hiking trails (24 miles), family and horse camping (no fee), fishing ponds. Open daily 6:00 am - 11:00 pm.

BOYD'S CRYSTAL ART GLASS COMPANY

Cambridge - *1203 Morton Avenue (off State Route 209 North) 43725. Phone: (740) 439-2077,* ***Web: www.boydglass.com****. Tours: Monday – Friday 7:00am – 11:00am and Noon – 3:30pm, 15 minutes. (September – May).* The Cambridge area became popular for glass manufacturing because of good sand and abundant wells of natural gas. Boyd's specialty is antique glass reproductions and collectibles. Typical shapes made are trains, airplanes, cars, small animals and Teddy the Tugboat. Watch molten glass being poured into one of 300 molds and put in a furnace. When they cool, they are hand-painted.

LIVING WORD PASSION PLAY

Cambridge - *6010 College Hill Road (2 miles west of State Route 209), 43725. Phone: (740) 439-2761. Hours: Thursday – Saturday 8:00 pm (Mid-June – Labor Day). Saturday Only 7:00 pm (September). Admission: $12.00 adult, $10.00 senior (60+), $6.00 child (under 12). Free Set Tours 7:15pm. Miscellaneous: Concessions, Gift Shop, Rain Checks, Free Parking.* Bible stories come to life before your eyes. Experience an evening back in the Holy Land, in 30 AD with an authentic representation of Old Jerusalem. Watch as Jesus and his disciples travel into Jerusalem, he is then crucified, and raises from the dead. The play is full of biblical animals and costumes, even chariots.

MOSSER GLASS

9279 Cadiz Road (I-77 exit 47. US 22 West)

Cambridge 43725

- Phone: (740) 439-1827, **Web: www.mosserglass.com**
- Tours: Monday-Friday 8:30am-10:30am and 12:30pm-3:00pm. No tours first 2 weeks in July and last 2 weeks in December. Best not to tour if it's hot outside as the plant is not air conditioned. FREE.

Mosser makes glass pitchers, goblets, lamps, figurines, auto parts (headlights), and paper weights. Your guide starts the tour explaining the glassmaking process from the beginning when glass powder (sand and cullet-broken glass) are heated to 2000 degrees F. in a furnace. Once melted, the molten glass is pulled on a stick and then iron molded or pressed, fire glazed and finally cooled in a Lehr which uniformly reduces the temperature of the object to prevent shattering. We saw them make old Ford car headlight covers and red heart shaped paperweights. They add selenium to make red glass. A little toothpick holder or doll's glass is typical of the free souvenir of this great tour!

SALT FORK STATE PARK RESORT

14755 Cadiz Road (7 miles Northeast of Cambridge on US 22)

Cambridge 43755

- Phone: (740) 439-2751 lodge or (740) 439-3521 park or (800) 282-7275 reservations, **Web: www.saltforkresort.com** or **www.dnr.state.oh.us/parks/parks/saltfork.htm**
- Admission: FREE

What a great, family-friendly outdoor resort with many hotel comforts! Everyone seems to spend at least a couple of hours each day at the Lodge area with overnight rooms, gift shops, indoor and outdoor pools & spa, fitness center, volleyball, basketball and tennis. The dining room serves breakfast, lunch and dinner in a rustic overlook setting (also, seasonal snack bars are available). The gameroom with multiple ping-pong and air hockey tables is downstairs. Fun family activities are planned seasonally (ie crafts, pool games, kid's bingo, family movies, bonfires, plus Parent's Night Out (once or twice a week). The cabins are where memories are made! Best for grade-schoolers and up (bunk beds) because they're right in the woods. The Nature Center is open with planned activities (seasonally, Wednesday-Sunday) and explorations. Bring your own boat to this beautiful lake (or rent one at Sugartree Marina (740) 439-5833 - Kids love the pontoon or speed/ski boats). Lots of camping, fishing, golfing, and well marked hiking trails too. A great place to kick back and create family memories!

ST HELENA III

***Canal Fulton** - 103 Tuscarawas Village Park (I-77 to Exit 111 Portage Street West, follow signs), 44614. Phone: (330) 854-3808 or (800) HELENA-3. Hours: Daily 1:00 – 3:00pm (Summer). Weekends 1:00 – 3:00pm (May, September, October). Admission: $5.00-$7.00 (age 3+).*

A one-hour horse drawn canal boat freighter ride with a narrative history of the canal system and the local area. Appearing as it did in the 1800's, the view also includes Lock IV, one of the few remaining working locks on old canal routes. Included in the tour is a Canal Museum with pictorial stories of colorful local history and canal memorabilia including tools used to build and repair canal boats.

CANTON BALLET

Canton - *605 North Market Avenue (Palace Theatre), 44702.* ***Web: www.cantonballet.com/ballet1.php****. Phone: (330) 455-7220.* Pre-professional training company performs with professional artists. Family shows like Wizard of Oz or the Nutcracker run $14.00-$22.00 for tickets.

CANTON CLASSIC CAR MUSEUM

Canton - *Market Avenue at 6th Street entrance, 44702. Phone: (330) 455-3603,* ***Web: www.cantonclassiccar.org****. Hours: Daily 10:00am – 5:00pm. Admission: $4.00-$6.00 (age 6+).* Housed in Ohio's earliest Ford-Lincoln dealership, this museum offers over 35 antique, classic and special interest cars displayed in the motif of flapper era Roaring 20's. Favorite exhibits are the Rolls Royce and celebrity cars including Queen Elizabeth's tour car, famous movie cars and Amelia Earhart's 1916 Pierce Arrow.

CANTON SYMPHONY ORCHESTRA

Canton - *2323 17th Street NW, 44702. Phone: (330) 452-2094,* ***Web: www.cantonsymphony.org***. Presents classical, holiday, pops, family and youth concerts / symphony.

PLAYERS GUILD THEATRE

Canton - *1001 North Market Avenue, 44702. Phone: (330) 453-7619,* ***Web: www.playersguildtheatre.com***. Family series presents plays based on award winning children's stories like Jungle Book and a Christmas Carol. Performances Thursday-Sunday.

MCKINLEY MUSEUM & DISCOVER WORLD

800 McKinley Monument Drive, NW (I-77 south exit 106, I-77 north exit 105, follow signs), **Canton** 44708

- Phone: (330) 455-7043, **Web: www.mckinleymuseum.org**
- Hours: Monday – Saturday 9:00am – 5:00pm, Sunday Noon – 5:00 pm (until 6:00 pm Summer). Closed major holidays.
- Admission: $6.00 adult, $5.00 senior (60+), $4.00 child (3-18).
- Miscellaneous: Planetarium.

McKinley Museum & Discover World (cont.)

After you park, take the 108 steps leading up to the bronze doors of the stunning McKinley Memorial where President William McKinley and his wife and children were laid to rest. A few steps away is the McKinley Museum where you can visit McKinley Hall, Historical Hall and the Street of Shops. Walk along the 19th Century Street of homes, general store, print shop, and doctor's office – all indoors on exhibit. Kid's eyes sparkle at the model trains and pioneer toys such as paper dolls and or mini cast- iron mini kitchen appliances. Last, but even more exciting for kids, is Discover World. A large dinosaur robot named "Alice" greets you and a real Stark County mastodon Bondo Betty is around the corner. Find hidden fossil drawers, make a fossil, look for the queen bee in a living beehive, touch a chinchilla, play a tune on tone pipes, visit Space Station Earth or be a weather forecaster – All in one afternoon!

PRO FOOTBALL HALL OF FAME

2121 George Halas Drive NW (I-77 and US 62)

Canton 44708

- Phone: (330) 456-8207, **Web: www.profootballhof.com**
- Hours: Daily 9:00am – 8:00pm (Memorial Day – Labor Day). Daily 9:00am – 5:00pm (Rest of Year). Closed Christmas Only.
- Admission: $12.00 adult , $8.00 senior (62+), $6.00 youth (14 & under), $30.00 family.
- Miscellaneous: Tailgating Snack Bar – over the counter / vending with Top Twenty Tele-trivia and QBI Call-the-Play Game. Special video presentations in the center of each room. "Located a football field away from the Hall of Fame" is The Stables Sports Restaurant (330-452-1230 or www.thestables.com).

If you're an NFL Football Fan, the anticipation builds as you enter the grounds of the sprawling Hall of Fame. At the top of the curving ramp upstairs you view the first 100 years of football with Pro Football's Birth Certificate and the oldest football (1895) available for display. Then hit some Astroturf and browse through Pro Football today and Photo Art Gallery (award winning, some amazing, photographs of football heroes in action). Older children look forward to the Enshrinement Galleries and Super Bowl Room. A newer addition to the Hall is Game Day Stadium. A 100-Yard film is shown in a two-sided rotating theater. Start at the Locker Room Show. Then the entire seating area rotates 180 degrees to the Stadium Show where you become part of a NFL game with a 2 story Cinemascope presentation. You see, hear and almost make contact with the players! What a rush!

HOOVER HISTORICAL CENTER

Canton - *1875 Easton Street NW (I-77 Portage Street/North Canton Exit), 44720.* ***Web: www.hoover.com****. Phone: (330) 499-0287, Tours: Tuesday–Sunday, 1:00, 2:00, 3:00 & 4:00pm. Closed holidays. Miscellaneous: Only known vacuum cleaner museum in the world. FREE.* See the Hoover Industry beginnings as a leather tannery. When automobiles came on the scene, W. H. Hoover searched for a new product. He bought the rights to inventor Murray Spangler's upright vacuum player cleaner and introduced it in 1908 - The Hoover Suction Sweeper Model O (On display). A short video details the history of the company. Guided tours of the farmhouse with include a display of antique vacuums. A favorite is the Kotten Suction Cleaner (1910) that requires a person to rock a bellows with their feet to create suction. An early 1900's electric vacuum weighed 100 pounds (and they advertised it as a portable!).

BLUEBIRD FARM TOY MUSEUM AND RESTAURANT

190 Alamo Road (at the bottom of the Square, take 332 south for two blocks, turn left on 3rd Street S.E.), **Carrollton** 44615

- Phone: (330) 627-7980, **Web: www.bluebird-farm.com**
- Hours: Tuesday- Sunday 11:00am - 4:00pm. Lunch served in restaurant. Dinner served on Friday and Saturday.
- Admission: Museum $2.00 adult, FREE child.
- Miscellaneous: Great reasonable gift ideas in the gift shop barn. Once every few months, they hold a Teddy Bear Tea. Christmastime is magical here.

A century old farmhouse restaurant featuring a fresh, daily menu of family-priced, old-fashioned dishes like ham loaf, swiss steak, and chicken casserole cooked only as Grandma could. Walk off your homemade dessert on the nature trail. The Toy Museum features playthings available to American children from the 1800's to the present (brightly, cleverly displayed). Look for some popular dolls like Raggedy Ann and Andy, Shirley Temple, Mickey and Minnie Mouse, and the beloved Teddy Bear...many made abroad. Ask for the scavenger hunt pages to play a game in the museum. This entire property is a wonderful haven for families...don't miss it when in Amish / Swiss area of Ohio!

ELDERBERRY LINE

Carrollton - *205 2nd Street (downtown, near SR 39 and SR 9) 44615. Phone: (330) 627-2282,* ***Web: www.elderberryline.com****. Hours: Saturday 11:00am, Sunday 1:00pm. (Mid-June – October). Admission: $12.00 adult, $9.00 child (2-12). Miscellaneous: No restroom on train. No cooling or heat. Elderberry Patch Gift Shop. 3 hours long including a one hour layover in Minerva.* The 14 mile trip (each way) between Carrollton and Minerva highlights some of Carroll County's most beautiful scenery, while giving passengers a nostalgic look at rail travel along a working railroad. The train crosses the historic "Great Trail" of the late 1700's, which opened the western frontier to the settlers of our young nation. The nickname "Elderberry Line" was given to the railroad in the 1890's due to the plentiful berry bushes that grow along the right of way.

MCCOOK HOUSE

Carrollton - *Downtown Square (west side of square), 44615.* ***Web: www.ohiohistory.org/places/mccookhse****. Phone: (330) 627-3345 or (800) 600-7172, Hours: Friday-Saturday 10:00am - 5:00pm, Sunday 1:00 - 5:00pm (Summers); Weekends only (Labor Day-mid October). Admission: $3.00 adults, $1.00 child (6-12). Miscellaneous: History of Carroll County lifestyles and industry portrayed upstairs - the clothing will appeal to girls.* The family earned the name of "Fighting McCooks" due to their extensive military service in the Civil War. Daniel McCook built this home and his family lived here until 1853. During the Civil War, Daniel's family contributed nine soldiers to the Union cause including 5 generals. Four of Daniel's family including Daniel himself died in the conflict. You're greeted by the painting in the front room. Each son and their father are portrayed. What's unique about the one son, John James I? In the hallway, you'll find an 1838 large map of Ohio. Can you find your home town or was it even around then? Look for the real tree trunk with cannon balls stuck in it from the Civil War.

ROSCOE VILLAGE

311 Hill Street (State Route 16 and 83, near US 36 - I-77 exit65))

Coshocton 43812

- Phone: (740) 622-9310 or (800) 877-1830
  Web: www.roscoevillage.com
- Hours: Daily, Most village shops open at 10:00 am Special events May – December. History Tour Buildings. Closed (January-February) for cleaning. Visitor Center daily 10:00am-5:00pm.
- Admission: "Living History Tour" $5.00-$10.00 (ages 5+). Just Browsing is FREE! Additional charge $3-$6.00 for canal boat ride.
- Tours: Daily 10:00am-3:00pm. Most beginning at 11:00am for 2 hours each. Summer tours are called Leisure Tours and are more self-guided.
- Miscellaneous: Monticello III Canal Boat-A horse drawn replica of an 1800's canal boat, offers narrated trips on the 1 1/2 mile restored section of the original Ohio-Erie Canal. 1 – 5:00pm daily from Memorial Day - Labor Day. Weekends only Labor Day to mid-October. Part of the Coshocton Park District (614) 622-7528.

Listed as "One of the 20 best sites to discover historic America" - it truly is a place that meets or exceeds your expectations. Experience life in a canal town with canal boat rides (for an additional fee) May through October. The Exhibit Hall is complete with realistic dioramas and working lock models. Watch craftsmen make brooms, weave or print. In the print shop, press your own bookmarks and postcards. Spend gobs of time in the General Store where you can play with and buy old-fashioned toys like harmonicas, paper dolls and wooden toys. Plan to have the kids bring their allowance (and you can too) because you won't be able to resist! Maybe take a lesson in the one-room school or see the trappings of the 1800's daily life in the doctor's house. The Johnson-Humrickhouse Museum is full of prehistoric American Indian tools and pottery or Ohio Pioneer house or Oriental decorative arts (Samurai swords).

During the summer, visit the Hillside where demonstrations of brick-making and woodworking take place. A family style restaurant, the rustic "Warehouse", was once a busy holding house for the transport of goods.

THE WILDS

14000 International Road (I-70 exit 155, Zanesville or exit 169, SR 83 - follow signs), **Cumberland** 43732

- Phone: (740) 638-5030, **Web: www.thewilds.org**
- Hours: Open Weekends (May 1 – Memorial Day & after Labor Day – October 31st). Wednesday – Sunday (Memorial Day – Labor Day). All hours when open 10:00am – 4:00pm.
- Admission: $12.00 adult, $11.00 senior(60+), $7.00 child (4-12). Parking fee $2.00.
- Tours: 1 hour tours in a shuttle bus - safari. School and Group Tours (20+) available almost any day (May – October).

Once a strip mine (donated by American Electric Power) it is now home to the International Center for the preservation of wild animals. Over 9000 acres of forest and grassland with 150 lakes is home to animals in a protected open range habitat (no pens, stables, and cages) designed to create an environment for reproduction. You'll see many animals you don't see in zoos like African gazelles, reticulated giraffes, mountain zebras, tundra swans and red wolves in herds. With lots of "tender loving care" and adaptation exercises, injured animals may now roam free. You might also see real wild horses that look like a rhinoceros and a horse. They are very strong and tough (yet beautiful to watch) animals.

TAPPAN LAKE RECREATION AREA

Deersville - *County Rd. 55, 84000 Mallarnee Road (12 miles Northwest of Cadiz off US 250), 44693. Phone: (740) 922-3649, **Web: www.mwcdlakes.com**.* Nature programs. 7,597 acres of camping, hiking trails, boating and rentals, fishing, swimming, visitor center, lodge or cabins and food service.

ATWOOD LAKE RESORT

Dellroy - *2650 Lodge Road (off SR 212 to SR 542 or off SR 39 entrance), 44620. Phone: (330) 735-2211 or (800) 362-6406,* ***Web: www.atwoodlakeresort.com***. Camping, hiking trails, boating & rentals, fishing, swimming, visitor center and winter sports. Beach with paddle boat rentals & food service. Dining and accommodations with indoor/outdoor pool at lodge. Comfortable, spacious 4 bedrm. cabins w/ trails! Summertime kids activities, too.

DENNISON RAILROAD DEPOT MUSEUM & CANTEEN

Dennison - *400 Center Street (off SR 250 or SR 36, Dennison exit to Second St.-turn right along tracks), 44621. Phone: (740) 922-6776 or (877) 278-8020,* ***Web: www.dennisondepot.org***. *Hours: Tuesday-Sunday 11:00am-5:00pm. Miscellaneous: Special train rides depart each season. Check website for events.* During W.W.II the Dennison Depot was located on the National Railway Defense Route. It was the main stopping point on the route because it was the exact mid-point between Columbus and Pittsburgh. One evening, a town's lady noticed the servicemen seemed sad, so she organized a few other friends to start a GI canteen. The community became so popular among the soldiers that it was called Dreamsville, USA. The canteen for WWII servicemen is now used as a museum of local history, a gift shop, an old fashioned candy counter and a theme restaurant. Lunch served at the Canteen Restaurant, a unique 1940s family restaurant offering Victory Garden Salads and Dreamsville Desserts (groups: ask about the 'hobo lunch' served in a souvenir bandana). Small admission to the museum includes kids being able to ring a steam locomotive bell, swing a lantern, climb a caboose and watch trains run on the model train layout.

BROAD RUN CHEESEHOUSE

Dover - *6011 County Road 139 NW (4 miles west of I-77, old SR 39), 44622. Phone: (330) 343-4108 or (800) 332-3358,* ***Web: www.broadruncheese.com***. *Admission: $1.50 per person (age 5+). Tours: Monday – Saturday (Mornings), by reservation usually. 20 minutes long with samples. Miscellaneous: Gift Shop with novelties, cheese and sausage.* Not just a window view but an actual tour of Swiss, Baby Swiss, Brick, and Muenster productions. They make 640,000 pounds of cheese from 8,000,000 pounds *(yes, pounds!)* of milk each year. After your factory tour you can sample cheese and as a souvenir, get an official cheesemaker paper cap (the one you wore during the tour). What happens to the cream that is separated off from the cheese? (hint: its made into another tasty product). Ever seen thick, warm milk cut into cubes? (forms "curds" and "whey"). What makes the holes?

WARTHER CARVINGS TOUR

331 Karl Avenue (I-77 to exit 83 to State Route 211 east)

Dover 44622

- Phone: (330) 343-7513, **Web: www.warthers.com**
- Hours: Daily 9:00am – 5:00pm (March – November)
  Daily 10:00am – 4:00pm (December – February)
- Admission: $8.50 adult, $4.00 student (6-17).
- Tours: Last tour begins one hour before closing.
- Miscellaneous: Tree of Pliers – 500 interconnecting pairs of working pliers carved out of 1 piece of walnut wood!
  Mrs. Warther's Button Collection – Over 70,000 in museum! Gift Shop and garden trails. Short videos throughout the tour keep it interesting.

A must see tour of the visions of a master craftsman! Mr. Warther started carving at age 5 with a pocketknife while milking cows and during breaks working at a mill. Before your tour begins, take a peek into the original 1912 workshop or at the display of wood carved postcards. A favorite carving of ours was the steel mill (3 x 5 feet) with moving parts depicting the foreman raising a sandwich to eat, and another worker sleeping on the job. The Abraham Lincoln Funeral Train has thousands of mechanized movements powered by a sewing machine motor. See models of steam locomotives and trains using mostly walnut, ivory, and arguto (oily wood) for moving parts which still run without repairs for over 60 years! He was dissatisfied with the knives that were available, so he developed his own line of cutlery, which is still sold today. The late Mr. Warther loved entertaining children with his carvings *(George actually met him in 1970)* and he would carve a pair of working pliers with just a few cuts in a piece of wood in only a few seconds! Now, one of the family members still carves pliers for each child visiting. This is "Where enthusiasm is caught, not taught." Truly amazing!

BEAVER CREEK STATE PARK

East Liverpool - *12021 Echo Dell Road (8 miles North of East Liverpool off State Route 7), 43920. Phone: (330) 385-3091,* ***Web: www.dnr.state.oh.us/parks/parks/beaverck.htm***. 3,038 acres of camping, hiking trails, fishing and winter sports. The park includes Little Beaver Creek, a state and national wild and scenic river, and acres of forest wilderness. The rich history of the area invites visitors to explore Gaston's Mill, pioneer village and abandoned canal locks.

MUSEUM OF CERAMICS

East Liverpool - *400 East 5th Street, 43920. Phone: (330) 386-6001or (800) 600-7880,* ***Web: www.ohiohistory.org/places/ceramics***, *Hours: Wednesday-Saturday 9:30am-5:00pm, Sunday and holidays Noon-5:00pm (May-December). Weekends only (March-April). Admission: $6.00 adult, $2.00 child (6-12).* The exhibits in the museum depict the growth and development of East Liverpool and its ceramic industry from 1840 to 1930, the period when the city's potteries produced over 50% of the ceramics manufactured in the United States. Displays cover good and bad times of the ceramic industry and the effects on its people. Life- sized dioramas of kiln, jigger and decorating shops with a collection of old and new ceramics make the museum easy to follow. Slide presentation.

LONGABERGER MUSEUM & FACTORY TOUR

5563 Raiders Road (on State Route 16)

Frazeysburg 43822

- Phone: (740) 322-5588, **Web: www.longaberger.com**
- Hours: Monday – Saturday 9:00am – 5:00pm. Sunday Noon - 5:00pm. Extended hours in the spring and summer and during special events. Closed holidays.
- Admission: FREE

- ❑ Tours: Arrive before 1:00 pm (Monday – Friday) to see actual production. No production on Saturday or Sunday. Weaving demonstrations daily in the Gallery with same setup as one of the factory stations.
- ❑ Miscellaneous: Their festivals at the Homestead are first class (check their website for events). Gift shops with tour baskets & eateries.

CORPORATE HEADQUARTERS: (State Route 16) Newark. A giant 7-story Market Basket design with towering heated handles (to melt the winter ice) on top and painted / stenciled to look like wood. Incredible!

HOMESTEAD: Gift shops with tour baskets for sale, lots of home furnishings and eateries. Their festivals are first class (check website for events). Tour a replica of the Longaberger Family Home where Dave grew up with his 11 brothers and sisters. JW's workshop may be toured also. The Make a Basket Shop (Crawford Barn) is where you can pay a fee to actually create your own hardwood maple Longaberger basket with the help of a Master artisan (takes one hour).

FACTORY TOURS: Fascinating tours and lots to see in this tiny little town. Longaberger - manufacturers high quality, handmade hard maple baskets. The one-quarter mile long factory is home to 1000 weavers who make over 100,000 baskets per week (each initialed and dated). It's best to watch a 13 minute video of the company's history and the manufacturing process that takes sugar maple logs (poached and debarked) that are cut and cuts them into long thin strips. You'll be mesmerized when you go upstairs to the mezzanine to view 400 crafters, each with their own station, weaving damp wood strips around "forms", Each basket takes about 20-30 minutes to make. Can you guess what a weaving horse is?

"LOOK, THINK AND DO CLUB". Ages 8 and up can adventure out into the local nature areas with a guide and provided backpack for each child (usually summertime and special events only). All children (any age) can romp around at the club's headquarters… "The Lookout Treehouse" (located within the Homestead). Listen to the owl and the sights and sounds of nature. Great gift ideas here too.

GNADENHUTTEN MUSEUM AND PARK

352 South Cherry Street (I-77 to SR 36 east)

Gnadenhutten 44629

- Phone: (740) 254-4143, **Web: www.tusco.net/gnaden**
- Hours: Monday-Saturday 10:00am-5:00pm, Sunday 1:00-5:00pm (June-August). Weekends only (September-October).
- Admission: $0.50-$1.00 donation.
- Miscellaneous: A 'friendly' cemetery tour on the premises. Look at the graves tombstone hands- why are they turned in different directions- what does it mean?

Gnadenhutten (Huts of Grace) was settled five months after Schoenbrunn on October 9, 1772. Joshua, a Moravian Mohican Elder, brought a large group of Christian Mohican Indians from Pennsylvania to this location. This settlement grew rapidly and the group worked hard and prospered, their standard of living was high for that era on the frontier, their cabins had glass windows, basements, they used pewter household utensils, they were adept in crafts and artwork, and loved music. It was here that the Roth child (1st white baby in this territory) was born, July 4, 1773. All went well until the Revolutionary War began and the English at Detroit wanted all Indians to fight against the Americans. The local Indians refused. When they would not leave, in September 1781, troops and Indian warriors rounded up all the Indians living in New Schoenbrunn, Gnadenhutten, and Salem and took them to Captives town. During the winter in the captive town many died of diseases. Permission to go home was granted to 150. They arrived back home in February 1782 and were gathering food and belongings, when Pennsylvania Militiamen under Colonel Williamson surrounded them. After a night of prayer and hymn singing, ninety men, women and children were massacred, then all cabins were set afire on March 8, 1782. Two boys escaped to warn others and to tell the story. See the sites of the two buildings where the Indians spent the night before their death. Those buildings, the Mission House and Cooper Shop (the actual basement foundation where one boy hid - it will take your breath away!), have been restored and are located on their original sites. The story of the massacre is told in the outdoor drama "Trumpet in the Land".

QUAIL HOLLOW STATE PARK

Hartville - *Congress Lake Road (2 miles North of Hartville), 44632.* ***Web: www.dnr.state.oh.us/parks/parks/quailhlw.htm.*** *Phone: (330) 877-6652.* Quail Hollow is a landscape of rolling meadows, marshes, pine and deciduous woodland trails surrounding a 40-room manor. Now called the Natural History Study Center, the former Stewart family home is primarily used for educational, nature-oriented and community activities. The home is open on weekends 1:00-5:00 pm. Bridle trails. 700 acres of hiking trails, winter sports.

GUILFORD LAKE STATE PARK

Lisbon - *(6 miles Northwest of Lisbon off State Route 172), 44432.* ***Web: www.dnr.state.oh.us/parks/parks/guilford.htm.*** *Phone: (330) 222-1712.* Guilford Lake State Park is a quiet fishing lake located in northeastern Ohio on the west fork of the Little Beaver Creek. The gentle rolling terrain of the area offers a serene escape for park visitors year round. 488 acres of camping, boating, fishing, swimming and winter sports.

ELSON FLOURING MILL

Magnolia - *261 North Main Street (SR 183, southwest edge of town), 44643. Phone: (330) 866-3353. Tours Every Thursday at 10:00 am and 2:00 pm, April through November. Admission is $2.00 per person.* Corn meal has been made at the mill since 1834 and can still be purchased today.

GUGGISBERG CHEESE FACTORY

5060 State Route 557 (Off State Route 39, I-77 exit 83)

Millersburg 44654

- Phone: (330) 893-2500, **Web: www.guggisberg.com**
- Hours: Monday-Saturday 8:00am – 6:00pm, Sunday 11:00 am – 4:00pm) (April – December). Monday-Saturday 8:00am – 5:00pm (December – March)

Home of the original Baby Swiss – you can watch through a window as cheese is being made (best time to view is 8:00 am – 2:00 pm weekdays). We learned milk is brought in the early mornings from neighboring Amish farms. Cultures and enzymes are added to form curd. Curd is pressed into molds and brine salted. Each cheese is aged at least a month for flavor. A short video is always playing that details this process if you can't view it personally.

ROLLING RIDGE RANCH

Millersburg - *3961 County Road 168 (State Route 62 to CR 168), 44654. Phone: (330) 893-3777. Hours: Monday – Saturday 9:00am – 1 hour before sunset.* Take a 2-mile safari ride in your own vehicle or a horse drawn wagon to see over 300 animals from 6 continents. Feed the animals from the vehicle and stop by the petting zoo before you leave.

YODER'S AMISH HOME

Millersburg - *6050 State Route 515 (between Trail and Walnut Creek), 44654. Phone: (330) 893-2541. Hours: Monday-Saturday 10:00am-5:00pm (mid-April thru October). Admission: Tours $3.50 Adult, $1.50 Children (under 12). Buggy Rides $2.00 Adult, $1.00 Children (under 12).* One home was built in 1866 and shows authentic furnishings from that period. Learn what a "hoodle stup" is. Then step into an 1885 barn with animals to pet. Most popular tends to be the turkeys – (Yes, you can try to pet turkeys!). Buggy rides are given by retired real Amish farmers who are personable and tell stories during the ride.

JOHN & ANNIE GLENN HISTORIC SITE & EXPLORATION CENTER

*New Concord - 68 West Main Street (I-70 to New Concord exit, across from library), 43762. Web: **www.johnglennhome.org**. Phone: (740) 826-3305, Hours: Wednesday-Saturday 10:00am-3:00pm, Sunday 1:00-4:00pm. Closed major holidays. Admission: $4.00 adult, $3.00 senior, $1.50 child (under 13).* John Glenn, astronaut and politician, spent his boyhood in this home that has been moved and restored to its late 1930's appearance as a museum dedicated to telling 20th century American history through the lives of John and Annie Glenn. John Glenn's brand of heroism is steeped in small-town values. These values, along with patriotism, public service, and commitment to family are interpreted at the museum. "Grit is the theme of the museum," according to The New York Times.

SCHOENBRUNN VILLAGE STATE MEMORIAL

State Route 259, East High Avenue (4 miles East of I-77 exit 81)

New Philadelphia 44663

- Phone: (330) 339-3636 or (800) 752-2711
  Web: www.ohiohistory.org/places/shoenbr
- Hours: Monday – Saturday 9:30am – 5:00pm. Sunday Noon – 5:00pm (Summer); Weekends Only (September and October)
- Admission: $6.00 adult, $2.00 child (6-12)
- Miscellaneous: Museum. Video orientation. Gift Shop. Picnic facilities. A special, interactive event is usually held one Saturday each month. Tape recorded tours available at no extra cost.

Take a self-guided tour of the reconstructed log building village founded by a Moravian missionary in 1772. The Moravian church founded Schoenbrunn ("beautiful spring") as a mission to the Delaware Indians. Being the first settlement in Ohio, Schoenbrunn claims the first civil code, the first church (learn about the love feast still occasionally held here, esp. near Christmas), and the first school. Problems associated with the American Revolution prompted Schoenbrunn's closing in 1777. Today the reconstructed village includes seventeen log buildings and gardens...many occupied by costumed interpreters demonstrating period crafts and customs.

TRUMPET IN THE LAND

New Philadelphia - *Schoenbrunn Amphitheatre (-77 to Exit 81), 44663.* ***Web: http://web.tusco.net/trumpet.*** *Phone: (330) 339-1132, Hours: Daily (except Sunday) 8:30 pm (mid-June to late August). Admission: $15.00 adult, $13.00 senior, $7.00 child (under 12). Miscellaneous: Read our write-up on Gnadenhutten to review more detailed history of this saga before you go.* In an Ohio Frontier setting (the first settlement at Schoenbrunn), meet historical characters like David Zeisgerber (missionary converting Indians), Simon Girtz (renegade), Captain Pipe (young warrior who hated white men) and John Heikewelder (explorer)...all vital historical figures in the founding of Ohio. The

Revolutionary War breaks out and Moravian Indian Christians would not take sides. Feel their stress and desires to try to remain neutral in a hostile environment. Sadly, in the end, American militia brutally massacre 90 Christian Indians at Gnadenhutten.

TUSCORA PARK

New Philadelphia - *South Broadway Street (I-77 to US 250 east) 44663. Phone: (800) 527-3387.* ***Web: www.tuscora.park.net****. Summertime hours: Weekday evenings, weekend Noon to dark.* The central feature is the antique big carousel or the summer showcase concert series or swimming pool. What draws little ones and families is also the Ferris wheel, 6-8 kiddie rides (including a train ride and mini roller coaster), batting cages and putt-putt - all at low prices. Most rides are 50 cents and activities are around $1.00. Great alternative to higher priced amusement "vacations".

USS RADFORD NATIONAL NAVAL MUSEUM

Newcomerstown - *228 W. Canal Street (I-77 exit 65, US 36 west, turn left on Canal St), 43832. Phone: (740) 498-4446,* ***www.ussradford446.org****. Hours: Tuesday-Saturday 12:30-3:00pm, Sunday 1:00-4:00pm (Memorial Day-Labor Day). Open other times by reservation. Admission: $2.00 adult, $1.00 child (Elementary School age).* The 446's Admirals, WW II souvenirs, 50 foot 3-D diorama "Rescue at Kula Gulf" with full size cruise ship, D.A.S.H. helicopter from Vietnam War (with radio controls), DesRon 21 ship displays, and the only part of USS Helena CL 50 left and items from pockets of men that abandoned ship.

HARRY LONDON CHOCOLATE FACTORY

North Canton - *5353 Lauby Road (I-77 Exit 113 Airport), 44720.* ***Web: www.harry-london.com****. Phone: (330) 494-0833 or (800) 321-0444. Tours: Monday – Saturday 9:00am – 4:00pm. (Actual production only on weekdays). Tour: 45 minutes – 1 hour. Reservations suggested (if group tour). Every half hour. Miscellaneous: Chocolate Hall of Fame, Candy Store.* Learn about cocoa beans and the history of chocolate (we didn't know the beans grow in pods on trunks of trees near the equator). Live the fantasy of making, molding, wrapping, and boxing chocolate candy, fudge, and butterscotch. Be sure to try a London Mint (money wrapped candy) or a London Buckeye. Small admission per person (age 6+).

MAPS AIR MUSEUM

North Canton - *5359 Massillon Road, Akron-Canton Airport (I-77 to Exit 113), 44720.* ***Web: www.mapsairmuseum.org***. *Phone: (330) 896-6332. Hours: Monday-Saturday 9:00am – 4:00pm and Wednesday evenings until 9:00pm. Admission: $2-4.00.* The staff here are pilots, mechanics, officers, and crew who desire to preserve the legacy of America's aviation heritage. Their slogan "Rebuilding History – One Rivet At a Time" really describes their dedication to acquire and renovate some of the world's greatest military aircraft. MAPS offers not just displays of mint condition aircraft, but also a truly unique "hands on" view of the restoration of some of the world's greatest aircraft by people who may have flown them years ago.

NATIONAL ROAD ZANE GREY MUSEUM

8850 East Pike (U.S. 40 / I-70 Norwich Exit)

Norwich 43767

- Phone: (740) 872-3143 or (800) 752-2602
  Web: www.ohiohistory.org/places/natlroad
- Hours: Monday – Saturday 9:30am – 5:30pm, Sunday & Holidays Noon – 5:00pm (May – September). Wednesday-Sunday (closed holidays) only (March, April, October and November).
- Admission: $6.00 adult, $2.00 child (6 – 12).

"Head West Young Man" in a Conestoga wagon as you explore the history of US-40 National Road. Built based on a concept of George Washington, it stretches between western territories in Illinois to the eastern state of Maryland. It was vital to the development of the frontier heading west and later called "America's Main Street". Play a game where children locate all the different types of bridges on this route (examples: the "Y" and "S" Bridge). The facility also commemorates author Zane Grey and his western novels and the area's ceramic heritage.

ROBINSON RANSBOTTOM POTTERY

Ransbottom Road (State Route22 south to State Route 93 south to County Road 102 east - Follow signs), **Roseville** 43777

- Phone: (740) 697-7355, **Web: www.ransbottompottery.com**
- Tours: Weekdays 9:00am - 2:00pm (except for 2 week plant shutdown in the summers and holidays).
  Guided - By Reservation, Self-guided tours are no appointment necessary. Weekends watch the video tour.
- Miscellaneous: Pot Shop Gift Shop with below-retail prices

Their clay is a special combination of top and bottom clay (what material lies in the middle but isn't used for pottery?). They use 27 tons of clay daily using the processes of casting, ram and spindle pressing, and jiggering. During the tour, you come very near the process, including hot kilns and large press machines. Stay in groups and hold onto small children. Talking with mold castors and watching clay being molded was most interesting. Also very interesting were the beehive kilns (look like brick igloos). Once the items were loaded, the man sealed the doorway with bricks. The pieces are left to heat dry for three days and then four days cooling. This kiln is used for large outdoor pieces (birdbaths, flower pots) that need slow hardening for durability against elements.

SENECAVILLE LAKE RECREATION AREA

Senacaville - *(3 miles Southeast of Senecaville on State Route 547), 43780. Phone: (740) 685-6013.* Nature programs. 7,613 acres of camping, hiking trails, boating and rentals, fishing, swimming, visitor center and cabins.

JEFFERSON LAKE STATE PARK

Steubenville - *(16 miles Northwest of Steubenville of State Route 43), 43944.* ***Web: www.dnr.state.oh.us/parks/parks/jefferso.htm.*** *Phone: (740) 765-4459.* In the sandstone bedrock can be found layers of coal which were formed by decaying swamp vegetation. 933 acres of camping, rough hiking trails, boating, fishing, swimming and winter sports.

CREEGAN COMPANY ANIMATION FACTORY

510 Washington Street (I-70 to State Route 7 North)

Steubenville 43952

- Phone: (740) 283-3708, **Web: www.creegans.com**
- Tours: Reservations Preferred. (45 minute tour). Monday – Friday, 10:00am-4:00pm. Saturday, 10:00am-2:00pm. Walking on three levels with stairs.
- Miscellaneous: Christmas Shop (year round). Retail store sells Creegan's most recent animated figures and scenery.

Start with the Craft Area where ribbon, yarn, and puppet props abound everywhere. Then, to the Art Department where workers paint faces on molded plastic heads and make costumes. (To make the plastic heads they use a machine press that uses molds to form faces out of sheets of plain white plastic.) In the sculpting area, shelves of hundreds of character head, feet, and hand molds line the walls and a woman sculpts new molds. Finally, peek inside some of the bodies of automated figures to view the electronics that produce body movements (some are a little scary for young ones). A costumed mascot (Beary Bear) greets and guides your pre-arranged tour of Animation "Behind the Scenes". Their theme is "We Make Things Move" and they're the nation's largest manufacturer of animated and costumed characters. (Some customers are Hershey Park and Disney World).

FERNWOOD STATE FOREST

Steubenville - *(north of SR-151, southwest of Steubenville), 43952. Phone: (330) 339-2205 (New Philadelphia office),* ***Web: www.dnr.state.oh.us/forestry/Forests/stateforests/fernwood.htm.*** *Open daily 6:00 am - 11:00pm.* 3,023 acres in Jefferson County. 3 mile hiking trail, several picnic areas, 22 family campsites (no fee).

JAGGIN' AROUND & WELSH JAGUAR CLASSIC CAR MUSEUM

Steubenville - *501 Washington Street (off Route 7 - Downtown), 43952.* ***Web: www.welshent.com/museum.htm****. Phone: (740) 282-1010.* Modern art deco décor restaurant serving lunch / dinner and kid's meals served in cardboard classic cars. Attached is the

Welsh Jaguar Classic Car Museum. See William Welsh's celebration of the "Glory Days of the Jaguar" that features classic XKs and XKEs. See a Mercedes Gull Wing and 60's Muscle cars.

STEUBENVILLE CITY OF MURALS

Steubenville - *501 Washington Street (CVB offices - maps), 43952. Phone: (740) 282-0938 or (800) 510-4442.* ***Web: www.steubenvilleoh.com****. Tours: Guided tours are available (admission) that includes other tourist spots in the area.* During a self-guided tour (free) you can see 25 giant full color (almost 3D) murals with the theme "Preserving a Piece of America" on the sides of downtown buildings. Each has its own name with some of the most interesting being Stanton Park, Ohio River Oil Company and Steam Laundry – these all "jump" right off the wall and appear almost like a photograph.

ALPINE HILLS MUSEUM

Sugarcreek - *106 West Main Street, 44681. Phone: (888) 609-7592. Hours: Daily 10:00am – 4:30pm, except Sundays (April – November). Extended summer hours. Donation accepted.* 3 floors of Swiss, German and Amish heritage. Many audio-visuals & push buttons "spotlight" parts of well-explained dioramas of an Amish kitchen, Swiss cheesehouse and a woodshop & printshop. Nearby, the best swiss steak & mashed potatoes in town are at the Swiss Hat restaurant – www.swisshat@tusco.net.

DAVID WARTHER MUSEUM

Sugarcreek - *1387 State Route 39 (In the Dutch Valley Complex) 44681.* ***Web: www.ivorybuyer.com/museum1.htm*** *Phone: (330) 852-3455. Hours: Monday-Saturday 9:00am-5:00pm (Closed major holidays). Admission: $4.00 (age 17+).* David Warther II is the grandson of Ernest Warther (see separate listing "Warther Carvings Tour"). He continues the legacy of carvings with a special emphasis on carving the theme "The History of the Ship" – solid legal ivory model ships. Even the rig lines are carved of ivory (one strand measures 1/10,000th of an inch in diameter). Know what "scrimshaw" is? David's workshop is on location (see him with next "work in progress"). Kids will absolutely love David's stories and his early boat carvings! Boat kits are for sale, too.

OHIO CENTRAL RAILROAD

Sugarcreek - *111 Factory Street, 44681. Phone: (330) 852-4676 or (866) 850-4676.* ***Web: www.amishsteamtrain.com****. Admission: $9.00 adult, $6.00 child (3-12). Tours: Monday-Saturday departures at 11:00am, 12:30pm, 2:00pm, 3:30pm (early May-end of October).* A one hour steam train ride through Amish Country. You can see farmers tilling their fields with horse and plow and doing other farm chores the old fashioned way. Just sit back and enjoy the peaceful Amish countryside from your passenger coach window.

COBLENTZ CHOCOLATE COMPANY

Walnut Creek - *4917 State Route 515 and State Route 39, 44687. Phone: (330) 893-2995 or (800) 338-9341. Hours: Monday – Saturday 9:00am – 6:00pm (June – October). Close at 5:00pm (November-May).* Watch through the kitchen windows as chocolate is stirred in large vats with automatic paddle stirs. Caramels, fruits, and nuts are hand dipped and layered on large trays to cool and dry. Also, see molds for chocolate forms used to create bars of barks and holiday shapes. Savor the sweet smell of fresh milk and dark chocolate as you decide which treats to buy. Our favorite was the chocolate covered Dutch pretzels with sprinkles or nuts on top.

ALPINE - ALPA

Wilmot - *1504 US 62, 44689. Phone: (330) 359-5454 or (800) 546-2572. Hours: Daily 9:00am - 8:00pm (Spring - Thanksgiving). Serving lunch and dinner beginning at 11:00am.* This is home of the "World's Largest Cuckoo Clock". The Guinness Book of World Records has it listed as 23 ½ feet high, 24 feet long and 13 ½ feet wide. Trudy, a life-size mannequin with a German accent, opens shutters to greet you. The Swiss Village Market has viewing windows (to watch cheese-making), restaurants and shops. Look for the 40-foot diorama with waterfalls and a moving train.

BUGGY HAUS

Winesburg - *County Road 160 (off Route 62), 44690. Phone: None (Amish). Hours: Monday – Saturday 8:00am – 5:00pm.* See the world's largest buggy or take a one hour guided tour of a working Amish buggy shop and three floors of warehouse and displays. You'll see over 500 units of buggies, carts, sleighs, and wooden riding horses for sale. Climb aboard them to test them out. Their tour includes the history and cultural differences of buggies around the country.

OHIO AGRICULTURAL RESEARCH AND DEVELOPMENT CENTER

1680 Madison Ave (off I-71 exit SR 83 or US 30), **Wooster** 44691

- Phone: (330) 202-3503 or (330) 263-3700
  Web: www.oardc.ohio-state.edu
- Hours: Monday – Friday 7:30am - 4:30pm (Summer). Monday – Friday 8:00am - 5:00pm (September – June).
- Admission: FREE
- Tours: Guided tours for groups of 10+ by appointment. Self guided maps at visitor center.

This center is the foremost, nationally known agricultural research Ohio State University facility with inventions to their credit such as crop dusting and adding vitamin D to milk. Many experiments on insects, greenhouses, honeybees and composting are going on. See how animals are raised, how the right wheat is important for successful bread making (maybe make some), how laser beams detect the size of water droplets in pesticide applications, and how a jellyfish gene can help soybean scientists. Most importantly, they teach you how agriculture impacts everyone-everyday. If self-guided tours are your option, you can see the Center which contains some activities for children such as a microscope and computer display as well as the bug zoo. You can also visit the 88 acre Secrest Arboretum which has many walking trails and a children's play area. This might spark the future scientist within your child.

WAYNE COUNTY HISTORICAL SOCIETY MUSEUM

Wooster - *546 East Bowman Street, 44691. Phone: (330) 264-8856,* ***Web:*** ***www.waynehistorical.org****. Hours: Wednesday – Sunday 2:00 – 4:30pm. Closed January and holidays. Admission $3.00 (age 15+).*

Early 1800's Carriage Barn, Log Cabin (early settlers home life), Schoolhouse (McGuffy Readers, dunce cap and stool, and potbelly stove, it accurately recreates the atmosphere of a late 1800's learning center), Indians, Women's Vintage Dress Shop, and Outdoor Bake Oven (typical of the massive outdoor ovens which were once found on virtually all German farms in the area during the 19th century).

LORENA STERNWHEELER

Zanesville - *Moored at Zane's Landing Park (West End of Market Street – I-70 to Downtown Zanesville Exit – Follow signs), 43701.* ***Web: www.visitzanesville.com/lorena.htm****. Phone: (740) 455-8883 or (800) 246-6303. Hours: Tuesday – Sunday at 1:00, 2:30, and 4:00pm (June – August). Weekends Only (September to mid-October). Admission: $6.00 adult, $5.00 senior, $3.00 child (2-12).* There was a mythical sweetheart of the Civil War named Lorena who inspired a song written by the famous Zanesvillian, Rev. Henry Webster. The 104' long, 59-ton boat was christened "Lorena" after that popular song. A one-hour cruise on the Muskingum River at a very reasonable rate.

MAPLETREE BASKETS

Zanesville - *705 Keen Street, 43701. Phone: (740) 450-8824 or (888) 2BASKET.* ***Web: www.mapletreebaskets.com****. Hours: Weekdays 8:00am-5:00pm. Saturday by appointment. Manufacturing tours given for groups of 12 or more by advanced reservation only.* Watch local artisans hand weave fine quality maple hard wood baskets.

MUSKINGUM RIVER PARKWAY STATE PARK

Zanesville - *(120 acres along 80 miles of the Muskingum River extending from Devola to Ellis Locks), 43702. Phone: (740) 452-3820,* ***Web: www.dnr.state.oh.us/parks/parks/muskngmr.htm****.* The Muskingum River is formed by the confluence of the Walhonding and Tuscarawas rivers in Coshoction flowing south through Zanesville where it joins the Licking River. The river travels 112 miles in all and its 10 locks are still hand-operated in the same manner as 150 years ago. Visitors are offered camping, hiking trails, boating, and fishing.

BLUE ROCK STATE PARK

Zanesville - *(12 miles Southeast of Zanesville off State Route 60 and County Road 45), 43720. Phone: (740) 674-4794,* ***Web: www.dnr.state.oh.us/parks/parks/bluerock.htm***. Rugged hills and rich green forests provide 350 acres of camping, hiking trails, boating, fishing, swimming and winter sports.

DILLON STATE PARK

Zanesville - *(8 miles west of Zanesville off State Route 146), 43830.* ***Web: www.dnr.state.oh.us/parks/parks/dillon.htm***. *Phone: (740) 453-4377.* The wooded hills and valleys of the area offer outdoor adventure with 7690 acres of camping, hiking trails, boating and rentals, fishing, swimming (sandy beaches), and winter sports. Family deluxe cottages with A/C and cable. Nearby, in the Blackhand Gorge, carved by the Licking River, a sandstone cliff bore a soot blackened (Black Hand Sandstone) engraving of a human hand. This mysterious petroglyph is thought to have served as a guide marker for Indians searching for Flint Ridge.

ZOAR VILLAGE

Zoar - *198 Main Street (State Route 212 – I-77 to Exit 93), 44697.* ***Web: www.ohiohistory.org/places/zoar.*** *Phone: (800) 262-6195 or (330) 874-3011. Hours: Wednesday – Saturday 9:30am – 5:00pm, Sunday – Holidays Noon – 5:00 pm (Summer). Weekends Only (April, May, September, October). Restricted hours for FREE Museum. Admission: $6.00 adult, $2.00 child (6-12). Miscellaneous: Video presentation first explains Zoar history. Probably best to tour as a group with an emphasis on early Ohio home and community life (w/German-American heritage) theme.* Zoar means "a sanctuary from evil". They, as a society of Separatists (separation between church and state), were known for their bountiful gardening designs based on the bible. The 12 block district of 1800's homes and shops include a dairy, bakery, museum, gardens, storehouse, tin shops, wagon shops, and blacksmith. They are actual original buildings in a real town of 75 families. Walk along streets dispersed with restored residences and shops for modern clients.

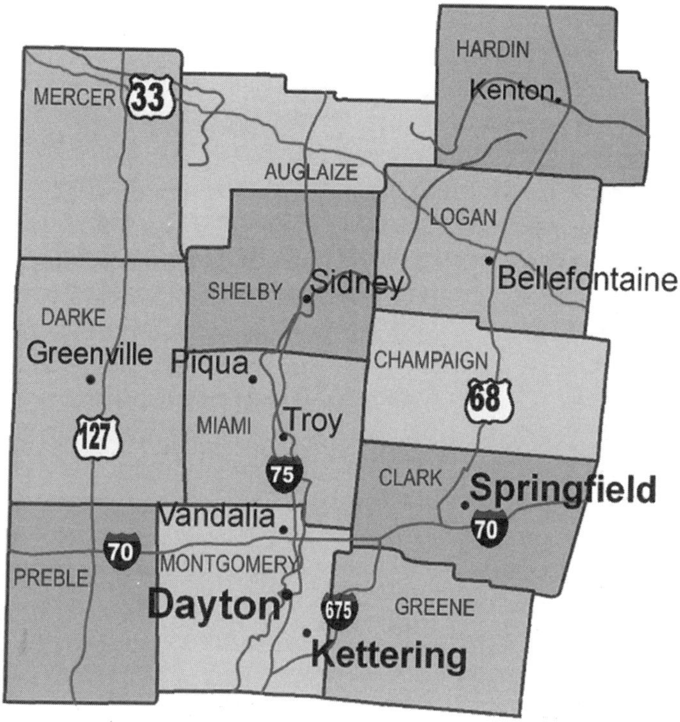

Chapter 3
Central West Area

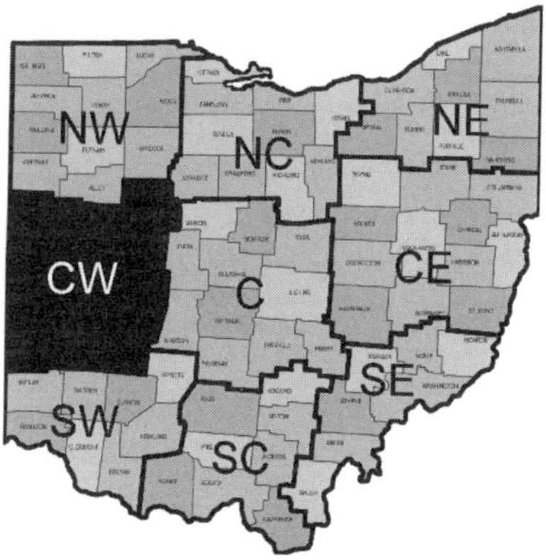

Our Favorites...

Blue Jacket / Tecumseh History

Boonshoft Museum of Discovery

Carillon Historical Park

Freshwater Farms

Piqua Historical Area

Sunwatch

United States Air Force Museum

Young's Jersey Dairy Farm

Tecumseh's Chair

ZANE SHAWNEE CAVERNS

Bellefontaine - *7092 State Route 540 (5 miles east of town), 43311.* ***Web: www.zaneshawneecaverns.org****. Phone: (937) 592-9592. Hours: Daily 9:00am - 5:00 pm. Admission: Caverns $7.00 adult, $4.00 child (under age 12). Museum $6.00 adult, $4.00 child. Cavern & Museum Combo Rate. Miscellaneous:There are a lot of extras like hayrides, gift shop, snack bar, and camping. Remember to dress appropriately because the temperature in the caverns is a constant 48-50 degrees F. The tour and slide show lasts about 45 minutes.* See crystals in objects formed like straws, draperies, and popcorn. They boast the only "cave pearls" found in Ohio. This property is now owned and operated by the Shawnee People. The Museum has artifacts from actual tribe members and some from prehistoric Indian digs (Hopewell, Ancient). Separate display cases give a special look to other Native American cultural areas including: Great Lakes Tribes, Northern Iroquois, Southwestern Tribes, Great plains, Southeastern Tribes and the Eskimo People. Also on display is the evolution of corn - Zea Maize to modern corn and Native American weapons along with several dioramas.

MERCER COUNTY HISTORICAL SOCIETY MUSEUM

Celina - *130 East Market Street, 45822. Phone: (419) 586-6065. Hours: Wednesday – Friday 8:30am – 4:00pm (summer), Sunday 1:00 – 4:00pm (October – April). Free.* Chronicles the past 200 years of Indian artifacts and antique transportation. Riley House. Nearby is the Courthouse and beautiful stairs where you look up at the colored glass dome.

CLIFTON MILL

75 Water Street (I-70 West to SR 72 South)

Clifton 45316

- Phone: (937) 767-5501, **Web: www.cliftonmill.com**
- Hours: Monday – Friday 9:00am – 4:00pm, Saturday – Sunday 8:00am – 4:00pm, Restaurant closes one hour earlier. (November-March). Weekdays 9:00am-5:00pm, Weekends 8:00am-6:00pm (April-October). Closed Christmas, New Year's, Easter & Thanksgiving Day. ** Please note December hours they close the restaurant at 2:00 pm and giftshop at 3:00 pm.

- ❑ Admission: Restaurant serves kids meals around $3.00-$5.00. Adult meals are double.
- ❑ Miscellaneous: Restaurant and store. Walk off your meal by parking down the road at Clifton Gorge Nature Preserve and "hiking" the small sand/gravel walkway past bridges and on platforms that give you a "crows nest" view of the gorge – beautiful!

A surprise treat tucked away in a small town where Woody Hayes grew up. Built in 1802 on the Little Miami River, it is the largest operating water powered gristmill in the nation. Before or after a yummy breakfast or lunch overlooking the river, take a self-guided tour for a small fee. There are 5 floors to view. The 3rd floor (main operations) is where you see how everything on the other floors above and below come together. The turbine takes the flowing water's energy to move a system of belts to the grindstones. As the stones rotate, raw grain is poured into the hopper, through a chute and into a space between the stones which grind it. The most interesting part of the tour is the belt to bucket elevators that are the "life of the mill" transporting grain and flour up and down 5 levels. Restaurant seating with a view of a waterwheel, river and covered bridge. Pancakes, mush, grits and bread are made from product produced at the mill. Best pork barbecue sandwich ever! Breakfast and lunch only. Be sure to buy some pancake mix to take home!

DAYTON SPORTS

Dayton -

DAYTON BOMBERS HOCKEY - Erwin J. Nutter Center, Fairborn. (937) 775-4747 or **www.daytonbombers.com**. East Coast Hockey League.

DAYTON DRAGONS BASEBALL - Fifth Third Field. (937) 228-BATS or **www.daytondragons.com**. Class A team.

PAUL LAWRENCE DUNBAR STATE MEMORIAL

219 N. Paul Lawrence Dunbar St (2 blocks N of 3rd St, E of US35), **Dayton** 45401

- ❑ Phone: (937) 224-7061 or (800) 860-0148
  Web: www.ohiohistory.org/places/dunbar
- ❑ Hours: Wednesday – Saturday 9:30am – 4:30pm, Sunday & Holidays Noon – 4:30pm (Memorial Day – Labor Day). Weekends Only (September, October).

- Admission: $3.00 Adult, $2.00 child (6-12).

The restored home of the first African American to achieve acclaim in American literature. From a young poet at age 6 to a nationally known figure (until his death at age 33 of tuberculosis), the guide helps you understand his inspiration especially from his mother and her stories of slavery. Personal belongings like his bicycle built by the Wright Brothers and a sword presented to him by President Roosevelt lead you to his bedroom where he wrote 100 novels, poems and short stories.

"We smile, but, O great Christ, our cries

To thee from tortured souls arise.

We sing, but oh the clay is vile

Beneath our feet, and long the mile;

But let the world dream otherwise,

We wear the mask!"

--Paul Laurence Dunbar

from the poem, We Wear the Mask

CITIZEN'S MOTORCAR PACKARD MUSEUM

Dayton - *420 South Ludlow Street – Downtown, 45402. Phone: (937) 226-1917. Hours: Tuesday – Friday Noon – 5:00pm, Saturday and Sunday 1:00 – 5:00pm.* See the world's largest collection of Packard automobiles in an authentic showroom. The art deco Packard dealership interior exhibits are spread through 6 settings, Included are the service area and a salesman's office with an old fan blowing and a radio playing early 1900's music.

DAYTON BALLET

Dayton - *140 North Main Street, 45402. Phone: (937) 449-5060.* ***Web: www.daytonballet.org***. Professional company performs new works by young American choreographers. (October – April)

DAYTON PHILHARMONIC ORCHESTRA

Dayton - *125 East First Street, 45402. Phone: (937) 224-9000.* ***Web: www.daytonphilharmonic.com***. Plays classical, pops, and Summer outdoor concerts.

DAYTON ART INSTITUTE

Dayton - *456 Belmonte Park North (I-75 exit 53B), 45405. Phone:* ***Web: www.daytonartinstitute.org****. (937) 223-5277 or (800) 296-4426. FREE.* Art collection spanning 5000 years. Experiencenter (features 20 hands-on activities) encourages interaction with art and experimentation with artistic elements of line, pattern, color, texture and shape.

WRIGHT CYCLE COMPANY

Dayton - *22 South Williams Street (off West 3rd Street), 45407. Phone: (937) 225-7705,* ***Web: www.nps.gov/daav/****. Hours: Monday - Saturday 8:30am - 4:30pm, Sunday 11:00am - 4:30pm (Summer). Wednesday - Sunday Only (Rest of year). Admission: Donation.* Actual site where the Wright Brothers had a bicycle business from 1895-1897 and developed their own brand of bicycles. On this site, they also developed ideas that led to the invention of flight almost 7 years later. We walked on the same floorboards that the brothers did and saw actual plans for a flying bicycle!

CARILLON HISTORICAL PARK

1000 Carillon Blvd. (I-75 to Exit 51),

Dayton 45409

- ❑ Phone: (937) 293-2841, **Web: www.carillonpark.org**
- ❑ Hours: Tuesday - Saturday 9:30am - 5:00pm. Sunday and Holidays Noon - 5:00pm (April thru October).
- ❑ Admission: $5.00 adult, $4.00 senior, $3.00 child (3-17). Special events priced higher.
- ❑ Miscellaneous: Museum Store sells period toys, snacks and candy. Wooded park with Ohio's largest bell tower, the Carillon Bell Tower (57 bells), also has many shaded picnic areas.

A must see - very comfortable and educational - over 65 acres of historical buildings and outdoor exhibits of history, invention and transportation. Called the "Little Greenfield Village" in Miami Valley and we definitely agree! Inventions like the cash register, innovations like flood control, and industries like Huffy Corporation are represented throughout the Park. Many of the oldest buildings from the early 1800's are represented too (tavern, home, school). As you enter most buildings, a

costumed guide will orient you to colorful stories of t
who once occupied them. The highlight of the collec
Wright Flyer III, the world's first practical airplane. Ou
Deed's Barn (learn about the Barn Gang and the big
started) and the rail cars that you can actually boarc
Smith is ritzy!

AULLWOOD AUDUBON CENTER AND FARM

Dayton - *1000 Aullwood Road, 45414. Phone: (937) 890-7360,* ***Web: www.audubon.org/local/sanctuary/aullwood/aacfhome.html****. Hours: Monday-Saturday 9:00am-5:00pm, Sunday 1:00-5:00pm. Closed holidays. Admission: $4.00 adult, $2.00 child (2-18).* The Discovery Room has more than 50 hands-on exhibits. Visitors can begin walks on five miles of hiking trails here. Around the building are special plantings of prairie and woodland wildflowers and a butterfly - hummingbird garden. The nearby Farm (9101 Frederick Pike) is the site of many special events. Cows, pigs, horses, chickens, turkeys, sheep, goats and barn swallows can all be found here if you come at the right time. The sugar bush, organic garden, herb garden and access to the trails are here.

BOONSHOFT MUSEUM OF DISCOVERY

2600 DeWeese Parkway (North of downtown I-75 to exit 57B, follow signs), **Dayton** 45414

- Phone: (937) 275-7431, **Web: www.boonshoftmuseum.org**
- Hours: Monday – Friday 9:00am – 5:00pm, Saturday 11:00am-5:00pm, Sunday Noon – 5:00pm. Closed major winter holidays.
- Admission: $7.50 adult, $5.50 senior, $5.00child (2-12). $1.00-$3.00 additional for Space Theater.
- Miscellaneous: With memberships here, you also can get free or discounted admissions to many museums in Ohio and surrounding states. Vending area. Discovery Shop.

Includes Museum of Natural History, Children's Museum plus Lasersphere (computer animated planetarium).

Boonshoft Museum of Discovery (cont.)

- ECOTREK - mastodon bones, desert animals (daytime vs. nighttime creatures using flashlights!), touch tide pool (ever seen a red sea cucumber? Touch one!), rainforest and treehouse within campsite and binoculars window views.
- WILD OHIO – An indoor zoo with small animals in natural surroundings. Visit the den of bobcat Van Cleve or a coyote, river otter, groundhog, fox or turtle.
- ANCIENT WORLD – Egyptian artifacts with 3000 year old mummy.
- SCIENCE CENTRAL – Inventions stations (water table w/ sticky water, airfort and force (tubes & funny windbag blower machines), chemistry lab, and a climbing discovery tower (nets, tubes & slide) provides hands on adventures.
- ZOOMZONE - interactives based on the PBS show, ZOOM. Send ideas to the show.
- KIDS' PLAYCE - baby garden, pioneer cabin, dig, slide & little creatures
- KIDSVILLE - a little village to play 'town'. Ever been a judge, or jury?

LEARNING TREE FARM

Dayton - *3376 South Union Road, 45418. Phone: (937) 866-8650,* ***Web: www.learningtreefarm.org****. Hours: Dawn to Dusk. Best weekdays when most facilities are open or during special programs. Admission: Hands on the Farm: $5.00 general self-guided. Special Programs: guided $7.00 general. $1.00 discount per person for groups (12+).* The history of the family which originally owned the farm, from their initial voyage to Ohio to the present day, has been researched and displayed. Visitors may tour the house, visit the farm animals, hike on the farm's land, and participate in hands-on activities like caring for animals, crafts, and sheep shearing. Special programs like "Finding Freedom on the Farm" highlights storytelling, quilts used by escaping slaves, clue game thru nearby land and daily activities of the safe house station.

SUNWATCH

2301 West River Road (I-75 to Exit 51, west on Edwin C. Moses Blvd., cross South Broadway, turn left), **Dayton** 45418

- Phone: (937) 268-8199, **Web: www.sunwatch.org**
- Hours: Tuesday – Saturday 9:00am – 5:00pm. Sunday and Holidays Noon – 5:00pm. (No one admitted after 4:30pm)
- Admission: $5.00 adult, $3.00 child (6-17) & senior (55+).
- Miscellaneous: Occasional Family Days are best. Orientation video suggested first.

Archaeological excavations at a site near the Great Miami River uncovered evidence of an 800-year-old village built by the Fort Ancient Indians. The reconstructed 12th Century Indian Village has self-guided tours of the thatched huts, gardens and artifacts of the lifestyle of a unique culture. In the museum exhibits study the trash pits - you can learn a lot from people's trash. Study their ancient calendars - can you tell the season? Some activities include story telling, archery,toys and games, harvesting, a multi-media presentation, and best of all, learn to tell time by charting the sun. See how the Indians used flint and bone to create jewelry and tools - then buy some as souvenirs.

COX ARBORETUM

Dayton - *6733 Springboro Pike, 45449. Phone: (937) 434-9005.* ***Web: www.metroparks.org****. Hours: Daily 8:00am to dusk. Visitor Center weekdays 8:30am - 4:30pm and weekends 1:00 - 4:00pm.* 170 acres including the nationally recognized Edible Landscape Garden. Every season has something special to offer, from spring's splashes of bright color to winter's textures. The Arboretum hosts nine specialty gardens. In addition to exploring gardens, hike trails through mature forests and colorful meadows.

UNITED STATES AIR FORCE MUSEUM

Wright Patterson Air Force Base (I-75 to State Route 4 East to Harshman Road Exit), **Fairborn** 45433

- Phone: (937) 255-3286, **Web: www.wpafb.af.mil/museum**
- Hours: Daily 9:00am - 5:00pm. Closed Thanksgiving, Christmas and New Years.
- Admission: FREE
- Miscellaneous: Largest Gift Shop imaginable. Concessions. IMAX THEATER - 6 story with hourly 40 minute space/aviation films-feel like you're flying with the pilots. Fee (937-253-IMAX) HUFFMAN PRAIRIE FIELD - Rte. 44 (937-257-5535). See where The Wright Brothers first attempted flight.

For the best in family entertainment / educational value, this museum is definitely a must see! You'll have a real adventure exploring the world's oldest and largest military aviation museum that features over 50 vintage WWII aircraft (even the huge 6-engine B-36) and 300 other aircraft and rockets. See everything from presidential planes, to Persian Gulf advanced missiles and bombs, the original Wright Brothers wind tunnel, to the original Apollo 15 command module. Look for the observation balloon (easy to find—just look up ever so slightly), Rosie the Rivetor and "Little Vittles" parachuted goodies. Discovery Hangar Five follows a common museum trend and focuses on the interactive learning of why things fly and different parts of airplanes. Continuous films played at stations throughout the complex (with chairs-take a break from all the walking). National Aviation Hall of Fame is next door. Morphis MovieRide Theater - actually move, tilt and shout.

FORT RECOVERY STATE MEMORIAL

Fort Recovery - *One Fort Site Street (State Route 49 and State Route 119), 45846. Web: www.ohiohistory.org/places/ftrecovr. Phone: (419) 375-4649. Hours: Daily Noon - 5:00pm (Summer). Weekends Only (May and September). Admission: $2.00 adult, $1.00 child (6-12).* The remaining blockhouses with connecting stockade wall are where General Arthur St. Clair was defeated by Indians in 1791. Later, in 1794, General "Mad" Anthony Wayne defended the fort successfully. A museum with Indian War artifacts and dressed mannequins is also displayed on the property.

BEAR'S MILL

Greenville - *Bear's Mill Road (5 miles East on US 36 then South) 45331, Phone: (937) 548-5112. Tours (self-guided): Weekends 11:00am – 5:00pm (April-November), Thursday- Sunday 11:00am – 5:00pm (December). Guided tours by appointment. Miscellaneous: Store-sells flours ground at the mill, gift baskets, handmade pottery.* Tour the mill built in 1849 by Gabriel Bear where grinding stones (powered by water flowing beneath the building) grind flour and meal. The process is slow and kept cool to retard deteriorating wholesome nutrients.

GARST MUSEUM, DARKE COUNTY HISTORICAL SOCIETY

Greenville - *205 North Broadway, 45331. Phone: (937) 548-5250. **Web: www.garstmuseum.org**. Hours: Tuesday – Saturday 11:00am – 5:00pm, Sunday 1:00 – 5:00pm. Closed January. Admission $1.00-$3.00 (age 6+).* The main features of the museum are Darke County's most-famous daughter sharp-shooter and entertainer Annie Oakley; world-traveler, broadcaster, author and adventurer Lowell Thomas; pioneering aviator Zachary Lansdowne; The Treaty of GreeneVille and much other history of the county including 30 individual room settings. Anthony Wayne, Native American artifacts and Village of shops, too.

CARRIAGE HILL FARM AND MUSEUM

Huber Heights - *7860 East Shull Road (I-70 to Exit 38 - State Route 201 north), 45424. **Web: www.metroparks.org**. Phone: (937) 879-0461. Hours: Monday - Friday 10:00am - 5:00pm, Saturday - Sunday 1:00 - 5:00pm. Admission: Donation. Miscellaneous: Picnic area, fishing, horseback riding, cross country skiing, hayrides and bobsled rides.* Stop at the Visitor Center for exhibits highlighting lifestyles of a century ago, a children's interactive center and the Country Store gift shop. The self-guided tour of an 1880's working farm is a great benefit to the community. The farm includes a summer kitchen, workshop, black smith and barns. Household chores and farming are performed as they were 100 years ago and a variety of farm animals fill the barn. They are best to visit when workers are planting or harvesting gardens.

INDIAN LAKE STATE PARK

Lakeview - *(US 33, 20 miles east of I-75), 43331. Phone: (937) 843-2717.* ***Web: www.dnr.state.oh.us/parks/parks/indianlk.htm.*** The present and much larger lake lies along one of the country's major avian migration routes. Indian Lake is an important resting stop for birds such as Canada geese, ducks, grebes, swans, egrets and herons. Many stay over the summer to nest. 6448 acres of camping, hiking trails, boating, fishing, swimming and winter sports.

LOCKINGTON LOCKS STATE MEMORIAL

Lockington - *5 miles North of Piqua-Lockington Road (I-75 to exit 83 West on State Route 25A), 45356. Phone: (800) 686-1535,* ***Web: www.ohiohistory.org/places/lockingt/index.html.*** *Hours: Daily Dawn to Dusk. Admission: FREE.* These stair step locks, among the best preserved in Ohio, were part of the Miami and Erie Canal System, which opened for navigation in 1845 and connected Cincinnati and the Ohio River to Toledo and Lake Erie. For several decades, the canal provided Ohio with valuable transportation and waterpower. View portions of five original locks (elevation adjusters for canal boats) and the aqueduct that lowered boats 67 feet into the Miami-Erie Canal.

MIAMISBURG MOUND

Miamisburg - *(I-75 to State Route 725 exit 42, follow signs), 45342.* ***Web: www.ohiohistory.org/places/miamisbur.*** *Phone: (937) 866-5632, Hours: Daily Dawn to Dusk. Miscellaneous: Park, Picnic tables and playground.* Take the 116 stairs up a 68-foot high and 1.5 acre wide mound built by American Indians. This is the largest conical burial mound in Ohio. Archaeological investigations of the surrounding area suggest that it was constructed by the prehistoric Adena Indians (800 BC - AD 100). The mound measures 877 feet in circumference.

WRIGHT B. FLYER

Miamisburg - *10550 Springboro Pike (State Route 741 – Dayton International Airport), 45342. Phone: (937) 885-2327. Hours: Tuesday, Thursday, and Saturday 9:00am – 2:00pm. Admission: Aircraft ride certificates may be purchased for $150.00. This entitles the certificate bearer to an orientation ride replicating the*

Wright Brothers' original flight patterns over Huffman Prairie! Otherwise, only donations. A group decided to build a flying replica of the first production aircraft ever built - the Wright Brothers B Model Airplane. The result is a fully operational flying aircraft that closely resembles the original Wright B Model that flew over Huffman Prairie in 1911. This hangar houses a flyable replica of the 1911 plane built by Wilbur and Orville Wright. They also have a half scale model of the plane and other aviation exhibits and souvenirs.

LAKE LORAMIE STATE PARK

Minster - *4401 Ft. Loramie Swanders Road (3 miles Southeast of Minster off State Route 66), 45865. Phone: (937) 295-2011.* ***Web: www.dnr.state.oh.us/parks/parks/lkloramie.htm***. One of the original canal feeder lakes, Lake Loramie State Park offers visitors a quiet retreat in rural Ohio. Swim from the sandy beach, hike along the old canal towpath, stay a night in a shaded campsite or boat the lazy waters of Lake Loramie.

BICYCLE MUSEUM OF AMERICA

New Bremen - *7 West Monroe Street (SR 274), 45869. Phone: (419) 629-9249,* ***Web: www.bicyclemuseum.com***. *Hours: Monday – Friday 11:00am - 5:00pm (til 7:00pm in the summer). Saturday 11:00am – 2:00pm. Admission: $3.00 adult, $2.00 senior, $1.00 student.* A department store has been converted into a showcase of the world's oldest bike (w/out pedals) to the Schwinn family collection (including the 1,000,000th bicycle made). High-wheelers to side-by-side doubles and quads. Celebrity bikes and bikes from balloon tire to banana seat bikes will amuse you.

ELDORA SPEEDWAY

New Weston - *13929 SR 118, 45362. Phone: (937) 338-3815.* ***Web: www.eldoraspeedway.com***. Fastest mile dirt track in the nation. U.S.A.C. Sprint, UMP Modifieds, and Stock Car racing. (April - October)

PIQUA HISTORICAL AREA TOUR

North Hardin Road (I-75 to exit 83 County Road 25A West to State Route 66 North), **Piqua** 45356

- Phone: (937) 773-2522 or (800) 752-2619
  Web: www.ohiohistory.org/places/piqua
- Hours: Wednesday – Saturday 9:30am – 5:00pm, Sunday and Holidays Noon – 5:00pm (Summer). Weekends Only (September and October).
- Admission: $6.00 adult, $2.00 child (6-12). Includes canal boat ride.
- Miscellaneous: Canal rides a few times during the afternoon.

Tour the Johnston Farm which includes an 1808 massive log barn which is probably the oldest such barn in Ohio. In the farmhouse, the kids will probably be most interested in the beds made of rope and hay filled sacks. Eight girls slept in one room (ages 2-20) and three boys in another. Many youth games of that time period are displayed. The Winter Kitchen is also very interesting – especially the size of the walk-in fireplace. The Farm buildings have costumed guides describing and interacting with youth as they demonstrate chores on the farm. Before you visit the canal, stop in the museum where excellent exhibits, inside and out, explain the treacherous job of building a canal and why. The General Harrison canal boat is powered by two mules which pull the boat down and back on a section of the Old Miami-Erie Canal (Cincinnati to Toledo). The cargo boat was once used to transport produce and meat at a speed limit of 4 MPH. The boats were fined $10.00 for speeding although many paid the fine and continued going 10 MPH. Once the railroads came, canals became obsolete.

KISER LAKE STATE PARK

Rosewood - *(17 miles Northwest of Urbana on State Route 235), 43070.* ***Web: www.dnr.state.oh.us/parks/parks/kisrlake.htm****. Phone: (937) 362-3822.* The rolling wooded hills and diverse wetlands add to the beauty of this scenic lake known for its clean, clear waters. 870 acres of camping, hiking trails, boating and rentals, fishing, swimming and winter sports.

CLARK STATE PERFORMING ARTS CENTER

Springfield - *300 South Fountain Avenue, 45501. Phone: (937) 328-3874.* ***Web: www.clarkstate.edu/pac/.*** Hosts national and regional performers, recording artists, Broadway shows, circuses, and Family Stages (Dinosaurs!) or Sunday Funday programs. (September- June)

BUCK CREEK STATE PARK

Springfield - *1901 Buck Creek Lane (4 miles East of Springfield on State Route 4), 45502. Phone: (937) 322-5284.* ***Web: www.dnr.state.oh.us/parks/parks/buckck.htm.*** Buck Creek State Park lies in a fertile agricultural area, rich in Ohio's history. The park's recreational facilities center around the 2,120-acre lake, offering endless water-related opportunities. The spotted turtle, a state endangered animal, is found in the area. The northernmost region of the park is an excellent area to observe waterfowl. The shallow waters provide a stopover for thousands of migrating ducks. Relatively rare songbirds of open meadows are also present including dickcissels, bobolinks and Henslow sparrows. The U.S. Army Corps of Engineers manages a visitor center and recreational site near the dam. The center provides displays, programs and dam operation tours. 4030 acres of camping, hiking trails, boating and rentals, fishing, swimming and winter sports. 26 family cabins with A/C.

ST. MARY'S FISH FARM

St. Mary's - *State Route 364 (East Side of Grand Lake), 45885. Phone: (419) 394-5170. Hours: Daily 7:00am - 3:30pm. FREE tours by appointment.* After boating or swimming on Grand Lake (man-made), wander through 52 acres of ponds where pike, catfish, etc. are raised. The farm is one of the only three in Ohio and is the only farm with a large mouth bass and yellow perch hatchery.

GRAND LAKE ST. MARY'S STATE PARK

St. Mary's - *834 Edgewater Drive (2 miles West of St. Mary's on State Route 703), 45885. Phone: (419) 394-3611.* ***Web: www.dnr.state.oh.us/parks/parks/grndlake.htm***. Nature programs. 14,000 acres of camping, boating and rentals, fishing, swimming, sport courts, putt-putt and winter sports. Ohio's largest inland lake.

SYCAMORE STATE PARK

Trotwood - *4675 N. Diamond Mill Road (1 mile North of Trotwood on State Route 49), 45426. Phone: (937) 854-4452.* ***Web: www.dnr.state.oh.us/parks/parks/sycamore.htm***. The meadows, woodlots and still waters of Sycamore State Park provide the perfect setting for picnicking, hiking, fishing and horseback riding. Snowmobiling. Bridle trails. 2,300 acres of camping, hiking trails, fishing and winter sports.

BRUKNER NATURE CENTER

Troy - *5995 Horseshoe Bend Rd. (Exit # 73 off of I-75, west on SR 55, 3 miles), 45373.* ***Web: www.tdn-net.com/brukner***. *Phone: (937) 698-6493. Hours: Daily 12:30 - 5:00pm. Hiking trails open dawn until dusk. Admission charged on Sunday.* This 164 acre nature preserve's attractions include 6 miles of hiking trails, a wildlife rehabilitation center and the interpretive center. The 1804 Iddings log house was built by the first settlers in Miami County. The Center's animal rehabilitation has over 65 permanent residents on display. The top floor contains a glass-enclosed vista room for watching and listening to birds as they feed. A ground-level viewing station for mammals also is available.

CEDAR BOG AND NATURE PRESERVE

Urbana - *980 Woodburn Road (off Route 68 North / I-70 to Springfield / off State Route 36), 43078. Phone: (937) 484-3744.* ***Web: www.ohiohistory.org/places/cedarbog***. *Hours: Wednesday - Sunday 9:00am - 4:30pm (April - September). Admission: $3.00 adult, $1.25 child (6-12).* A bog is a remnant of the Ice Age (glaciers and mastodons) and public tours take you to the boardwalk over this bog. Below you'll see the black, wet, slimy muck and chilly dampness created by a constant water table and cool springs. In contrast, see excellent orchid, prairie and woodland wildflowers.

FRESHWATER FARMS OF OHIO

2624 US 68 (north of downtown circle)

Urbana 43078

- Phone: (937) 652-3701 or (800) 634-7434
  Web: www.fwfarms.com
- Store Hours: Monday-Saturday 10:00am-6:00pm. Closed major holidays.
- Tours: FREE. Self-guided tour
- Miscellaneous: Bring a cooler if you plan to purchase any fish. Supplies for ponds at home - compatible fish, frogs. Produces several hundred thousand trout sold to premium restaurants. The Douglas Inn (111 Miami St., 937-653-5585) downtown Urbana serves this wonderful fresh trout in a historic early 1800s bldg.

Start your tour by petting a sturgeon fish. Why can you touch them, but not catfish? They raise rainbow trout that are bred in large water tanks. Farmer Smith, a marine biologist with a doctorate in nutrition, and his father (an engineer), developed a system of tracks and tanks using re-circulated pure cleaned water. The fish are really spoiled with a special diet and solar-heated hatchery. View the spring water "ponds" with gravel bottoms (outside) and put a quarter in the machine to get fish food to feed the fish. Other newer exhibits of live fish are the jumbo freshwater shrimp and their "loopy" eyes! These fish are really spoiled, aren't they?

NEIL ARMSTRONG AIR AND SPACE MUSEUM

Wapakoneta *- 500 South Apollo Drive (I-75 to Exit 111), 45895. Web: www.ohiohistory.org/places/armstron. Phone: (419) 738-8811 or (800) 860-0142. Hours: Monday – Saturday 9:30am – 5:00pm. Sunday Noon – 5:00pm. Closed Winter Holidays. Admission: $6.00 adult, $2.00 child (6-12).* The museum honors Neil Armstrong (a Wapakoneta native) and other area aeronauts (like the Wright Brothers) and their flying machines. After greeted by a NASA Skylaneer flown by Armstrong in the early 1960's, trace the history of flights from balloons to space travel. Look at the Apollo crew spacesuits or watch a video of lunar space walks.

In the Astro Theater, pretend you're on a trip to the moon. Another favorite is the Infinity Cube – 18 square feet covered with mirrors that make you feel like you've been projected into space. Blast OFF!

MAC-O-CHEE AND MAC-O-CHEEK CASTLES (PIATT CASTLES)

State Route 245 (Route 33 West to State Route 245 East)

West Liberty 43357

- Phone: (937) 465-2821, **Web: www.piattcastles.com**
- Hours - (Each Castle): Daily, Noon – 4 pm (April – October), 11:00 am – 5:00 pm (Summer).
- Admission: $8.00 adult, $7.00 senior (60+),$6.00 student (13-21), $5.00 child (5-12). Prices listed are for each castle. Discount combo prices for both castles.
- Miscellaneous: Hands-on activities for families (summer).

Castles in Ohio? Catch the eerie, yet magnificent old castles furnished with collections ranging from 150-800 years old. Both castles were built in the mid-1800's and give a good sense of what the lifestyle of the upper-class Piatt brothers family was like. This tour is very manageable for school-aged (pre-schoolers not suggested) children and includes lots of land to explore outside. Telling friends they were in a castle is fun too. Because the furniture is original, the homes have an old smell and the rooms look frozen in time. Ceiling paintings and the kitchen/dining area were most interesting.

MAD RIVER THEATER WORKS

West Liberty - *319 North Detroit, 43357. Phone: (937) 465-6751.* ***Web: www.madrivertheatre.org***. Their purpose is to create and produce plays that explore the concerns of rural people and to perform these works for multi-generational, primarily rural audiences. They interview local residents and research historical issues with contemporary relevance (ie. John Henry, slavery, Casey Jones). This material is used to craft plays with music that are drawn from and produced for the people of the rural Midwest.

OHIO CAVERNS

West Liberty *- 2210 East State Route 245 (I-70 to US 68 north to SR 507 east), 43357.* ***Web: www.cavern.com/ohiocaverns.*** *Phone: (937) 465-4017, Hours: Daily 9:00am – 5:00pm (April – October). 9:00am – 4:00pm (November – March). Admission: $9.50 Adult, $5.00 Children (5-12). Historic tour costs more. On the premises is a park and gift shop.* This tour is a 45 minute guided regular or historic tour of the largest caves in Ohio. The temperature here is 54 degrees F. constantly so dress appropriately. Look for the Palace of the Gods and stalagmites that look like cacti or a pump.

NATIONAL AFRO-AMERICAN MUSEUM AND CULTURAL CENTER

Wilberforce *- 1350 Brush Row Road (off US 42 - Next to Central State College), 45384.* ***Web: www.ohiohistory.org/places/afroam.*** *Phone: (800) BLK-HIST. Hours: Tuesday - Saturday 9:00am - 5:00pm. Sunday 1:00 - 5:00pm Admission: $4.00 Adult, $1.50 Children.* Wilberforce was a famous stop on the Underground Railroad and became the center (Wilberforce University) for black education and achievements. The University was the first owned and operated by Afro-Americans. Best feature is the "From Victory to Freedom - the Afro-American Experience of 1950 - 1960's".

BLUE JACKET

Caesar's Ford Park Amphitheater (SR 35 to Jasper Road, south to Stringtown Road), **Xenia** 45385

- Phone: (937) 376-4318 or (877) 465-BLUE
  Web: www.bluejacketdrama.com
- Hours: Tuesday – Sunday at 8:00pm (Mid–June – Labor Day). Dinner at the Pavilion 5:30-7:30pm. Backstage guided tours at 4:00 & 5:00pm
- Admission: $9.00 - $15.00 adult, $8.00-$13.00 senior, 6.00-$8.00 child (1-12). $3.50 Adult, $2.00 child additional for backstage tour. Picnic Basket Dinners are ~$5.00-$9.00 per person and yummy and filling.
- Tours: Backstage guided tours at 4:00 and 5:00pm. Members of the cast whimsically teach you the theatrical effects (like revolving stages and underground tunnels) and tricks to make it look real! Suggested for children to ward against fright during drama.

- ❑ Miscellaneous: During dinner, they present Blue Jacket 101 (learn basic, interesting history) and a Frontier Musical Review. These are something not normally presented at these dramas and they're FREE. This keeps the kids from getting bored before the show and everyone is in the mood to watch and learn! The Holiday Inn Xenia is closeby for overnight lodging (Main St., 937-372-9921).

Over two hour outdoor drama recounts the true story of a pure white man adopted by Indians. Named for the unique clothes he wore at the time of his capture, Duke was named Blue Jacket. Blue Jacket became a Shawnee Indian Chief and fought to keep the land and heritage from frontiersmen like Daniel Boone, Simon Kenton and whites. To add life to the drama, they use live horses, real muskets, cannons, lots of flaming arrows and torches. Horses thunder across the stage in the largest horse charge in outdoor drama during the siege of Ft. Boonesborough. Lots of Ohio Territory history here (and good explanations of why each character acted as they did). This family drama is not only for everyone in the family, but has multiple threads of Blue Jacket's family life. The acting is filled with enough humor to keep from getting too serious.

GREENE COUNTY HISTORICAL SOCIETY MUSEUM

Xenia - *74 Church Street (near center of town), 45385. Phone: (937) 372-4606. Hours: Tuesday – Friday 9:00am-Noon, Saturday and Sunday, 1:00 – 3:00 pm (Summer). Weekends Only (Rest of Year). Admission: Donations suggested.* Restored Victorian home and 1799 James Galloway log house where Tecumseh tried to "woo" Rebecca Galloway (actually view the chair Tecumseh sat in near the fireplace!). First, pick herbs from a 1700's garden, smell them and then try to enter the front door of the log house. No door knob or latch? How did they open the door and why? The Carriage House has a wonderful display of farm equipment, general store (candy), china, books, furniture, toys, railroad exhibit, and school. In the Big House, easily explore the many rooms looking for old-fashioned toys, the kiddie potty, or, the old hair crimpers and curling irons - try one - how does it work?

KIL-KARE SPEEDWAY

Xenia - *1166 Dayton-Xenia Road, 45385. Phone: (937) 426-2764.* ***Web: www.kilkare.com***. NHRA drag-racing on a ¼ mile strip. NASCAR stock car racing on a 3/4 mile oval track. (April-August)

JOHN BRYAN STATE PARK

Yellow Springs - *3790 State Route 370 (2 miles Southeast of Yellow Springs on State Route 370), 45387. Phone: (937) 767-1274.* ***Web: www.johnbryan.org***. 750 acres of camping, hiking trails, fishing and winter sports. The Clifton Gorge is a limestone gorge cut by the river (a national natural landmark). Rent-a-Tepee is for a truly unique camping adventure. Tepees are spacious, sleep as many as five adults or a family of six, and feature weatherproof construction. Canvas tepees are anchored on wooden platforms. Each comes equipped with a cooler, foam sleeping pads, cots, a lantern, propane stove, broom and dustpan. Fee is $27.00 per night.

YOUNG'S JERSEY DAIRY FARM

6880 Springfield-Xenia Road (On Route 68, off I-70)

Yellow Springs 45387

- Phone: (937) 325-0629, **Web: www.youngsdairy.com**
- Hours: Daily 10:00am – 10pm (April-October). Open later in the summer and closes earlier in the winter.
- Admission: Grounds are FREE. Each activity is between $2.00-$5.00 per person.
- Tours: Scheduled groups Monday – Friday (April – October). $3.00 Children – FREE for Teachers and Chaperones. FARM TOURS: This one hour tour starts with a short video (and farm petting ducks, rabbits and chicks) that follows the farming process: from feeding the cows (amazing how much food they need - 25 gallons of water, over 100 lbs. of hay and grain), milking the cows, bottling the milk (quickly chilled to 35 degrees) and making the ice cream (what's their secret? see the operations thru the processing window), to selling the milk and ice cream in the store and restaurant. The children then visit the animals in the barn. The children see what a cow eats, feed the goats (why can't they bite?), and visit with the other farm animals. The next step is a wagon ride. Finish the tour with some homemade ice cream.

The Dairy store began in 1960 and is still operated by members of the Young family. Udders and Putters Miniature Golf, Driving Range, Batting Cage, Corny Maze (a 3 acre corn field maze open weekends, August thru October), Wagon Rides & Moo-ver & Shaker Barrel Cart rides on weekends, Petting Area – Baby Jersey (pretty-faced calves) cows, pigs and sheep; Water Balloon Toss (summertime). Go to the petting area and then the wagon ride with a treat at the end in one of the restaurants. Our family has fallen in love with this farmplace amusement park!

MARMON VALLEY FARM

Zanesfield - *7754 SR 292 (off US 33 northwest, exit Mad River Mountain Area), 43360.* ***Web: www.marmonvalley.com****. Phone: (937) 593-8051. Hours: Call for details.* Winter and summer activities are available at Marmon Valley Farm. They have live farm animals and a fun barn with rope bridges, rope swings and barn games. Hiking and horseback riding (year-round trail rides, on ponies, or in the indoor arena) are available. If it's very cold, try ice-skating. When there's snow, you may want to take your sled along for some great sled riding hills. Their barn dances and hayrides are designed to build relationships and learn about the Lord through bible study. There's a swimming hole and small boatcraft too. Overnights combine activities with just enough time left to wander and make new friends.

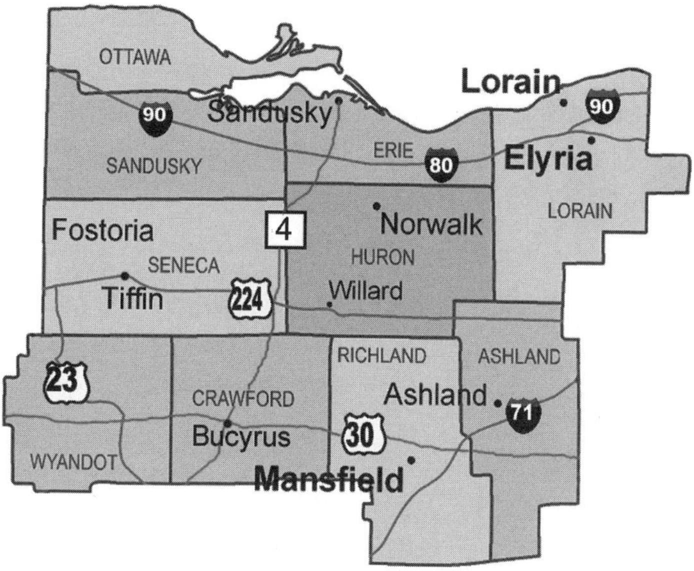

Chapter 4
North Central Area

Our Favorites...

Carousel Magic !

Crystal Cave

Great Bear Lodge & Waterpark

Jones Potato Chips

Kelley's Island

Living Bible Museum

Mohican Area

Thomas Edison's Birthplace

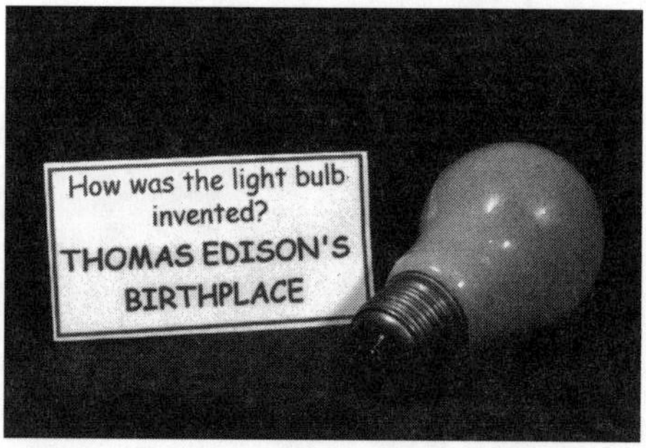

How was the light bulb invented?
THOMAS EDISON'S BIRTHPLACE

LYME VILLAGE

Bellevue - *5001 State Route 4 (south of SR 113), 44811. Phone: (419) 483-4949.* ***Web: www.lymevillage.com****. Hours: Tuesday - Saturday 11:00am - 4:00pm, Sunday 1:00-4:00pm (Summer). Sunday only (May and September). Admission: $7.00 adult, $6.00 senior (60+), $3.00 child (6-12). Tours are 1-2 hours. Discounts for partial tours. Miscellaneous: Gift Shop and concessions. Best to visit during special events.* This 19th Century Ohio Village includes the Wright Mansion, Annie Brown's log home that she owned for 82 years (early Ohio settler exhibits inside), a blacksmith shop, schoolhouse, barns, a church, and the Cooper-Fries general store. All original buildings were moved to this location. Of special interest is the National Museum of Postmark Collector's Club (with the world's largest single collection of postmarks) in a restored post office.

MAD RIVER & NKP RAILROAD SOCIETY MUSEUM

Bellevue - *233 York Street (Just South of US 20), 44811. Phone: (419) 483-2222.* ***Web: www.onebellevue.com/madriver****. Hours: Daily 1:00 – 5:00pm (Memorial Day - Labor Day). Weekends Only (May, September, October) Admission: $3.00 adult, $1.00 child (3-12).* Look for steam engines, diesel engines, or the huge snow plow. Once you find them, browse through their collections of full-scale locomotives, cabooses, and mail cars – many that you can climb aboard. Tour guide volunteers are usually retired railway personnel who are knowledgeable and excited to tell you stories about the old railway days.

SENECA CAVERNS

Bellevue (Flat Rock) - *15248 Twp. Road 178 (SR 4 off turnpike, south of SR 269), 44828. Phone: (419) 483-6711.* ***Web: www.senecacavernsohio.com****. Hours: Daily 9:00am - 7:00pm (Summer). Weekends 10:00am - 5:00pm (May, September, October). Admission: $9.50 adult, $7.50 senior(62+), $5.00 child (5-12). Miscellaneous: Light jacket is suggested as the cave is a constant 54 degrees F.* Take a one hour tour of the 110 foot deep limestone cave with many small rooms, seven levels and the "Ole Mist'ry River". The cave is actually an earth crack discovered by two boys out hunting in 1872. To make the tour really fun, stop by Sandy Creek Gem Mining and let your little explorers pan for gems.

COOPER'S MILL APPLE BUTTER & JELLY FACTORY

Bucyrus - *1414 North Sandusky Avenue (U.S. Route 30 bypass and State Route 4), 44820. Phone: (419) 562-4215. Hours: Open Monday - Saturday 8:30am-6:00pm. Admission: FREE. Tours: Monday-Friday 9:00am-11:30am and Noon-3:30pm. Miscellaneous: Farm Market - taste test jellies and homemade fudge.* Jelly Factory tour lets you watch fruit spreads being made the old fashioned way. With "Grandma" recipes, watch the cooking of fine jams and apple butter.

CATAWBA ISLAND STATE PARK

Catawba Island - *(off State Route 53), 43452. Phone: (419) 797-4530.* ***Web: www.dnr.state.oh.us/parks/parks/lakeerie.htm***. A fishing pier, launch ramp, picnic shelter and picnic areas can be found here. Swimming is permitted at your own risk.

WILDWOOD WATERPARK

Columbia Station - *11200 East River Road (Route 252), 44028. Phone: (440) 236-3944. Hours: Daily Daytime. (Mid June – Labor Day). Admission: $8.00-$10.00 (ages 5+).* A waterpark in the woods with sandy beaches and waterslides, paddle boats, miniature golf, and canoe rides.

HICKORIES MUSEUM, LORAIN COUNTY HISTORICAL SOCIETY

Elyria - *Lorain County, 509 Washington Avenue (North of Broad Street), 44035. Phone: (440) 322-3341.* ***Web: www.lchs.org***. *Tours: Tuesday – Saturday 1:00pm & 2:30pm. Admission.* 1894 Tudor home built by inventor Arthur Garford (padded bicycle seat). Large amount of hickory trees.

HAYES PRESIDENTIAL CENTER

1337 Hayes Avenue (Rt. 6), Spiegel Grove, **Fremont** 43420

- Phone: (419) 332-2081 or (800) 998-7737
  Web: www.rbhayes.org
- Hours: Monday - Saturday 9:00am - 5:00pm, Sunday and Holidays Noon - 5:00pm

- ❑ Admission: $6.00 adult, $5.00 senior (60+), $2.00 child (6-12) Home or Museum. Combo prices offered to tour both.
- ❑ Miscellaneous: Museum Store

Disputed Election? Contested Florida votes? Popular vote vs. Electoral College vote? It all happened in 1876 with the campaign of Rutherford B. Hayes. The iron gates that greet you at the entrance were the same gates that once stood at the White House during the Hayes administration. The 33-room mansion estate was the home of President and Mrs. Rutherford B. Hayes and is full of family mementos, private papers and books. They give you the sense he dedicated himself to his country. The museum displays the President's daughter's ornate dollhouses and the White House carriage that the family used. As 19th President, Hayes contended with the aftermath of Reconstruction in the South, the problems of our black citizens, and the plight of the American Indian.

KELLEY'S ISLAND STATE PARK & STATE MEMORIALS

(reached only by ferry or boat), **Kelley's Island** 43452

- ❑ Phone: (419) 746-2546 or (419) 797-4530 (Rock) or (419) 797-4025 (Grooves), **Web: www.dnr.state.oh.us/parks/parks/lakeerie.htm**
- ❑ Hours: Daylight hours.
- ❑ Admission: FREE

Six miles of hiking trails lead to scenic vistas, historic sites and two nature preserves, North Pond Nature Preserve, and the North Shore Nature Preserve, offering excellent locations for watching wildlife. Picnic areas, a picnic shelter, launch ramps, fishing access areas and a 100-foot swimming beach are also available. The islands were formed during the glacial period when massive ice sheets entered Ohio. Glaciers gouged and scoured the bedrock; their tremendous weight left deep depressions which filled with meltwater, forming the Great Lakes. GLACIAL GROOVES STATE MEMORIAL is a must see and a great way to study Ohio geology. Located on the north side of the island, the largest easily accessible grooves were formed when ice once covered solid limestone bedrock. Looking safely over fence, you see a giant groove passage that seems unbelievable. Placards along the trail detail the history of glaciers moving through the area. Prior to the War of 1812, the Lake Erie Island region had been occupied by Ottawa and Huron (Wyandot) Indian tribes. A testimony to their existence on the islands is carved in INSCRIPTION ROCK STATE MEMORIAL. The flat-topped limestone slab displays carvings of animals and human figures. Discovered partly buried in the shoreline in 1833, the 32 feet by 21 feet rock is now entirely exposed (protected by a roof and viewing platform). Archaeologists believe the inscriptions date from sometime between AD 1200 and 1600.

LAKESIDE

Lakeside (Marblehead) - *236 Walnut Avenue, 43440.* ***Web: www.lakesideohio.com****. Phone: (419) 798-4461 or (866) 9-LAKESIDE. Chautaqua – like resort with programs in a historic enclave on Lake Erie. (June – September).* The entire area is a Christian family retreat of shops, eateries, entertainment, lectures, worship services and family-rated movies. Daily, weekly and season pass admission prices are charged (avg. $10.00 per person per day-ages 10+).

MID OHIO SPORTS CAR COURSE

Lexington - *Steam Corners Road (I-71 exit SR 97 or SR 95, follow signs), 44904. Phone: (419) 884-4000 or (800) MID-OHIO,* ***Web: www.midohio.com****.* Indy Car, Sport Car, AMA Motorcycles, Vintage Car Races. General, Weekend, Paddock (walk through garages & see drivers) passes available. Weekends (June – mid September)

LANDOLL'S MOHICAN CASTLE RESORT

Loudonville – *561 Twp. Rd 3352, 44842. Phone (800) 291-5001.* ***Web: www.landollsmohicancastle.com*** Stay overnight in a castle with royal family suites or cottages! *(cottages coming soon)*. Euro-gardens and cobblestone paths lead into the 30 miles of hiking/golf cart trails. Indoor pool with cave & waterfall, dining. Rooms with fireplaces, Jacuzzis, mini-kitchens, heated tile floors, and complimentary euro-style continental breakfast. Carriage rides also available around property. An enchanted family experience!

MOHICAN STATE PARK RESORT

Loudonville - *3116 State Route 3, 44842. Phone: (419) 994-4290 or (419) 938-5411 Resort.* ***Web: www.mohicancamp.com*** *or* ***www.mohicanresort.com****.* Nature programs, scenic, bike rentals, bridle trails. 1,294 acres of camping, hiking trails, boating and rentals, fishing and winter sports. Most people come to stay at riverfront family cabins (with A/C, fireplaces and cable) or the Lodge rooms (with indoor/outdoor pools, sauna, tennis, basketball and shuffleboard facilities). Family playground activity center. Among the resort's most popular attractions are birds of prey presentations conducted by experts from the Ohio Bird Sanctuary. Nearby activities include visiting Amish country, four canoe liveries, Pleasant Hill Marina, Mohican Water Slide, five golf courses, two horse stables, downhill ski resorts Snow Trails and Clear Fork and the Mid-Ohio Sports Car Course...and the famous Malabar Farm.

ARTS & SCIENCE DISCOVERY CENTER

Mansfield - *75 North Walnut Street Richland Academy, west of carousel, downtown), 44902. Phone: (419) 522-8224.* ***Web: www.richlandacademy.com****. Hours: Monday-Thursday 10:00am-7:00pm, Friday-Saturday 10:00am-4:00pm. Admission: $2.00 to Discovery Center.* Showcases techno-art - hands-on. Play a gas-powered Fire Organ or follow the perpetual motion Wave Machine. Call before your visit for the daily activity and performance schedule. The Academy also has performances in black box theatre, recitals, musicals, choral concerts, and children's plays.

CAROUSEL MAGIC! FACTORY & RICHLAND CAROUSEL PARK

44 West 4th Street(behind the Gift Horse) (I-71 Exit State Route 13 North to downtown), **Mansfield** 44902

- Phone: (419) 526-4009 factory or (419) 522-4223 carousel
  Web: www.carouselmagic.com
- Admission: Factory Tour $4.00 adult, $1.00 child (5-12). Carousel $1.00 – (2) ride tokens.
- Tours: Factory Tuesday-Saturday 10:00am – 4:00pm. 30-45 minutes long. (Memorial Day-December 23, except Thanksgiving). Reservations necessary for parties of 10 or more.

Watch the wood carousel horses being made starting from a "coffin box" with a hollow center, then the carving with special tools, and finally the painting. The artisans casually show off their skill. Why do some carousels run backwards? Why were they built in medieval times? Now that you know how they're made, walk over to the wonderful carousel in the center of town (Main & Fourth Street-indoor/outdoor style - open daily). For lunch, stop at the Coney Island Diner on Main Street with its genuine old-time tables, stools and "Blue Plate" specials.

JOHNNY APPLESEED HERITAGE CENTER

Mansfield - *124 North Main Street, 44902. Phone: (800) 642-0388.* ***Web: www.jahci.org.*** Outdoor Historical Drama focusing on Johnny Appleseed as a unique national hero as a humanitarian, philanthropist and conservationist. It will focus on his wanderings all across Ohio, Pennsylvania, Indiana, Illinois and Kentucky in the early 1800's, planting apple seeds and sharing his love and faith. Opens June 2003.

MANSFIELD PLAYHOUSE

Mansfield - *95 East Third Street, 44902. Phone: (419) 522-8140 or (419) 522-2883 tickets.* ***Web: www.mansfieldplayhouse.com.*** Community and guest artists present adult and youth productions. (September-May)

MANSFIELD SOLDIERS AND SAILORS MEMORIAL BUILDING MUSEUM

Mansfield - *34 Park Ave West, 44902. Phone: (419) 525-2491. Hours: Saturday-Sunday 1:00-5:00pm. Donations accepted.* The building was built in 1888 and is the oldest continuously used memorial building in the state of Ohio. The museum houses artifacts of military history of Richland County as well as civil and natural history artifacts.

MANSFIELD SYMPHONY ORCHESTRA

Mansfield - *138 Park Avenue West, Renaissance Theatre, 44902. Phone: (419) 522-2726.* ***Web: www.rparts.org.*** *Student pricing.* Performs classical works, opera, pops, ballet (holiday Nutcracker) and special events in restored Renaissance Theatre. Summer musical and outdoor concerts.

OHIO BIRD SANCTUARY

Mansfield - *3773 Orweiler Road (west of Lexington off SR 97, turn north on Bowers Rd, then east), 44903. Phone: (419) 884-HAWK.* ***Web: www.ohiobirdsanctuary.org****. Hours: Visitors Center open Wednesday, Friday, Saturday & Sunday 10:00am-4:00pm. Trails open daily during daylight hours, restricted winter hours, and group tours by reservation (small fee).* The Ohio Bird Sanctuary is located on the headwater of the Clearfork River. The marsh and old growth forest offers great birding and hiking. Enjoy seeing birds up close at the birds of prey or by walking through the songbird aviary. The Sanctuary is also a wildlife rehabilitation for native bird species. Groups can schedule "Falcon & Friends", a live bird presentation. Picnic tables, gift shop. FREE.

JONES POTATO CHIPS

Mansfield - *265 Bowman Street (I-71 to US 30 west to US 39 south to Bowman St), 44905. Phone: (419) 522-2988.* ***Web: www.joneschips.com****. Admission: FREE. Tours: By appointment, Monday through Friday between the hours of 9:00am and 1:00pm. Tours last 35-45 minutes.* Warm potato chips! The automated equipment processes volumes of potatoes each day into hand-cooked wavy style *(marcelled)* chips. Machines peel, slice, salt and package the fresh potato chips. They make 8000 lbs. of chips per day!

LIVING BIBLE MUSEUM

500 Tingley Avenue (I-71 to US 30 West to State Route 545 North)

Mansfield 44905

- Phone: (419) 524-0139 or (800) 222-0139
  Web: www.livingbiblemuseum.org
- Hours: Monday – Friday 10:00am – 5:00pm, Saturday 10:00am-7:00pm, Sunday 2:00-7:00pm (April – December). Weekends Only (January – December).
- Admission: $4.50 adult, $4.25 senior, $3.50 youth (6-18), $20.00 family. This is the price per museum. Discounts for 2+ museum tours. There are 4 museums: Life of Christ, Miracles of The Old Testament, Christian Martyrs, or Christian History.

- ❑ Miscellaneous: Gift Shop. Collection of rare bibles and religious woodcarvings.

The only life-size wax museum in Ohio – it features figures from the Old and New Testaments (non-denominational). Featured stories include the Life of Christ, Jonah and the whale, and Adam and Eve. The tour guide takes you through dimly lit hallways that add a theatrical, dramatic effect. Your personal tour guide will assist you through dioramas from the Bible, each with its own audio text, music, and some with special effects. At the end of the tour you will be left emotional (a small chapel is available to reflect).

KINGWOOD CENTER

Mansfield - *900 Park Avenue West (I-71 exit State Route 30), 44906.* ***Web: www.virtualmansfield.com/kingwood/index.htm****. Phone: (419) 522-0211. Hours: 8:00am-30 minutes before dusk.* Forty-seven acres of gardens, woods and ponds surrounding the King French Provincial mansion. Greenhouses with a specialty of tulips and perennials and short hiking trails are family friendly.

MANSFIELD FIRE MUSEUM

Mansfield - *(2 miles west of downtown on W. Fourth Street), 44906. Phone: (419) 529-2573 or 800/211-7231.* ***Web: www.mansfieldfiremuseum.org****. Hours: Saturday-Wednesday 1:00-4:00pm (June 1-September 1). Weekends only (September 1-June 1). FREE.* A museum of fire fighting history with reproductions of a turn-of-the-century fire station. Hear the antique alarm bell that alerted the firemen and you can almost see the horses leave their stable to be hitched to the hose wagon.

OHIO STATE REFORMATORY

100 Reformatory Road (I-71 to SR 30 west & SR 545 North)

Mansfield 44906

- ❑ Phone: (419) 522-2644, **Web: www.mrps.org**
- ❑ Hours: Sunday 1:00-4:00pm (Mid-May to September).
- ❑ Admission: $5.00 per person per tour.

- Tours: Phone Reservations Preferred. Children under 9 and pregnant women should use caution because of stairs and lead-based paint. 45 minutes. Daily group tours (10+) by appointment. Groups by reservation only

A castle prison? Well, maybe from the outside only. This 1886 structure was built as a boy's reformatory. The original cellblocks and offices remain intact and were used to film 4 major motion pictures including "The Shawshank Redemption" and Air Force One. What does the architecture have to do with spiritual reform? The East Cell Block houses the world's largest free-standing steel cell block - 6 tiers. Tours to choose from:

- <u>TOWER TOUR</u> - Travel the length of the East Cell Block. Wind your way to the top of a guard tower. Visit the Catholic Chapel high up in the Central Block. This most strenuous tour involves extensive stair climbing.
- <u>DUNGEON TOUR</u> - Venture into the dark and dingy "Hole" in the detention wing. Take a trip through the strange and narrow basement corridors. Check out the mysterious "Hot Box". Hear the story of the seven-foot Jesus.
- <u>HOLLYWOOD TOUR</u> - See the Shawshank Warden's Office and Andy Dufresne's escape tunnels. Hazard a trip into the sinister "Hole". View the 1886 West Cell Block used as a Russian prison in Air Force One. Visit the Hollywood wall. This tour involves extensive stair climbing.
- <u>"EASY TIME" TOUR</u> - See the Visiting Room and hear the stories. Get a glimpse into a prisoner's life in both the East and West Cell Blocks. View a video and hear prison stories from a second floor room in the Warden's residence. This is the least strenuous tour.

<u>BOOKMASTERS</u>

Mansfield (Ashland) - *2541 Ashland Road, 44905. Phone: (419) 281-8549 ask for plant manager.* ***Web: www.bookmasters.com****. Tours: Monday – Friday 10:00am – 2:00pm. Appointment necessary. Group size (6 – 40).* While visiting, kids will learn step-by-step how books (like the "Kids Love" books) are produced.

Start by seeing what materials are needed, then see the pre-press division, the printing area (with huge, monster-like printers), and the final book binding area. See all phases of books being made through production and view finished books at the end of the tour.

MALABAR FARM STATE PARK

4050 Bromfield Road (I-71 to Exit 169, follow signs)

Mansfield (Lucas) 44843

- Phone: (419) 892-2784, **Web: www.malabarfarm.org**
- Admission: Big House Tour, $3.00 adult,$1.00 child (6-18). Tractor Drawn Wagon Tour, $1.00 (6+)
- Tours: Begin at 11:00am, last tour at 3:00pm.
- Miscellaneous: Malabar Inn. 1820's stagecoach stop restaurant. (Special note to grandparents… Humphrey Bogart & Lauren Bacall were married on these beautiful grounds).

A writer and lover of nature, Louis Bromfield, dreamed of this scenic land and home. It is still a working farm and the place where Bromfield discovered new farming techniques. The guides at the Big House tell captivating stories. Bridle trails, fishing, hiking trails, camping and winter sports are also available park-wide. During seasonal events, kids can watch harvesting or planting, ride an authentic wagon, or help with daily chores @ 3:30pm. Easy to understand farm exhibits (even milk a mechanical cow!)

EAST HARBOR STATE PARK

Marblehead - *(8 miles East of Port Clinton on State Route 269), 43440.* ***Web: www.dnr.state.oh.us/parks/parks/eharbor.htm****.* *Phone: (419) 734-4424.* Nature programs. 1,152 acres of camping (large campground), hiking trails, boating, fishing, swimming (sandy beaches) and winter sports.

KELLEYS ISLAND FERRY BOAT LINES

Marblehead - *510 W. Main Street, 43440. Phone: (419)798-9763 or (888)225-4325.* ***Web: www.kelleysislandferry.com****.* Daily passenger and automobile transportation to Kelleys Island from Marblehead, departing every half-hour during peak times. Available year-round, weather permitting. Admission fees.

MARBLEHEAD LIGHTHOUSE STATE PARK

Marblehead *43440. Phone: (419) 798-4530 or (800) 441-1271, Web:* **www.marbleheadpenisula.com**. *Hours: Monday-Friday 1:00-5:00pm (June-August). On Saturdays there are pioneer demos at the lightkeeper's house.* The oldest working lighthouse on the Great Lakes. Marblehead Point has been known for having the roughest weather along Lake Erie. To warn ships of the danger of being dashed against the rocks by winds from the north, the federal government constructed the Marblehead Lighthouse in 1821. Built of native limestone, it is the oldest light in continuous operation on the Great Lakes. The reflector lamp originally burned whale oil, lard oil, coal oil, and now it's electric.

PREHISTORIC FOREST & MYSTERY HILL

8232 East Harbor Road - State Route 163 (8 miles East of Port Clinton off State Route 2), **Marblehead** 43440

- Phone: (419) 798-5230, **Web: www.prehistoricforest.com**
- Hours: Daily 10:00am – 7:30pm (June – August). Weekends Only (May and September).
- Admission: $5.00-$7.00 (4 and over).
- Miscellaneous: Sleeping cabins (w/AC) available to rent.

Learn the eating habits and lifestyles of dinosaurs in a forest full of them. Take a walk through a volcano, dig for dinosaur footprints and bones or get your picture taken with Reggie, the 14' Python snake! Also included is the Reptile House (live pythons, lizards, and alligators) and Mystery Hill (the "Illusion of Nature" House where water runs uphill and chairs stick to the walls). Be sure to volunteer for the fun demonstrations at Mystery Hill. Also, the T-Rex now "follows" you, the Stenonychosaurus is the brainest, and the dinosaurs are pretty much life-size!

TRAIN – O – RAMA

Marblehead - *6732 East Harbor Road (Route 161 East), 43440. Phone: (419) 734-5856.* ***Web: www.trainorama.net****. Hours: Monday – Saturday 11:00am – 5:00pm, Sunday 1:00 – 5:00pm. Admission: $5.00 adult, $4.00 senior, $3.00 child (4-11). Miscellaneous: Train Gift Shop.* Ohio's largest operating model train display open to the public.

EDISON BIRTHPLACE MUSEUM

North Edison Street (off State Route 250, Downtown, near exit 7 off Turnpike), **Milan** 44846

- Phone: (419) 499-2135, **Web: www.tomedison.org**
- Hours: Tuesday – Saturday 10:00am – 5:00pm, Sunday 1:00 – 5:00pm (Summer). Tuesday – Sunday 1:00 – 5:00pm (April- May and September – October). Wednesday-Sunday 1:00-4:00pm (February-March and November-December). Closed Easter.
- Admission: $5.00 adult, $4.00 senior (60+), $2.00 child (6-12).
- Miscellaneous: The Milan Historical Museum Complex is across the street.

Edison was born here in 1847 and raised in this home until age 7. The original family mementos give you a feeling of being taken back in time. The room full of his inventions (he had 1,093 American patents) gives you a sense of his brilliance! Most famous for his invention of the light bulb and phonograph (1st words recorded were "Mary had a little lamb"), you may not know he was kicked out of school for being a non-attentive/slow learner! So, his mother home-schooled him. Part of the Edison family belongings include slippers, Derby hat, cane, Mother Edison's disciplinary switch (still hanging in the original spot in the kitchen), butter molds and "Pop Goes the Weasel" yarner. Two practical inventions of the time you'll want to see are the pole ladder (a long pole that pulls out to a full size ladder) and the slipper seat (a cushioned little seat, low to the ground, so it is easier to put your slippers or shoes on). Ask about one of our favorite Edison inventions...the Power Nap!

MILAN HISTORICAL MUSEUM

10 Edison Drive (off SR 113, Turnpike exit 118)

Milan 44846

- Phone: (419) 499-2968, **Web: www.milanhist.org**
- Hours: Tuesday - Saturday 10:00am - 5:00pm, Sunday 1:00 - 5:00pm (Summer). Tuesday - Sunday 1:00 - 5:00pm (April, May, September, October)
- Admission: $5.00 adult, $4.00 senior, $2.00 child (6-12).
- Miscellaneous: Gift Shop with video and slide presentations. Provide excellent school tour packets of study.

Tour includes several buildings in a complex featuring different themes like the Galpin Home of local history, dolls, toys and a collection of mechanical banks. There are several other homes along with a blacksmith and carriage shop and everything you might want to buy from the 1800's is sold in the general store. Be sure to add this to your visit to Edison's Home, one block away.

OBERLIN HERITAGE TOUR

Oberlin - *73 South Professor Street, James Monroe House (State Route 38 and State Route 511), 44074. Phone: (440) 774-1700.* ***Web: www.oberlinheritage.org/visit.html.*** *Hours: Tuesday, Thursday, Saturday 10:30am and 1:30pm. Admission: $4.00 adult, child FREE w/adult.* The Underground Railroad, former politicians' and professors' homes (workshop of aluminum history and study student life around campus through the years), and a little red school house with collection of lunch pails and McGuffey Readers.

MOHICAN-MEMORIAL STATE FOREST

Perrysville - *3060 County Road 939, 44864. Phone: (419) 938-6222,* ***Web: www.dnr.state.oh.us/forestry/Forests/stateforests/mohican.htm.*** *Open daily 6:00am - 11:00pm.* 4,498 acres in Ashland County. Hiking trails (24 miles), bridle trails (22 miles), "Park & Pack" camping sites (10), snowmobile trails (7 miles - weather permitting), state nature preserve. Also War Memorial Shrine and Mohican State Park is adjacent.

AFRICAN SAFARI WILDLIFE PARK

267 Lightner Road (Off State Route 2 exit SR 53, follow signs)

Port Clinton 43452

- Phone: (419) 732-3606 or (800) 521-2660
  Web: www.africansafariwildlifepark.com
- Hours: Daily 10:00am-5:00pm (April, May, September, October). Daily 9:00am-7:00pm (Memorial Day-Labor Day)
- Admission: $10.00 - $16.00 per person (summer). $3.00 discount (spring & fall). Admission ages 3+.
- Miscellaneous: Safari Grill and gift shop. Jungle Junction Playland and petting zoo.

See more than 400 animals (including llamas, alpacas, and zebras) as they wander freely around your vehicle as you drive through a 100-acre park. This is the only drive through safari park in the Midwest. The giraffe lean their long necks over to check you out through your car windows. The friendliest animals are the camels and ponies and you can ride them, too (at no additional charge). The ugliest are probably the warthogs. Another favorite is the "Porkchop Downs" pig races. Boy, do they snort loud when they're trying to win!

CRANE CREEK STATE PARK & MAGEE MARSH WILDLIFE AREA

Port Clinton - *(Rte. 2, west of Port Clinton), 43452. Phone: (419) 898-0960.* ***Web: www.dnr.state.oh.us/odnr/parks/cranecrk.htm****. Hours: Open dawn to dusk, year-round.* Sportman's Migratory Bird Center. Walk the boardwalk trails or climb the observation tower.

GREAT LAKES POPCORN COMPANY

Port Clinton - *115 Madison Street (downtown), 43452.* ***Web: www.GreatLakesPopcorn.com****. Phone: (419) 732-3080 or (866) 732-3080. Hours: Daily 10:00am-5:00pm (Sunday 11:00am-5:00pm). Extended Seasonal hours. Tours are available for school-age children.* Look for the bright red & white awning and listen for the "island music" as you and your children find this fun adventure! See popcorn popped and coated and sample many varieties of popcorn including "Bubble Gum", "Root Beer", "Jelly Bean" and "Wild Walleye". The "Popcorn Tasting Station" is where kids and families alike can sample any, or all, of the 30 plus flavors.

JET EXPRESS

Port Clinton - *5 North Jefferson Street (docks at foot of Perry Street Bridge, SR 163), 43452. Phone: (800) 245-1JET.* ***Web: www.jet-express.com****. Admission: Average $10.00 each way. (April-October).* Indoor and outdoor seating on the fastest catamaran to Islands. 22 minute trip with some boat facts weaved in. Nice ride and the docks are located right in the hub of activity. Free parking nearby or parking fee at terminal.

ALASKAN BIRDHOUSE WILDLIFE AREA

Put-In-Bay - *Meechen Road, 43456. Phone: (419) 285-9736. Hours: 11:00am-5:30pm (Seasonally). Admission: $2.00-3.00 per person (age 6+).* Narrated tours of North American Wildlife including grizzly bears, moose, geese, walleye fish, whales, cranes, quails, and ducks. Over 100 stuffed pelts of animals are displayed in their natural habitats.

AQUATIC RESOURCE CENTER

Put-in-Bay - *Peach Point, 43456. Phone: (419) 285-3701 or (419) 625-0062. Hours: Tuesday-Saturday 11:00am - 6:00pm. (May - August). Admission: FREE.* The Ohio Division of Wildlife invites kids to learn about fish and fishing. Live fish exhibits, hands-on displays and public fishing supplies.

CRYSTAL CAVE & HEINEMAN'S GRAPE JUICE WINERY

Catawba Avenue, **Put-in-Bay** 43456

- ❑ Phone: (419) 285-3412
- ❑ Hours: Daily (early May - Late September). Call for schedule.
- ❑ Admission: $5.00 adult, $1.50 child (6-11).

Although you may be hesitant to have children tour a winery, they really put emphasis on the grapes (varieties, flavor, color, etc.) and the chemistry of making juice. Did you know they use air bags to press the juice out of grapes? The Crystal Cave (located below the factory) is well worth the visit! You'll walk right into the world's largest geode! Every crystal (mostly bluish green) has 14 sides. We promise a WOW on this one! A complimentary glass of juice or wine is offered at the end of the tour.

LAKE ERIE ISLANDS MUSEUM

Put-in-Bay - *441 Catawba Avenue, 43456. Phone: (419) 285-2804, **Web: www.leihs.org**. Hours: Daily 11:00am – 5:00pm (May, June and September). Daily 10:00am – 6:00pm (July and August). Admission: FREE.* Boating, sailors, and shipping industry artifacts. Video shown is an excellent trip to the past. Why did so many Grand Hotels burn? What are the major industries on the island...a hint...one is a fruit! Usually live displays of Box Turtles, Painted Turtles, and island snakes can be seen at the wildlife building. Look for ship models scattered throughout.

MILLER BOAT LINE

Put-in-Bay - *Catawba Point (SR 2 to Route 53 north), 43456. **Web: www.millerferry.com**. Phone: (800) 500-2421 or (419) 285-2421.* Service to Put-in-Bay and Middle Bass Island. Low rates and most frequent trips.

PERRY'S CAVE

Put-in-Bay - *979 Catawba Avenue (South Bass Island, 1/2 mile from town), 43456. **Web: www.perryscave.com**. Phone: (419) 285-2405. Admission:$6.00 adult, $2.50 child (6-12). Tours: Daily 10:30am - 6:00pm. Tours leave every 20 minutes in the summer. Fewer times rest of year. Miscellaneous: War of 1812 mini-golf. Antique car museum.* Inside the cave you'll see walls covered with calcium carbonate (the same ingredient in antacids) that has settled from years of dripping water. Rumor says Perry kept prisoners and stored supplies in the cave during the Battle of Lake Erie. At the Gem Mining Company, buy a bag of sand at the gift shop. Take the bag outside to the mining station and dig through it to find gems. Compare your stones to a display in the survey stations.

PERRY'S VICTORY AND INTERNATIONAL PEACE MEMORIAL

93 Delaware Avenue, **Put-In-Bay** 43456

- Phone: (419) 285-2184, **Web: www.nps.gov/pevi**
- Hours: Daily 10:00am - 7:00pm (Mid-June - Labor Day). Daily 10:00am - 5:00pm (Late April - Mid-June & September and mid-October).

- ❑ Admission: Observation Deck by elevator, $3.00 per person (age 17 and up). Must climb two flights of stairs first.

Built of pink granite, 352 feet high and 45 feet in diameter, this memorial commemorates the Battle of Lake Erie and then the years of peace. Commodore Perry commanded the American fleet in the War of 1812. In September of 1813 he defeated the British and Perry then sent his famous message to General William Henry Harrison "We have met the enemy and they are ours". Interpretive actors outside chat with you on busy days and weekends. The new Visitors Center facility has extensive exhibits, an auditorium featuring a film with surround sound, and an expanded bookstore. The exhibits will tell the story of the Battle of Lake Erie, the War of 1812, construction of the monument and the international peace that it represents. A live feed camera system will provide views from the top of the monument enabling those who are unable or decide not to make the trip to the observation deck to witness the view.

PUT-IN-BAY TOUR TRAIN

Put-In-Bay - *(South Bass Island), 43456. Phone: (419) 285-4855.* ***Web: www.put-in-bay-trans.com****. Hours: Daily 10:00am–5:00pm (Memorial Day – Labor Day). Weekends Only (May and September). Admission: $8.00 adult, $1.50 child (6-11).* A one-hour narrated tour of the island. Departing every 30 minutes, the train trolley allows passengers to depart and re-board (without additional cost) at any time. The train stops at caves and museums. Younger ones will want to get off near downtown at Kimberly's Carousel for an old-fashioned ride for a buck.

CAPTAIN GUNDY'S PIRATE ADVENTURE

Sandusky - *Jackson Street Pier, 44870. Phone: (419) 625-3193.* Set sail for high sea adventure on the El Loro, docked in downtown Sandusky. This one-hour adventure scouts the waters of Sandusky Bay and Lake Erie for pirates' treasure. Hear tales of Bay and Great Lakes history.

CEDAR POINT

State Route 4 (I-80 to Exit 118 or 110. Follow Signs)

Sandusky 44870

- Phone: (419) 627-2350, **Web: www.cedarpoint.com**
- Hours: Vary by season. May – October.
- Admission: $20.00-$44.00, Small children (under 48") – General (ages 4-59). Separate admission for Soak City and Challenge Park. Combo, 2 day & Starlight rates. Parking $8.00.
- Miscellaneous: Stroller rental. Picnic area. Food Service. Miniature golf.

More rides than most other parks in the world! The amusement extravaganza on the shores of Lake Erie includes 15 Roller Coasters and:

- SOAK CITY – wave pool, water slides, Adventure Cove, Eerie Falls (get wet in the dark), swim-up refreshment center.
- CHALLENGE PARK – Rip cord Sky coaster (fall 150 feet and then swing in a 300-foot arc. Grand Prix Raceway.
- SPLASH - high dive act in Aquatic Stadium.
- LIVE SHOWS – 50's, Motown, Country, Ice Shows.
- CHAOS – turn sideways & upside down at the same time.
- MILLENIUM & MAGNUM XL - tallest and best coasters.
- WICKED TWISTER - speed so fast you float on air.
- CAMP SNOOPY - with piped-in kids music and child sized play like Red Baron airplanes, Woodstock's express family coaster, Peanuts 500 Speedway. Also Sing-along Show with Peanuts characters.

GOODTIME I

Sandusky - *(docked at Jackson Street Pier), 44870. Phone: (419) 625-9692 or (800) 446-3140.* ***Web: www.goodtimeboat.com****. Admission: $13.00 - $23.00 (ages 4 and up). Tours: Depart 9:30am, Arrive back 6:30pm (Memorial Day-Labor Day).* Island hopping 40-meter sight seeing cruise to Kelley's Island and Put-In-Bay. Stop for awhile at each island.

GREAT BEAR LODGE & INDOOR WATERPARK

4600 Milan Road (SR250) (Ohio Turnpike, exit 7, north on SR250)

Sandusky 44870

- Phone: (419) 609-6000 or (888) 779-BEAR
  Web: www.greatbearlodge.com
- Hours: Waterpark daily 9:00am-10pm. Wristbands are good day of arrival until closing the next day. Checkout is 10:30am.
- Admission: Lodge room suites include 4-6 waterpark passes. Rooms vary from $169-$300+ per night. Additional waterpark passes $15.00 each.
- Miscellaneous:All suites: Family, KidCabin (log cabin in room with bunk beds), microwave, refrigerator (you can bring food and snacks for meals), hair dryer, coffee maker (with real coffee mugs), and private balcony. Arcade and outdoor pools, gift shops. Bring Coast Guard approved swim vests for non-swimmers (limited number of vests available at park, too).

Well, we've gone to explore this family-friendly resort several times....and the verdict...we are always VERY impressed! Even though it's a resort...it still was comfy for the both kids and parents. The multi-story giant log cabin is a place you check into and don't want to leave for a couple of days! Bring you own food to prepare (microwave style) or eat in one of two on site restaurants - GITCHIE GOOMIE GRILL (fishing lodge grill with good sandwiches, appetizers, salads, and light entree menu). LUMBER JACK'S COOK SHANTY has a logging camp theme with food served in bowls and dishes at the table (pass it around family style please). All the kid's menu prices for both restaurants are around $5.00 and includes beverage & dessert (oooh that Moose Tracks Ice Cream....). BEAR TRACK LANDING Indoor Waterpark is the highlight! The minute you step into the Outdoor/Northwoods ambiance (and gently heated, no musty or chlorine smell-they ozonate the water) you have hours of fun. FORT MACKENZIE is in the middle and it's a big thrill to stand under its 48 foot tall tipping water tower bucket that dumps 1000 gallons of water on the structure and splashes thrill seekers below. If you don't scream from excitement there, you're sure to on the giant inner tube slides (best for elementary ages and up). In 5 pools (all ages levels), 7 waterslides, and the water fort you'll find watchful and helpful lifeguards - there for safety and are excellent for crowd control. With a little planning of resources, you will get your money's worth in memories and fun for sure! Even fun for grandparents, as we found out recently with kids and grandma having just as much fun. If your family wants to spread out more, try the Royal Bear Suites w/more spacious layout and a separate bedroom. The Outdoor Water Area (open seasonally) is a 68,000 gallon pool with a geyser & water basketball.

ISLAND ROCKET

Sandusky - *101 W. Shoreline Drive, 44870. Phone: (419)627-1500 or (800)854-8121.* ***Web: www.islandrocket.com****. Admission: $23.00-$29.00 per adult, round trip.* Ride the Rocket! Sandusky's fastest ferryboat now has direct service to Cedar Point, Kelleys Island, and Put-in-Bay. Frequent departures from downtown Sandusky make the Rocket convenient and fun for the whole family. Enjoy both Kelleys Island and Put-in-Bay with one of the island-hopper passes; reservations recommended.

LAGOON DEER PARK

Sandusky - *1502 Martins Point Road,State Route 269 (between State Route 2 and US 6), 44870. Phone: (419) 684-5701.* ***Web: www.sanduskyfunspots.com/deerpark****. Hours: Daily 10:00am – 6:00pm (May-mid-October). Admission: $6.75 adult, $3.75 child (3-12).* Pay Fishing available in stocked lake. Hand feed and pet hundreds of deer, llamas, miniature donkeys and other tame species. Altogether, They have 250 exotic animals from Europe, Japan, Asia, South and North America. Approximately 75 baby animals are born here each year.

MERRY-GO-ROUND MUSEUM

West Washington and Jackson Streets (State Route 6, downtown)

Sandusky 44870

- Phone: (419) 626-6111, **Web: www.merrygoroundmuseum.org**

- Hours: Monday - Saturday 11:00am - 5:00pm. Sunday Noon - 5:00pm (Summer). Weekends Only (January & February). Wednesday - Sunday (Rest of the Year).
- Admission: $4.00 adult, $3.00 senior (60+), $2.00 child (4-14). Includes carousel rides.
- Miscellaneous: Gift Shop

This colorful, bright, big museum was the former Post Office. Once inside, you'll see all sorts of carousel memorabilia and history. Next, tour the workshop to watch craftsman make carousel horses with authentic "old world" tools. Finally, ride the Herschel 1930's indoor merry-go-round.

SOUTH BASS ISLAND STATE PARK

South Bass Island – *43452. Phone: (419) 285-2112.* ***Web: www.dnr.state.oh.us/parks/parks/lakeerie.htm.*** A summer ferry takes you to explore over 35 acres on South Bass Island. Camping, boating, fishing, swimming and winter sports.

INDIAN MILL

Upper Sandusky – *State Route 23 and State Route 67 to Route 47 (along the banks of the Sandusky River), 43351. Phone: (419) 294-3349 or (800) 600-7147.* ***Web: www.ohiohistory.org/places/indian.*** *Hours: Friday – Saturday 9:30am – 5:00pm, Sunday 1:00 – 6:00pm (Memorial Day – October). Admission: $1.00 Adult, $.50 Youth (6-12).* In a scenic location along the Sandusky River, Indian Mill, built in 1861, is the nation's first educational museum of milling in its original structure. The restored three-story structure replaces the original one-story building that the U. S. government built in 1820 to reward the loyalty of local Wyandot Indians during the War of 1812. Many exhibits are placed around the original mill machinery. The restored miller's office displays the history of milling from prehistoric times to the present.

WYANDOT COUNTY HISTORICAL SOCIETY

Upper Sandusky – *130 S 7th Street, 43351. Phone: (419) 294-3857.* ***www.wyandotonline.com/wchs/pages/wyandot_county_museum.htm*** *Hours: Thursday – Sunday 1:00 – 4:30pm (May – October). Small Admission.* An 1853 mansion with displays including American Indian and pioneer days, antique toys and clothing. Also school house. Featured in the schoolhouse are lunch pails from 1880 - 1910, wooden desks with attached chairs, old maps and teaching materials, as well as a pot bellied stove.

INLAND SEAS MARITIME MUSEUM & LIGHTHOUSE

Vermillion - *480 Main Street (3 blocks North of State Route 60 / US 6), 44089. Phone: (440) 967-3467 or (800) 893-1485. Web: **www.inlandseas.org**. Hours: Daily 10:00am – 5:00pm. Admission: $6.00 adult, $5.00 senior (65+), $4.00 child (6-16), Family $14.00.* The museum celebrates adventures of the Great Lakes including models, photographs, instruments, a steam tug engine, and a 1905 pilothouse. Special artifacts are the timbers from the Niagara (Admiral Perry's 1812 ship) and an 1847 lighthouse built with a 400 foot catwalk to the mainland. Take the family on a unique underwater adventure as an interactive exhibit lets you dive the Great Lakes shipwreck of your choice.

FINDLEY STATE PARK

Wellington - *(3 miles South of Wellington on State Route 58), 44090. **Web: www.dnr.state.oh.us/parks/parks/findley.htm**. Phone: (440) 647-4490.* Once a state forest, Findley State Park is heavily wooded with stately pines and various hardwoods. The scenic hiking trails allow nature lovers to view spectacular wildflowers and observe wildlife. One area of the park is set aside as a sanctuary for the Duke's skipper butterfly, an extremely rare insect. Nature programs. Bike rental. 931 acres of camping, hiking trails, boating and rentals, fishing, swimming and winter sports.

CELERYVILLE, BUURMA VEGETABLE FARMS

Willard - *4200 Broadway (Route 224 West to Route 103 South to Celeryville), 44890. **Web: www.buurmafarms.com**. Phone: (419) 935-3633. Hours: Weekdays (June – September) just watching. Tours: 20+ people required.* Judged one of the best industrial tours in the state, this is a 3000-acre organic "muck" vegetable garden. On tour you'll see greenhouses, celery and radish harvesting machines in action, and vegetable processing (cleaning, pruning) and packaging. You'll love the facts and figures it takes to produce veggies. Truly unique!

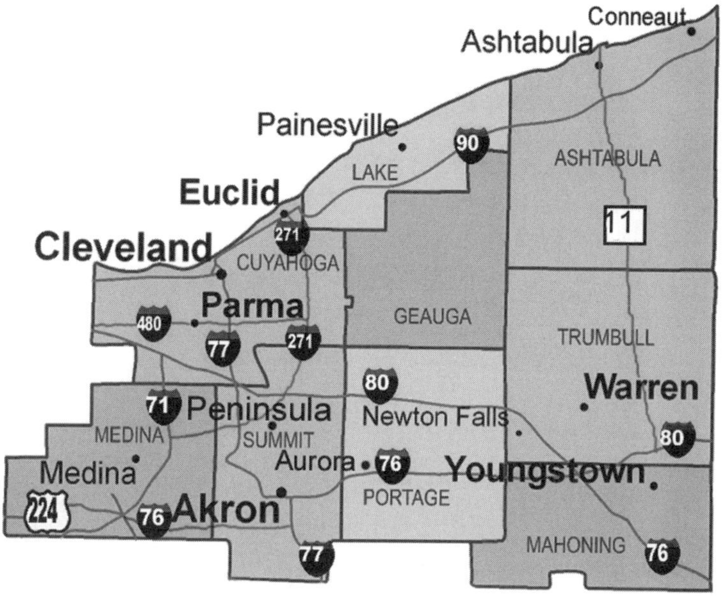

Chapter 5
North East Area

Our Favorites...

Cleveland Museum of Natural History

Cuyahoga Valley National Park & Train

Fairport Marine Lighthouse

Hale Farm & Village

Inventor's Hall of Fame

Lake Farm Park

Malley's Chocolates

Mill Creek Park

Canal Lock in Cuyahoga Valley

STAN HYWET HALL

Akron - *714 North Portage Path (I-77 or I-71 to State Route 18, follow signs into town), 44303. Phone: (330) 836-5533.* ***Web: www.stanhywet.org****. Hours: Daily 10:00am – 4:30pm (April – December). Tuesday-Saturday 10:00am-4:00pm, Sunday 1:00-4:00pm (February-March). Admission: $10.00 adult, $6.00 child (6-12). Miscellaneous: Museum Store, Carriage House Café. Special event Nooks and Crannies tour is more of an adventure into secret passages and doors.* Want to pretend you're visiting old rich relatives for tea – this is the place. The long driveway up to the home is beautifully landscaped. You can park right next to the home and carriage house (vs. a block away) and are greeted as an invited guest. The actual family photographs of the Seiberling Family (Frank was the co-founder of the Goodyear Tire and Rubber Company) scattered throughout the home make you feel as if you know them. Stan Hywet means "stone quarry" referring to the stone quarry the house was built on and the stone that was supplied for building. Being an English Tudor, it is rather dark inside with an almost "castle-like" feeling (the detailed wood panels and crown molding are magnificent). Try to count the fireplaces (23) and discover concealed telephones behind the paneled walls.

AKRON ZOOLOGICAL PARK

Akron - *500 Edgewood Avenue (Perkins Woods Park), 44307. Phone: (330) 375-2525.* ***Web: www.akronzoo.com****. Hours: Daily 10:00am – 5:00pm (April-October). Daily 11:00am-4:00pm (November-March). Closed New Year's Day, end of October, Thanksgiving, Christmas Eve and Christmas Day. Admission: $7.50 adult, $6.00 senior, $5.00 child (2-14). Small parking fee. Reduced winter admission.* A medium-sized zoo (over 300 animals) featuring Monkey Island, The River Otter Exhibit, and an Ohio Farmyard petting area. Visit the Asian Trail with Tiger Valley, the red pandas, and the barking deer. The newest exhibit "Wild Prairie" includes prairie dogs and black-footed ferrets.

AKRON AEROS

Akron - *Canal Park, downtown. 44308. Phone: (330) 253-5151 or (800) 97-AEROS.* ***Web: www.akronaeros.com***. Minor league baseball with ticket prices ranging $6-9.00. AA affiliate of the Cleveland Indians. Special events like Little League Nights and fireworks.

AKRON ART MUSEUM

Akron - *70 East Market Street, 44308. Phone: (330) 376-9185.* ***Web: www.akronartmuseum.org***. *Hours: Daily 11:00am-5:00pm. Free.* An intimate setting for discovering beautiful, new art dating from 1850 to the present. Kids "Drop-in" programs allow for hands-on exploring contemporary art. The Sculpture Courtyard serves as an outdoor gallery with large-scale sculptures.

AKRON CIVIC THEATRE

Akron - *182 S. Main Street, 44308. Phone: (330) 535-3179.* ***Web: www.akron-civic.com***. *Admission.* The ornate interior features a mighty Wurlitzer organ and resembles a Moorish garden complete with blinking stars and moving clouds. The theater features first-rate productions, films and concerts like Fantastic Fridays. Group tours of the theater are available and are interesting for all ages.

AKRON SYMPHONY ORCHESTRA

Akron - *17 North Broadway (performances at E.J. Thomas Performing Arts Hall on Univ. of Akron campus), 44308. Phone: (330) 535-8131.* ***Web: www.akronsymphony.org***. Professional orchestra offers pops, classical and educational concerts. Family Series of concerts, Picnic Pops in the Park and Youth Symphony. (September – July)

NATIONAL INVENTORS HALL OF FAME

221 South Broadway Street (off State Route 18, Downtown)

Akron 44308

- Phone: (330) 762-4463, **Web: www.invent.org**
- Hours: Tuesday – Saturday 9:00am – 5:00pm, Sunday Noon – 5:00 pm. Closed major holidays.

- Admission: $7.50 adult, $6.00 senior (65+) and youth (3-17), $25.00 family.
- Miscellaneous: Hall of Fame (4 floors of exhibits) with open architecture with 5 tiers of steel and windows. Next door is Quaker Square shops and the Depot Diner, a former Railway Express Train and model train display sit-down lunch and dinner (330) 253-5970.

Start with the Inventor's Workshop. A sign says it all - "This is a place to mess around. No rights. No wrongs. Only experiments and surprises!" This is honestly the most hands-on, exploring creativity area we've visited in Ohio. Kids' (and adults') minds open before your eyes. Therefore, plan to spend at least 2 hours exploring. In the wood shop you can actually work with a hammer, nails, and saws (all real) to build a mini boat, house, or new instrument. A favorite exhibit was the "untitled" (metal grasses) which was sculpted of iron powder and danced to music in a magnetic field. Also see the animation area where we each made our own "Toy Story" type movies.

WEATHERVANE PLAYHOUSE

Akron - *1301 Weathervane Lane, 44313. Phone: (330) 836-2626.* ***Web: www.weathervaneplayhouse.com***. Offers mainstage and children's productions, Youth Theatre shows, Spring Puppet show (ex. Our Town, Fiddler on the Roof).

GOODYEAR WORLD OF RUBBER

Akron - *1144 East Market Street (Downtown, Goodyear Hall, 4th floor of headquarters), 44316. Phone: (330) 796-7117.* ***Web: www.goodyear.com***. *Hours: Monday-Friday 8:00am-4:30pm. Tour: Introductory film (by request) of tire production. 1 hour. Groups of 10 or more should call ahead for a reservation. FREE.* Discover how Charles Goodyear vulcanized rubber in his kitchen in a replica of his workshop. Other attractions include a simulated rubber plantation (hands on), Indy race cars, an artificial heart, a moon buggy, history of blimps, history of the trucking industry, and of course an array of Goodyear products. Everyone leaves knowing about at least one unusual new product made from rubber to tell his or her friends about.

PORTAGE LAKES STATE PARK

Akron - *5031 Manchester Road (SR 93), 44319. Phone: (330) 644-2220.* ***Web: www.dnr.state.oh.us/parks/parks/portage.htm.*** The wetlands of the park attract thousands of geese and waterfowl during spring and fall migration periods. Mallards, wood ducks and Canada geese nest in the wetlands each year. In addition, woodcock, heron, hawks, owls, red fox, beaver and muskrat are often sighted. 4,963 acres of camping, hiking trails, boating, fishing, swimming and winter sports.

SUMMIT COUNTY HISTORICAL SOCIETY / JOHN BROWN HOME / PERKINS STONE MANSION

Akron - *550 Copley Road, 44320. Phone: (330) 535-1120.* ***Web: www.neo.rr.com/Summit_County_Historical_Society/.*** *Hours: Wednesday - Sunday 1:00-4:00pm. Closed January and February.* The fight to free slaves governed abolitionist John Brown's life from his hometown days in an 1830's house to the 1859 raid on Harpers Ferry (WV). The house features photos from the time, a reconstruction of a canal boat captain's quarters and changing exhibits about the area. Just across the street is the Perkins Mansion with a décor illustrating Akron and Summit County's history.

OHIO BALLET

Akron - *354 East Market Street, 44325. Phone: (330) 972-7900.* ***Web: www.ohioballet.com.*** Professional company performs at E.J. Thomas Hall in Akron and Ohio Theatre in Cleveland. Produces free outdoor performances in summer.

PYMATUNING STATE PARK

Andover - *Lake Road (6 miles Southeast of Andover off SR 85), 44003.* ***Web: www.dnr.state.oh.us/odnr/parks/parks/pymatuning.*** *Phone: (440) 293-6329.* Nature programs. 17,500 acres of camping, hiking trails, boating and rentals, fishing, swimming and winter sports. Family cabins.

ASHTABULA ARTS CENTER

Ashtabula - *2928 West 13th Street, 44004. Phone: (440) 964-3396.* ***Web: www.ashartscenter.org.*** *GB Community Theatre*

(September-April). Host of other drama, dance & musical performances (Music Man). Workshops for kids on seasonal themes.

GREAT LAKES MARINE & COAST GUARD MUSEUM

1071 Walnut Blvd. (Point Park in Ashtabula Harbor),

Ashtabula 44004

- Phone: (440) 964-6847, **Web: www.ashtcohs.com/ashmus.html**
- Hours: Thursday-Sunday Noon-5:00pm (June-August). Weekends only (May and September).

Holds treasures of the Great Lakes. Housed in the former residence of the Lighthouse Keepers and the Coast Guard Chief, built in 1898. Contains models, paintings, marine artifacts, photos of early Ashtabula Harbor and ore boats and tugs, miniature hand-made brass tools that actually work, and the world's only working scale model of a Hulett ore unloading machine. Expansive view of the harbor from the hill. Feel like you're captain of the high seas in the actual pilothouse from the steamship.

HUBBARD HOUSE & UNDERGROUND RAILROAD MUSEUM

Ashtabula - *Walnut Boulevard and Lake Avenue, 44004. Phone: (440) 964-8168.* ***Web: www.ashtcohs.com/ashmus.html****. Hours: Friday - Sunday and Holidays Noon - 6:00pm (Summer).1:00 - 5:00pm (September and October). Donations accepted.* A northern terminal that was part of the pathway from slavery to freedom in the pre Civil War era.

COVERED BRIDGE PIZZA

Ashtabula, North Kingsville and Andover - *SR 85 or US 20, 44114. Phone: (440) 969-1000 or (440) 224-0497 or (440) 293-6776. Open Daily for Lunch/Dinner. Moderate prices. Casual.* Actual covered bridges with built-in pizza shops! Located in the heart of Ashtabula County (area features 14 covered bridges that can be toured). Historical pictures of the history of each bridge is displayed on the walls of the shop.

SIX FLAGS WORLDS OF ADVENTURE

1060 Aurora Road, St. Rte. 43 (9 miles north of Turnpike Exit 13)

Aurora 44202

- Phone: (330) 562-8303 or (877) 989-3389
  Web: www.sixflags.com
- Hours: Open 10:00 am. Closes after dark. Weekends Only (May, September, October).
- Admission: ~$40.00 General (over 48"). Half price for kids (under 48") and Seniors (61+). Kids age 2 and under FREE. $8.00 for Parking.
- Miscellaneous: Lockers and changing rooms. Paddleboat and Aquacycle rentals. Stroller and wagon rental. Picnic area. Food service. Towel rental. Proper swimwear required. Swimwear available in gift shops. Restaurants.

Take a ride on a backward loop or 13-story plunge roller coaster. Water play at Hurricane Harbor: 2-½ acre pool with surfs, water chutes, wet slides, toboggan run, or white water rapids. Little ones can splash in mini-waterfalls and slides (even a feeding area for babies). Turtle Beach is a 5-story tree house with 150+ water gadgets to shoot. Newer rides are the Superman mega coaster, the Villain, Knight Flight (long, floorless coaster) or the X-Flight (flying coaster). Also Batman Stunt Show, Bugs Bunny appearances, Looney Tunes Boom Town (family soft play area), and Shipwreck Falls boat ride. The Sea Life Park is home of the famous killer whale. See shows with entertaining trained dolphins, sea lions, penguins, sea otters and walruses. There's lots of other sites to see like the water ski show, dolphin habitat, life-size dinosaurs and "Pirates" silly 3D movie. Another exhibit is Shark Encounter in an arched tank that goes overhead making it look like sharks are surrounding you or Tiger Island of big cats.

MAGICAL THEATRE COMPANY

Barberton - *565 W. Tuscarawas Avenue, 44203. Phone: (330) 848-3708.* Northeast Ohio's only professional resident and touring theater for children and families. They produce theatre to enhance the educational growth of young people and their families (ex.

Snow White and Seven Dwarfs or Peter Rabbit). They have a strong outreach to groups and schools.

HALE FARM AND VILLAGE

2686 Oak Hill Road (I-77 exit 226 or I-271 exit 12 (Rte. 303), follow signs), **Bath** 44210

- Phone: (330) 666-3711 or (800) 589-9703
  Web: www.wrhs.org/sites/hale.htm
- Hours: Wednesday - Saturday 11:00am - 5:00pm. Sunday Noon - 5:00 pm. (Memorial Day – October). Special Weekends (November-March).
- Admission: $12.00 adult, $10.00 senior (60+), $7.00 child (3-12)
- Miscellaneous: Museum Shop (you can purchase crafts made on site) and Snack Bar. Map and sample questions to ask towns people provided. Summer Family Fundays are old-fashioned fun geared towards kids. Remember, authentic dirt roads throughout the village.

Tour a living museum with original buildings moved to the area to form a village. Jonathan Hale moved to the Western Reserve from Connecticut and prospered during the canal era building an elaborate brick home and farm typical of New England. The gate house prepares guests with an orientation movie, then begin your adventure around the homestead area with an old-fashioned sawmill and wood shop. Period tools and machines provide wood- working demonstrations. Other barns serve as shops for a blacksmith, candle or broom-maker and basket maker (look for their fly-swatter). The Hale House (bricks made on site by Hale family and still made today) has pioneer cooking (and sampling!) demonstrations. Across the street, visit with mothers, daughters, sons and fathers (they are 1st person 1848) as they share with you thoughts of the day. You will feel like you're part of mid-1800's life as crops are planted and harvested, meetings attended, letters written, textiles spun, barters made, and church and school attended. Kids are asked to help with chores and schoolwork. Maybe you'll even get to "knead" the dough for bricks (w/your feet!) or card wool or roll clay marbles. Samples of crafts worked on are given to the kids as souvenirs. We liked the mix of some buildings set in the present, some set in Wheatfield Township 1848 - it's amusing and interesting.

HUNTINGTON BEACH RECREATION AREA

Bay Village - *Cleveland MetroParks, along the Lake Erie coast, 44140. Phone: (440) 871-2900.* Lake Erie Nature And Science Center. Hiking trails, boating, fishing, swimming, food service.

NOAH'S LOST ARK ANIMAL SANCTUARY

Berlin Center - *8424 Bedell Road (off SR 224), 44401. Phone: (330) 584-7835.* ***Web: www.noahslostark.com****. Hours: Tuesday-Friday, 10:00am-5:00pm, Saturday-Sunday 10:00am-5:00pm (May-August). Weekends only (September-October). Admission: $6.50 adult, $5.00 child (2-17).* One of Ohio's largest breeders of ostrich invite you to tour the Exotic Animal Park. The facility is dedicated to providing a permanent safe haven for unwanted and abused Exotic animals. Hands-on interaction with unusual, uncommon international animals (camels, pot-bellied pigs, antelope). Wagon rides thru farm. Newly constructed large cat compound featuring Tigers, Lions, Ligers, Servals, Leopards, Caracals and Bobcats.

CUYAHOGA VALLEY NATIONAL PARK

15610 Vaughn Road (I-271 exit 12, Rte. 303)

Brecksville 44141

- ❑ Phone: (216) 524-1497 or (800) 257-9477 or (800) 445-9667
  Web: www.nps.gov/cuva/index.htm or **www.dayinthevalley.com**
- ❑ Hours: Visitor Center open at 9:00am-5:00pm. Park hours vary by season.
- ❑ Miscellaneous: Hale Farm & Village & Cuyahoga Valley Scenic Railroad all within park. See separate listings in this chapter for details. No overnight camping within the park, however some is available near the perimeter.

Visitors enjoy picnicking, hiking, bike trails, bridle trails, winter sports, golf, fishing, and ranger-guided programs. Some of the park attractions are:

- ☐ CANAL VISITOR CENTER: Permanent exhibits illustrate 12,000 years of history in the valley, including the history of the Ohio & Erie Canal. The canal-era building once served canal boat passengers waiting to pass through Lock 38. A 20-minute slide program about the park is shown by request. (Canal Road 1.5 miles south of Rockside Road. Access off Hillside Road).
- ☐ LOCK 38 DEMONSTRATIONS: Learn about the canal days in the museum and watch the canal lock demonstrations held afternoons every weekend during the summer and periodically in early fall. "Hoooooo!" is the command that mule drivers shouted as they approached Twelve-mile Lock. Step back in time and relive the canal era along the Ohio & Erie Canal. Imagine riding in a boat being raised or lowered in the old stone lock. Join volunteers and park rangers in 19th-century dress as they operate Lock 38.
- ☐ OHIO & ERIE CANAL TOWPATH TRAIL: Once a mode of transportation of goods and people, the canal (dry and overgrown in places) makes for a nice path for over 19 miles of biking, hiking, running or walking. As you enjoy the Towpath Trail each summer, you may chance upon musicians playing banjo, harmonica, and other instruments.
- ☐ FRAZEE HOUSE: Constructed in 1825 and 1826, the same years the northern section of the Ohio & Erie Canal was built. It is an example of an early, Federal-style Western Reserve home and features exhibits relating to architectural styles, construction techniques, and the Frazee family (east side of Canal Road, 3.5 miles south of Rockside Road in Valley View).
- ☐ BRANDYWINE FALLS: A boardwalk trail allows a close view of the roaring water (best after lots of rain).
- ☐ THE LEDGES OVERLOOK: Hikers can climb to the top of the valley walls to view lots of greenspace.
- ☐ BOSTON STORE: 1836 gas station store functions as a museum with exhibits on canal boat construction.

MAPLESIDE FARMS

294 Pearl Road, US 42 (on US 42, between Rte. 82 and Rte 303 off I-71 exits), **Brunswick** 44212

- Phone: (330) 225-5576 or 225-5577 store. **Web: www.mapleside.com**
- Hours: Open daily for lunch and dinner. Closed Mondays November-August.
- Tours: Scheduled. Minimum 12 people. $4.00-$6.00 per person.Teachers are FREE. Monday-Friday (Labor Day-October)
- Miscellaneous: Gift shop, bakery and ice cream parlor.

They harvest over 20,000 bushels of apples each year from 5,000 apple trees. Many of the 20 different varieties are kept fresh in controlled atmosphere storage so they can be enjoyed year around (what's the secret?). Apple tree orchard view at the restaurant. Try yummy apple fritters and dishes with pork and apples. Even their side dishes are "apple-related" like: Waldorf Salad, homemade applesauce or escalloped apples. Fall group tours of the orchards include sample apples (some picked, some from packing room); a tour of apple orchards and production areas with explanation of growing and processing apples; a cup of cider and bakery; a visit to Harvest Hideout playland; and a small pumpkin for each child. Everything you ever wanted to know or never knew about apples!

CENTURY VILLAGE MUSEUM & COUNTRY STORE

Burton - *14653 E Park Street (State Route 87 and State Route 700), 44021.* ***Web: www.geaugalink.com/geaugahistory****. Phone: (440) 834-1492. Admission: $5.00 adult, $4.00 senior, $3.00 child (6-12). Tours: Tuesday-Sunday 10:30am,1:00 and 3:00pm (May - October). No 10:30am tour on weekends.* Tour the magnificent century homes on the Village grounds, hear stories of early settlers, and view a collection of 9,000 toy soldiers. A restored community with 12 buildings (log cabin, church, barns, schoolhouse, marshal's office and train station) containing 19th Century historical antiques and a working farm. Best to attend during Apple Syrup Festivals, Civil War Festival, or Pioneer School Camp.

YELLOW DUCK PARK

Canfield - *10590 Columbiana Canfield Road (3 miles north of SR1, on SR 46), 44406. Phone: (330) 533-3773.* ***Web: www.yellowduckpark.com****. Hours: Daily 11:00am-8:00pm (Summer). Admission: $7.00-$10.00 (Ages 5+). Season passes or daily admission.* Yellow Duck Park is a "family" swim club and picnic fun land that offers a wide range of family fun attractions. The park consists of 42 acres of wooded and well trimmed lawn areas. Shaded picnic areas encircle a wide variety of both wet and dry attractions and activities in a family atmosphere. Enjoy a family swim club, Little Tikes Beach, Yellow Duck and Jackrabbit Waterslides.

PIONEER WATERLAND AND DRY PARK

Chardon - *10661 Kile Road (off US 6 or SR 608/US 322), 44024. Phone: (440) 951-7507,* ***Web: www.pioneerwaterland.com****. Hours: Daily 10:00am – 8:00pm (Memorial Day – Labor Day). Admission: $15.95 and up. Dry activities are a few additional dollars each. Less than 40" tall FREE. Miscellaneous: Picnic Area, Food Service, and Video Arcade.* Little ones frequent the toddler play area and waterland. Others can explore the water slides, paddleboats, inner tube rides, volleyball nets, Indy raceway, batting cages, miniature golf or driving range. All adjoining a chlorinated crystal clear lake with beaches.

CHILDREN'S MUSEUM OF CLEVELAND

10730 Euclid Avenue University Circle (I-90 to MLK exit 177)

Cleveland 44106

- Phone: (216) 791-KIDS, **Web: www.museum4kids.com**
- Hours: Tuesday-Sunday 10:00am-5:00pm (except Christmas and New Years).
- Admission: $5.00 adult, $4.50 senior(65+), $4.50 child (18 months - 15).

The Children's Museum of Cleveland offers innovative and educational exhibits for children. Splish! Splash! features a two-story climbing structure that is designed to teach basic principles of the water cycle (fun to climb into). Also in this area is the News

Channel 5 Kids' Forecast Center (predict weather, then present it before camera). Put on an apron & splash play in Water Works. Bridges to Our Community features areas that are joined together by bridges. Kids pretend to shop, bank, pump gas or drive a bus. Build with blocks or create art here, too. The Big Red Barn area is a child's book brought to life- infants & preschoolers play with lots of chutes and ladders. Temporary exhibits might be covering tools or trains or sand. Summer camps. Best for kids under 10.

CLEVELAND BOTANICAL GARDEN

11030 East Blvd. (University Circle, I-90 to MLK exit)

Cleveland 44106

- Phone: (216) 721-1600, **Web: www.cbgarden.org**
- Hours: Monday - Saturday 9:00am - dusk and Sunday Noon - dusk. (Hershey Children's Garden closes at 5:00pm.)
- Admission: FREE

Display gardens changing each season (best April-October for color). Most like the Knot Garden and the newer areas: the spiny desert of Madagascar and the cloud forest of Costa Rica. With its wheelchair-accessible tree house, dwarf forests, scrounger garden, worm bins and watery bog, Hershey Children's Garden is an exciting destination for families. Lots of adventure paths to explore and splash in water spouts. Flowers in a bathtub - oh my!

CLEVELAND CENTER FOR CONTEMPORARY ART

Cleveland - *8501 Carnegie Avenue (2nd floor of Playhouse Complex), 44106.* ***Web: www.contemporaryart.org****. Phone: (216) 421-8671 Hours: Tuesday-Saturday 11:00am-6:00pm. Admission: FREE.* Displays of avant-garde paintings, sculpture, drawings, prints, and photographs by regional and national artists. From Warhol to Lichtenstein, Christo to Grooms - and every season they continue to tap into new trends.

CLEVELAND MUSEUM OF ART

Cleveland - *11150 East Boulevard, 44106. Phone: (216) 421-7340 or (888) 262-0033.* ***Web: www.clevelandart.org****. Hours: Tuesday, Thursday, Saturday & Sunday 10:00am-5:00pm. Wednesday & Friday 10:00am-9:00pm. Admission: FREE general admission, charge for parking and special exhibits. Miscellaneous: Café open daytime.* See collection of objects from all cultures and periods including European and American paintings, medieval, Asian, Islamic, pre-Columbian, African masks, Egyptian mummies and Oceanic art. The kids really like the Armor Court (knights in shining armor).

CLEVELAND MUSEUM OF NATURAL HISTORY

1 Wade Oval Drive (University Circle, I-90 and Martin Luther King Dr. exit), **Cleveland** 44106

- Phone: (216) 231-4600 or (800) 317-9155, **Web: www.cmnh.org**
- Hours: Monday - Saturday 10:00am – 5:00pm, Sunday Noon – 5:00pm. Also, Wednesdays open until 10:00pm (September – May only). Closed holidays.
- Admission: $6.50 adult, $4.50 youth (7-18) and senior (60+), $3.50 child (3-6).
- Miscellaneous: Gift shop. Modern Planetarium and interactive pre-show activities(extra fee) plus Observatory open Wednesday evenings. Live animal shows daily. Café lunch. Parking fee.

Meet "Happy" the 70 foot long dinosaur or "Lucy" the oldest human fossil. Look for real dino eggs and touch real dino bones! Highlights of Ohio Natural History are: Johnstown Mastodon -- A long-ago Ohio resident; Dunkle - this fearsome 16-foot-long armored fish with huge self-sharpening jaws is a native Clevelander found in the shale of the Rocky River Valley; Ringler dugout-the oldest well-dated watercraft ever found in North America (found in 1976 in Ashland, OH); Soil - look at NE Ohio vs. Southern Ohio soil; the Glacier that Covered Cleveland; the Diorama of Moundbuilders - shown in layers depicting what might be found (excellent examples-the most spectacular mounds were found in Ohio); or the Wildlife Center & Woods (outside, partially enclosed) where natural habitats are home to raptors (owls, hawks), songbirds, turkey, river otters, fox and many other species found in the state. The lower level has Ohio Botany, Ohio Birds & Insects and Ohio Ecology. In the Discovery Center (a favorite explore), kids can use microscopes or view live insects and reptiles. Lots of touch and feel toys and games. "Planet e" is an interactive area featuring actual footage from NASA space missions projected onto a large viewing monitor. Your "spacecraft" can take you to planets and moons in the solar system and launch a probe. Or, experience an earthquake in Ohio – are we ready? Kids visiting here are first amazed at the large scale of the prehistoric skeletons and also love that many prehistoric artifacts came from Ohio. As you might have guessed, you need several hours or many visits to explore every corner of this place!

CLEVELAND ORCHESTRA

Cleveland - *11001 Euclid Avenue, 44106. Phone: (216) 231-1111 or (800) 686-1141.* ***Web: www.clevelandorchestra.com***. Concerts in beautiful Severance Hall (September-May), outdoors at Blossom Music Center (Summer). The COYO (Cleve. Orchestra Youth Orchestra) performs concerts also. Family Concerts are specially designed for children 6 and older. These narrated concerts are structured around a theme and include collaborative artist such as young musicians, singers, dancers and actors.

CLEVELAND PLAYHOUSE

Cleveland - *8500 Euclid Avenue, 44106. Phone: (216) 795-7000.* ***Web: www.clevelandplayhouse.com***. America's longest running regional theatre presents contemporary and classical children's series plays during the school year.

CLEVELAND SIGNSTAGE THEATRE

Cleveland - *8500 Euclid Avenue, 44106. Phone: (216) 229-2838.* ***Web: www.signstage.org***. Performances combine the beauty of sign language, mime and the theatre to create cultural experiences shared by deaf and hearing people.

WESTERN RESERVE HISTORICAL SOCIETY MUSEUM

10825 East Boulevard, University Circle (I-90 to MLK exit 177)

Cleveland 44106

- Phone: (216) 721-5722, **Web: www.wrhs.org**
- Hours: Monday – Saturday 10:00am – 5:00pm, Sunday Noon – 5:00pm.
- Admission: $7.50 adult, $6.50 senior, $5.00 student (age 6+).
- Miscellaneous: Look for the new Crawford Museum of Transportation & History open 2004. We strongly suggest Tour at Two (Monday-Friday @ 2:00pm) hands-on programs and guided tours for families.

Cleveland's oldest cultural institution boasts a tour of a grand mansion recreating the Western Reserve from pre-Revolution War to the 20th Century. The look (but mostly don't touch) displays include: farming tools, clothing and costumes (displayed with cute artifacts of the time) and over 150 classic automobiles (Cleveland built cars, oldest car, and heaviest car) and airplanes. Look for an original Morgan Traffic Signal (native Clevelander) or the Tinkerbelle - the smallest sailboat to cross the Atlantic.

CLEVELAND LAKEFRONT STATE PARK

Cleveland - *8701 Lakeshore Blvd., NE (off I-90, downtown), 44108.* ***Web: www.dnr.state.oh.us/parks/parks/clevelkf.htm.*** *Phone: (216) 881-8141.* Cleveland Lakefront State Park provides natural relief to the metropolitan skyline. Sand beaches, tree-lined picnic areas and panoramic views of the lake are found within the park along the Lake Erie shoreline. The annual Erie fish catch nearly equals the combined catches of all the other great lakes. Dominant species are perch, smallmouth and white bass, channel catfish, walleye and freshwater drum. 450 acres of boating and rentals, fishing, swimming, and winter sports.

CLEVELAND METROPARKS ZOO & RAINFOREST

3900 Wildlife Way (I-71 exit Fulton Road or East 25th Street)

Cleveland 44109

- Phone: (216) 661-6500, **Web: www.clemetzoo.com**
- Hours: Daily 10:00am – 5:00pm. Until 7:00pm Weekends (Summer). Closed only Christmas and New Year's Day.
- Admission: $8.00 adult (12+), $4.00 child (2-11). Free Parking. Free zoo only admission for Cuyahoga county residents on Mondays. Discount winter rates.
- Miscellaneous: Outback railroad train ride, camel rides and adventure rides are $1.50-$3.00 extra. Concessions and cafes. Zoo trams run daily for FREE.

A rainforest with animal and plant settings like the jungles of Africa, Asia, and South America is the most popular exhibit to explore. The rainforest boasts a storm every 12 minutes, a 25-foot waterfall, and a walk-through aviary. Altogether, the whole zoo holds thousands of animals from all continents including Africa and Australia. Wolf Wilderness is a popular educational study exhibit where you can view thru a giant window the wolves acting "naturally" in the day and night. The Australian Adventure has a kookaburra station, wallaby walkabout and koala junction (55 ft. treehouse and play area with petting yard).

LOLLY THE TROLLEY TOURS

1831 Columbus Road (Station: Powerhouse @ Nautica, west bank of Flats), **Cleveland** 44113

- Phone: (216)771-4484 or (800)848-0173, **www.lollytrolley.com**
- Hours: Early morning or afternoon departures. More available on weekends (even early evening).
- Admission: $7.00-$10.00 (1 hr.) or $10.00-$15.00 (2 hr.).
- Tours: 1 or 2 hours, Reservations Required. 1 hour tour is suggested for preschoolers

- ❑ Miscellaneous: Lots of specialty tours with Cleveland authors traveling along to sites or Holiday Tours (see Seasonal & Special Events).

"Lolly the Trolley", an old fashioned bright red trolley, clangs its bell as you take in over 100 sights around the downtown area. The tour includes Cleveland's North Coast Harbor featuring the world's only Rock & Roll Hall of Fame and Museum and the Great Lakes Science Center; Downtown Cleveland; The Warehouse District, The Flats, a river port by day and a bustling entertainment center by night; Ohio City, with both Victorian homes renovated by "urban homesteaders"; and the West Side Market, one of the world's largest indoor/outdoor food and produce markets; Playhouse Square; University Circle, a focal point for cultural educational and medical institutions. Your tour concludes with a brief stop at the Rockefeller Greenhouse and a drive along the Lake Erie shoreline back to the station. A great way to show off the city to visitors or get an overview of sites to decide which you want to visit.

TOWER CITY CENTER OBSERVATION DECK

Cleveland - *50 Public Square, 42nd Floor, Terminal Tower, 44113. Phone: (216) 621-7981. Hours: Weekends 11:00am - 4:30pm (Summer), 11:00am - 3:30pm (Rest of Year). Admission: $2.00 adult, $1.00 child (6-16).* The 42nd floor deck offers a full view of the city (best if you choose a clear day) with a few displays of the history of the Terminal Tower and downtown.

CLEVELAND BROWNS

Cleveland - *Browns Stadium Downtown, Lakefront, 44114. Phone: (440) 891-5050 or (440) 224-3361 tours.* ***Web: www.clevelandbrowns.com***. NFL Football, New Dawg Pound. Largest scoreboard in NFL Football. Kids Club. Tours by appointment give you facts and figures plus a peek at locker rooms and press boxes. Tickets begin at $30.00. (September-December)

GOOD TIME III

825 East 9th Street Pier (Behind Rock & Roll Hall of Fame)

Cleveland 44114

- Phone: (216) 861-5110, **Web: www.goodtimeiii.com**
- Admission: $15.00 adult, $14.00 senior, $9.00 child (age 2+).
- Tours: Daily Noon, 3:00pm, Sundays at 6:00pm (mid-June to Labor Day). Weekends (Friday-Sunday) only in May and September.
- Miscellaneous: Food Service Available. Lower deck is air-conditioned and heated.

The quadruple-deck, 1000 passenger boat takes a two hour excursion of city sights along the Cuyahoga River and Lake Erie. The word Cuyahoga is Indian for "crooked". You'll see tugboats and the largest yellow crane boats in the country. See all the industry in the Flats including concrete, pipe, transportation, limestone, and coke businesses. Collision Bend used to be so narrow that many boats got tangled up. Since then, they have dredged the curve and it's now very wide.

GREAT LAKES SCIENCE CENTER

601 Erieside Avenue (E 9th Street and I-90, North Coast Harbor, Downtown), **Cleveland 44114**

- Phone: (216) 694-2000, **Web: www.glsc.org**
- Hours: Daily 9:30am – 5:30pm.
- Admission: $6.00-$8.00. Memberships Available. Omnimax additional $6.00-$8.00. Discount combo tickets.
- Miscellaneous: Gift Shop OmniMax Theater – 6 story domed screen image and sound. Pizza Hut Express, Great Lakes Grill and Bytes sandwich restaurants on location.

Over 300 interactive exhibits – especially fun on the second floor. Pilot a blimp, test your batting skills, or bounce off the walls in the Polymer Funhouse. The science playground museum focuses on the Great Lakes region and its environment(Sick Earth, Cloud Maker, Nitrogen Fixation). Young lab scientists (guests) can create a tornado or create light. Virtual Sports, Electric Shows & one of the largest video walls east of the Rockies.

NAUTICA QUEEN

Cleveland - *1153 Main Avenue (West Bank Flats), 44114.* ***Web: www.nauticaqueen.com****. Phone: (216) 696-8888 or (800) 837-0604, Hours: Monday – Thursday Noon, 7:00pm; Friday Noon, 7:30 pm; Saturday 11:00am, 7:30pm; Sunday 11:00am, 4:00pm (April-December). Reservation Required. Admission: $13.00-18.00 child (Adult prices are about double).* 3 Hour Dinner Cruise or 2 hour Lunch/Brunch Cruise. Many cruises include entertainment with special themes.

ROCK AND ROLL HALL OF FAME MUSEUM

Cleveland - *One Key Plaza (9th Street exit north, downtown waterfront), 44114. Phone: (216) 781-ROCK or (800) 493-ROLL,* ***Web: www.rockhall.com****. Hours: Daily 10:00am - 5:30pm (open until 9 p.m. on Wednesdays). Closed Thanksgiving and Christmas. Admission: $18.00 adult (13-59), $14.00 senior (60+), $11.00 youth (9-12). Free Museum admission for children 8 and under with the purchase of an adult admission.* As parents reminisce, kids will probably giggle, at most of the many exhibits including: Rock & Roll and the Media, It's Only Rock & Roll, Cinema (documentary films), Induction Videos, Radio Station and the Hall of Fame. Please check in with Visitor's Services before you explore here - they'll let you know which areas have PG and above ratings - you'll know which areas to overlook.

U.S.S. COD

1809 East 9th Street (North Marginal Road next to Burke Lakefront)

Cleveland 44114

- Phone: (216) 566-8770, **Web: www.usscod.org**
- Hours: Daily 10:00am - 5:00pm (May - September).
- Admission: $5.00 adult, $4.00 senior (62+), $3.00 student (under 6 Free).
- Miscellaneous: Recommend airport parking lot.

We started our visit at the Aristotle periscope on shore that gives you a view of Lake Erie and puts you in the mood to explore the WW II submarine that sank enemy shipping boats. The ninety-man crew lived in cramped quarters - an amazing reminder of the price of freedom. The eight separate compartments, tight quarters, ladders to climb and plenty of knobs to play with give an authentic feeling of submarine life. The best part of this tour is the fact that the sub was actually used in wartime and still remains pretty much the same as during wartime…very authentic presentation.

WILLIAM G. MATHER MUSEUM

Docked at 1001 East 9th Street Pier (Northcoast Harbor)

Cleveland 44114

- Phone: (216) 574-6262
  Web: http://little.nhlink.net/wgm/wgmhome.html
- Hours: Daily 10:00am - 5:00pm, except Sunday Noon - 5:00pm (Summer). Weekends (Friday-Sunday) Only (May, September, October).
- Admission: $5.00 adult, $4.00 senior(60+), $3.00 youth (5-18).
- Miscellaneous: Best for preschoolers and older because of dangerous spots while walking. Films play continuously. After your visit, have lunch or dinner at Hornblowers Restaurant (216-363-1151). An actual barge restaurant on the water.

The floating Mather is an iron boat once used to carry ore, coal and grain along the Great Lakes. Little eyes will open wide in the 4 story engine room and they will have fun pretending to be the crew (or maybe guests) in the cozy sleeping quarters or the elegant dining room. Group tours are treated to programmed learning fun in the Interactive Cargo Hold area. Make a sailor hat or a boat made from silly putty (why does a boat float?). Learn to tie sailors' knots with real rope or pretend you're at sea as you move the ship's wheel. In the pilothouse area, kids use navigation charts, working radar, and a marine radio to plan a trip.

CLEVELAND CAVALIERS

Cleveland *- Gund Arena, 44115. Phone: (216) 420-2200.* ***Web: www.nba.com/cavs***. Professional Basketball. (September – April).

CLEVELAND INDIANS

Cleveland *- 2401 Ontario (Jacobs Field), 44115. Phone: (866) 48-TRIBE.* ***Web: www.indians.com***. *$7.00-$27.00 tickets. (April –*

October). Tours (fee of $4.50-$6.50) include Kidsland, a press box, a suite, a dugout, a fun video...lasts one hour (Monday-Saturday 10:00am-2:00pm, some summer Sundays) Professional Baseball. Kids Club.

CLEVELAND ROCKERS

Cleveland - *Gund Arena, 44115. Phone: (216) 263-ROCK.* ***Web: www.wnba.com/rockers****. Tickets range from $10.00-$20.00.* WNBA women's basketball.

DANCING WHEELS

Cleveland - *Cuyahoga Community College Theatre, Metro Campus, 44115.* ***Web: www.gggreg.com/dancingwheels.htm****. Phone: (216) 432-0306.* Dancing Wheels is one of the first professional modern dance companies in the United States. The company, comprised of dancers with and without disabilities, uses modern dance and wheelchair choreography. Productions such as "The Snowman".

MALLEY'S CHOCOLATES

13400 Brookpark Road (I-480 and West 130th street)

Cleveland 44135

- Phone: (216) 362-8700 or (800) 835-5684
  Web: www.malleys.com
- Admission: $3.00 (age 3+)
- Tours: Monday-Friday 10:00am –3:00pm (By Appointment). Also some Saturdays. Strollers allowed, No cameras. 60 minute tour, 15-50 person limit.

See and hear about the story of chocolate from a professional at Malley's family business (since 1935). We learned it takes 400 cocoa beans to make one pound of chocolate. You'll watch them roast nuts, dip chocolates, and wrap goodies along with samples at the beginning and end of the tour (plus a candy bar to take home). They sell one half million pounds per year with the most sales at Easter, then Christmas, then Valentine's Day. Allow time to shop in their factory store.

NASA GLENN RESEARCH VISITOR CENTER

21000 Brookpark Road (I-480 to Exit 9, next to Cleveland Hopkins Airport, Lewis Field), **Cleveland** 44135

- Phone: (216) 433-2000, **Web: www.grc.nasa.gov**
- Hours: Weekdays 9:00am – 4:00pm. Saturday & Holidays 10:00am – 3:00pm, Sunday 1:00 – 5:00pm. Closed major winter holidays.
- Admission: FREE
- Tours: Available, call for details

The interactive exhibit space called the Aero Adventures houses displays on a space shuttle, satellites, zero gravity chamber, wind tunnels, and space environmental tanks. The Apollo Command Module (used on Skylab 3) is the most popular area. Look for the moon rock and space suit used by astronauts (audio explanation) and tribute to John Glenn. ACTS satellite control room and the space shuttle live broadcasts are a great reason for frequent visits.

MEMPHIS KIDDIE PARK

Cleveland *-10340 Memphis Avenue (I-71 to West 117th/Memphis Avenue Exit), 44144. Phone: (216) 941-5995.* ***Web: www.memphiskiddiepark.com****. Hours and Admission: 10:00am-8:00pm, seasonal. Pay per ride (~$1.00 each). Discounts for books of tickets.* With many of the original rides still in place, Memphis Kiddie Park is truly a landmark of the Cleveland area which has thrilled generations of children. Memphis Kiddie Park consists of eleven miniature amusement rides, a concession stand, an arcade, and an eighteen hole miniature golf course. The park is mainly for youngsters anywhere from about a year old on up to around eight. Little tots rides like a ferris wheel, roller coaster (our little girl's first!) and carousel.

CONNEAUT HISTORICAL RAILROAD MUSEUM

Conneaut - *363 Depot Street and Mill Street (East of Route 7), 44030.* ***Web: www.nrhs.com/chapters/conneaut.htm****. Phone: (440) 599-7878. Hours: Daily Noon – 5:00pm (Memorial – Labor Day). Admission: Donation.* Old New York Central depot with relics from the Ashtabula Bridge Disaster of 1876 and large displays of lanterns, timetables, passes and old photos. Climb aboard the steam engine and caboose on exhibit.

MOSQUITO LAKE STATE PARK

Cortland - *1439 SR 305 (10 miles North of Warren off State Route 305), 44410.* ***Web: www.dnr.state.oh.us/odnr/parks/parks/mosquito.*** *Phone: (330) 637-2856.* Bridle trails. 11,811 acres of camping, hiking trails, boating and rentals, fishing, swimming at sandy beach and winter sports. Near the lake, look for the 12 bald eagles that reside in the area.

FAIRPORT MARINE MUSEUM

129 Second Street (I-90 to SR 44 north to SR 2)

Fairport Harbor 44077

- Phone: (440) 354-4825, **Web: www.ncweb.com/org/fhlh**
- Hours: Wednesday, Saturday, Sunday and Holidays. 1:00 – 6:00pm (Memorial Weekend – Labor Day)
- Admission: $2.00 adult, $1.00 senior and student. Under 6 – FREE.

Pretend you're on a sea voyage as you explore an old pilothouse with navigation instruments, maps and charts and a large ship's wheel. Find out what number of whistles you use to indicate the ship's direction. This room is large enough to really romp around. The highlight of this museum has to be the real lighthouse (although it's a steep climb up and out to the deck). After you proudly climb the 69 steps, catch your breath with a beautiful view of Lake Erie. Our favorite lighthouse & museum combo!

ERIEVIEW PARK

Geneva-on-the-Lake - *5483 Lake Road (I-90 to Geneva Exit 218 to State Route 531), 44041. Phone: (440) 466-8650.* ***Web: www.ncweb.com/biz/erieview.*** *Hours: Daily 2:00 - 10:00pm (Memorial Day – Labor Day). Weekends only (Mother's Day to Early June). Admission: "Day Pass" $7.00-$15.00, Individual rides are ~$2.00. No admission into park to walk around.* Located on the "strip" with 20 old-fashioned classic rides, kiddie rides, bumper cars and water slides. Food service and picnic areas.

GENEVA STATE PARK

Geneva-on-the-Lake - *Padanarum Road (Shore of Lake Erie), 44041.* ***Web: www.dnr.state.oh.us/odnr/parks/jparks/geneva.htm****. Phone: (440) 466-8400.* 698 acres of camping, hiking trails, boating and jet ski rentals, fishing, swimming at sandy beach, winter sports. Large cottages.

AC & J SCENIC RAILROAD

Jefferson - *State Route 46 to East Jefferson Street (Rte. 11 north, exit @ Rte. 307 west), 44047. Phone: (440) 576-6346.* ***Web: www.acjrailroad.com****. Hours: Weekends departing 12:30, 2:00, and 3:30 pm. (mid-June - October). Admission: $8.00 adult, $7.00 senior (60+), $5.50 child (3-13).* Ride on a 1951 Nickel Plate train with a bright red caboose on a one hour ride through woodlands and farmland. Stop halfway at a staging yard for coal and iron ore in Ashtabula Harbor. Gift shop / concessions.

JEFFERSON DEPOT

Jefferson - *147 E Jefferson Street (SR 46 and downtown), 44047.* ***Web: www.members.tripod.com/jeffersonhome****. Phone: (440) 293-5532. Hours: Sunday 1:00-4:00pm (June-October). Admission: $2.00 donation accepted.* Travel back in time to the 1800's Costumed kinfolk will let you peek back into the past! See the ornate 1872 LS&Ms Railroad Station on the National Register, the quaint 1848 "Church in the Wildwood," 1849 Church barn, 1918 Caboose, 1838 Spafford One-Room School House, Hohn's General Store, Early Pharmacy and 1888 House.

VICTORIAN PERAMBULATOR MUSEUM

Jefferson - *26 East Cedar Street (off State Route 46), 44047.* ***Web: www.webspawner.com/users/carriage/****. Phone: (440) 576-9588. Hours: Wednesday & Saturday 11:00am – 5:00pm (Summer Only). Saturdays only (September-May). Admission ~ $3.00.* First of all, do you know what a perambulator is? If you were like us, we just had to know! Answer…a baby carriage. Two sisters have collected and displayed almost 140 carriages dating from the mid- 1800's to the early 1900's. Some are shaped like swans, gondolas, seahorses, and antique cars (made from wicker, which was the Victorian style). This is supposedly the nation's only baby carriage museum.

KENT STATE UNIVERSITY MUSEUM

Kent - *East Main & South Lincoln Streets (Rockwell Hall) 44242. Phone: (330) 672-3450.* ***Web: www.kent.edu/museum****. Hours: Wednesday-Saturday 10:00am-4:45pm. Sunday Noon-4:45pm. Admission. Miscellaneous: Pufferbelly Train Depot Restaurant (330-673-1771) nearby.* Features work of the world's greatest artists and designers. Fashion, ethnic costumes, and textiles are highlighted along with whimsical artifacts from that time.

HOLDEN ARBORETUM

Kirtland - *9500 Sperry Road, 44094. Phone: (440) 946-4400.* ***Web: www.holdenarb.org****. Hours: Tuesday – Sunday 10:00am – 5:00pm. Small admission over age six.* 3000 acres of gardens and walking trails (focus on woody plants). Butterfly garden, ponds. Guided or self-guided hikes begin at Visitors Center.

LAKE FARMPARK

8800 Chardon Road (I-90 to SR 306 south to SR 6 east)

Kirtland 44094

- Phone: (800) 366-FARM, **Web: www.lakemetroparks.com**
- Hours: Daily 9:00am - 5:00pm. Closed Mondays (January-March) and all major holidays.
- Admission: $6.00 adult, $5.00 senior (60+), $4.00 child (2-11)
- Miscellaneous: Gift Shop. Restaurant. Comfortable walking or tennis shoes are best to wear on the farm. Wagon rides throughout the park are included. Wagon rentals are available. Barnyard - ostriches, poultry, sheep petting. Pony rides are $2.00. Seasonal events are fantastic (see last chapter)! Part of Lake Metroparks (28 parks in Lake County – nature, bikeway, 2 golf courses, beach)

Not really a farm - it's a park about farming (and the cleanest farm you'll ever visit!). Most of their focus is to discover where food and natural products come from. In the Dairy Parlor, you can milk a real cow and make ice cream from the cow's milk. Wander over to the Arena and watch the sheep show or a horse show. What products can be made with the help of sheep? - How about feta cheese from their milk and yarn from their wool coats. Use special brushes to clean their wool and then spin some by hand. Some of the cutest exhibits are the babies...look for them all around the Arena. Exhibits are ready to be played with all day in the Great Tomato Works. A giant tomato plant (6 feet wide with 12-ft. leaves) greets you and once inside the greenhouse, you can go down below the earth in the dirt to see where plants get their start. Sneak up on a real honeybee comb, but mind the words on the sign, "DO NOT DISTURB - HONEYBEES AT WORK". This visit generates lots of questions about the food you eat. Great learning!

MAILBOX FACTORY

Kirtland - *7857 Chardon Road (US 6), 44094. Phone: (440) 256-MAIL.* ***Web: www.mailboxfactory.com****. Hours: Tuesday - Friday 8:00am - 6:00pm, Saturday 9:00am - 5:00pm.* You can't miss this place! As you approach the workshop, finished decorative mailboxes are adorning the lawn and many boxes and totem poles (yes!) are works in progress. Owner Wayne Burwell used to drive a snow plow and occasionally knocked down mailboxes during his work. When he replaced them, he did it with such a unique mailbox that others on the street became envious. Now his livelihood is making mailboxes shaped like cows (with a cowbell), pelicans, trucks, flamingoes, or a "pig box". Let your imagination run...A must see!

LAKE MILTON STATE PARK

Lake Milton - *(1 mile South of I-76 off State Route 534), 44429.* ***Web: www.dnr.state.oh.us/parks/parks/lkmilton.htm****. Phone: (330) 654-4989.* Lake Milton's reservoir offers the best in water-related recreation. Boating, swimming and fishing are popular. The scenic shoreline provides a habitat for waterfowls and shorebirds for visitors to enjoy. 2,856 acres of boating, fishing, swimming and winter sports. At the beach are scenic cruises with live narration of history of the lake and Craig Beach Village. (330) 547-5555 or **www.miltoncruises.com**. 1 hour long, ~$6.00-$7.00 per person.

BECK CENTER FOR THE CULTURAL ARTS

Lakewood - *17801 Detroit Avenue, 44107. Phone: (216) 521-2540.* ***Web: www.lkwpl.org/beck/.*** Visual and performing arts center offers children's theatre with productions like "Alice in Wonderland" and "The Hobbit".

MAGICAL FARMS

Litchfield - *5280 Avon Lake Road (SR 83), 44253. Phone: (330) 667-3233.* ***Web: www.alpacafarm.com.*** *Hours: 9:00am-4:30pm, and other times by appointment. Closed Christmas, New Year's Day and Thanksgiving. Tours: Daylight hours, daily, by appointment.* Second largest alpaca breeding farm in North America. With over 50 barns and sheds, a visit to Magical Farms is not only a learning experience...it's an adventure. It's an opportunity for hands-on training and lots of fun interacting with the animals. Picnic sites and gift shop, too.

TENDER SHEPHERD FARMS

Lodi - *7434 Lafayette Road, 44254. Phone: (330) 948-4218.* ***Web: http://home.neo.rr.com/tsfpacas.*** Alpaca farm with over 40 acres to tour. Learn about their care and fiber products made from their fur.

ZOO-4-U

Madison - *5414 River Road, 44057. Phone: (440) 428-6556. Hours: Tuesday-Sunday 11:00am-4:30pm (May 1 - October 31). $6.00 per person (age 4+).* Exotic and rare domestic petting zoo. 150 different kinds of animals that you can handle, pet and ride. Playground, picnic area & pony rides.

ELM FARM - AMERICAS ICE CREAM & DAIRY MUSEUM & PARLOR

Medina - *1050 Lafayette Road (US 42, 2 mile south of the Square, near the water tower), 44258. Phone: (330) 722-3839.* ***Web: www.elmfarm.com.*** *Hours: Monday-Saturday 11:00am-6:00pm, Sunday Noon-5:00pm. Extended hours for parlor. Fewer hours in the winter. Admission: $2.00-3.50 (age 6+).* The dairy farm dates back to the early 1900's. They started manufacturing ice cream in the 50's. The parlor serves the treats and light lunch foods in a soda fountain theme. In the back, they have a museum that features displays showing the way dairies used to operate and lots of dairy inventions through the years (ie. Jack Frost freezer, 20's & 30's Popsicle molds). The interactive areas and collection of full-size rare trucks and milk bottles demonstrates a great deal about the history behind Elm Farm and the dairy industry.

MEDINA COUNTY HISTORICAL SOCIETY JOHN SMART HOUSE MUSEUM

Medina - *206 North Elmwood Street and Friendship Street, 44258. Phone: (330) 722-1341. Hours: Tuesday and Thursday 9:30am – 5:30pm. First Sunday of Month 1:00 – 4:00pm.* East Lake style home. Victorian, Civil War, pioneer and Indian artifacts. Life-size photographs of real "giants", Anna Julian and Martin Bates (also boots and helmet).

GARFIELD'S LAWNFIELD NATIONAL HISTORIC SITE, JAMES A.

8095 Mentor Avenue (I-90 exit Rte. 306, turn right 2 miles East on US 20), **Mentor** 44060

- Phone: (440) 255-8722, **Web: www.wrhs.org/sites/garfield.htm**
- Hours: Monday-Saturday 10:00am - 5:00pm, Sunday Noon - 5:00pm (May-October). Weekends only (Nov.-April).
- Admission: $7.00 adult, $6.00 senior (60+), $5.00 child (6-12).
- Miscellaneous: Gift Shop. Summer Fun Programs (weekdays at 2:00pm) are recommended for hands-on. If touring with school-aged kids, ask for the Young People's club worksheet of puzzles & games. Not recommended for preschoolers. Garfield Birthplace Site & Monument east of Cleveland (440-248-1188 & 216-421-2665).

The Victorian farmhouse mansion was the home of President James A. Garfield. Notice the tiles in the dining room fireplace were painted by family as a craft project. The walk-in safe is neat (contains the wreath sent to his funeral by the Queen of England). Like to drape your legs over the side of a chair? Catch Garfield's office Reading Chair. Who killed him and why? A great museum explains his politics and death. Shortly after his election, an opponent at a railroad station in Washington D.C. assassinated him. See the video showing his life as a preacher (he strongly believed in Divine Providence), teacher and lawyer plus Garfield's campaign on the front porch of his home in 1880. Journalists standing on the lawn covering the campaign nicknamed the property "Lawnfield". Other structures on the 7.82 acre site include the carriage house (visitor center), the campaign office, the 75-foot tall pump house/windmill and barn. Be sure to spend as much time in the Visitors Center as on tour.

MIDDLEFIELD CHEESE HOUSE

Middlefield - *State Route 608, 44062. Phone: (440) 632-5228 or (800) 32-SWISS.* ***Web: www.middlefieldcheese.com****. Hours: Monday – Saturday 7:00am – 5:30pm. FREE admission.* Over 20 million pounds of Swiss cheese are produced here each year. Your tours begins with the film "Faith and Teamwork" describing the cheese-making process. Then wander through the Cheese House Museum with Swiss cheese carvings, antique cheese-making equipment, and Amish memorabilia. Lastly, sample some cheese before you buy homemade cheese, sausage and bread.

PUNDERSON STATE PARK RESORT

Newbury - *(2 miles East of Newbury off State Route 87), 44065. Phone: (440) 564-2279 park or (440) 564-9144 lodge,* ***Web: www.dnr.state.oh.us/parks/parks/punderson.htm*** *or* ***Web: www.pundersonmanorresort.com****.* Nature programs. Tennis. 996 acres of camping, hiking trails, boating and rentals, fishing, swimming and winter sports. Family cabins with A/C and fireplaces. Punderson Manor House Resort has indoor/outdoor pools, tennis, basketball, toboggan and winter chalet.

MAHONING VALLEY SCRAPPERS

Niles - *111 Eastwood Mall Blvd. (Cafaro Field), 44446. Phone: (330) 505-0000.* ***Web: www.mvscrappers.com****.* Class A baseball team with concerts and special family events. Tickets start at $6.00. (late June - early September).

NAT'L MCKINLEY BIRTHPLACE MEMORIAL & MUSEUM

Niles - *40 North Main Street (SR 46 to downtown), 44446. Phone: (330) 652-1704,* ***Web: www.mckinley.lib.oh.us****. Hours: Monday - Thursday 9:00am - 8:00pm. Friday and Saturday 9:00am - 5:30pm, Sunday 1:00 - 5:00pm (September - May Only). FREE* The classic Greek structure with Georgian marble which houses a museum of McKinley memorabilia. Also see artifacts from the Civil War and Spanish-American War. McKinley was the 25th President and the first to use campaign buttons. He was assassinated in office.

HEADLANDS BEACH STATE PARK

Painesville - *State Route 44 (2 miles Northwest of Painesville), 44060.* ***Web: www.dnr.state.oh.us/parks/parks/headlnds.htm****. Phone: (440) 881-8141.* The trademark of Headlands Beach State Park is its mile-long natural sand beach, the largest in the state. In addition to its popularity during the summer season with picnickers and swimmers, the area is home to many plant species typically found only along the Atlantic Coast. 125 acres of hiking trails, fishing, swimming and winter sports.

PAINESVILLE SPEEDWAY

Painesville - *500 Fairport Nursery Road, 44077. Phone: (440) 354-3505.* ***Web: www.painesvillespeedway.com****.* 1/5 mile asphalt track. Sportsmen, Figure 8, Trophy Stock and Factory Four.

CUYAHOGA VALLEY SCENIC RAILROAD

Cuyahoga Valley National Recreation Area (Independence Depot is off I-77 exit 155, follow signs), **Peninsula** 44264

- ❑ Phone: (330) 657-2000 or (800) 468-4070, **Web: www.cvsr.com**
- ❑ Hours: Departs Wednesday – Sunday, Morning and early Afternoon (June – October). Weekends, Morning and early Afternoon (Rest of the Year)
- ❑ Admission: $11.00 - $20.00 adult, $10.00 - $18.00 senior, $7.00 - $12.00 child (3+). Reservations are highly recommended.
- ❑ Miscellaneous: Gift Shop Car/Concession Car, Park Ranger /Volunteer available for transportation or nature information. Main train trips depart from Independence, Peninsula & Akron.

- ❑ Bring a picnic lunch to eat in transit or at a stopover. Wheelchair car available. See Seasonal & Special Events Chapter for great holiday trains including visits from "Thomas the Tank Engine".

Ride in climate controlled coaches built between 1939 and 1940 on the very scenic 2 - 6 ½ hour ride to many exciting round trip destinations. Meadowlands, pinery, marsh, rivers, ravines, and woods pass by as you travel to Hale Farm and Village, Quaker Square, Inventor's Hall of Fame, Akron Zoo, Canal Visitor Center, Stan Hywet Hall or just a basic scenic tour (best if small kids take shorter trips or one's with layovers). Narration of views and history of changes in the area included. The Canal Limited is the only excursion which begins at the depot in Peninsula on a trip north to Canal Visitor Center. The center is a restored house on the Ohio & Erie Canal. Learn about the canal days in the museum and watch the canal lock demonstrations held every weekend during the summer and periodically in early fall. This is a fun way to spend the day family style (grandparents too!) and see one other attraction along the way. Be sure your little engineers get a blue or pink cap to wear along the trip as a memory of their first train ride!

TINKER'S CREEK STATE PARK

Portage - *Aurora-Hudson Road (2 miles West of State Route 43), 44266.* ***Web: www.dnr.state.oh.us/parks/parks/tinkers.htm.*** *Phone: (330) 296-3239.* Herons, ducks, geese and beaver can be found in the spring-fed waters, while cattail, buttonbush and swamp white oak line the shores of this beautiful park. 60 acres of hiking trails, fishing trails, swimming and winter sports.

PORTAGE COUNTY HISTORICAL SOCIETY

Ravenna - *6549 North Chestnut Street, 44266. Phone: (330)296-3523.* ***Web: www.history.portage.oh.us.*** *Hours: Tuesday, Thursday & Sunday 2:00-4:00pm.* Besides the Lowrie-Beatty museum, the society's 12-acre site includes the Carter House, an early pioneer homestead, John Campbell Land Grant Office, 1810-1811 the Mahan Barn, an 1810 New England-type barn, Ford Seed Company Museum, housed in an old photographer's studio, an Advance-Rumely Steam Traction Engine, the unique Proehl-Kline Clock Tower housing the 1882 Portage County Courthouse Seth-Thomas clock & courthouse bell; & various farm buildings.

WEST BRANCH STATE PARK

Ravenna - *5708 Esworthy Road (5 miles East of Ravenna off State Route 5), 44266. Phone: (330) 296-3239.* ***Web: www.dnr.state.oh.us/parks/parks/westbrnc.htm***. Nature programs. Bridle trails. 8,002 acres of camping, hiking trails, boating and rentals, fishing, swimming and winter sports.

DOVER LAKE WATERPARK

Sagamore - *7150 West Highland Road (access I-77, I-271, SR 303 or SR 82), 44067. Phone: (330) 467-SWIM or 655-SWIM (Akron),* ***Web: www.DoverLake.com***. *Hours: Daily 11:00am-7:00pm (Mid-June thru mid-August). Admission: $13.00-$16.00 per person (40" and under are free). Parking $3.00.* 7 mountain slides, tube rides, speed slides, kiddie playland, wave pool, paddleboats and a nice small lake and beach.

SHAKER HISTORICAL MUSEUM

Shaker Heights - *16740 South Park Boulevard (off I-271), 44120.* ***Web: www.ohiohistory.org/places/shaker***. *Phone: (216) 921-1201. Hours: Tuesday – Friday and Sunday 2:00 – 5:00pm. FREE.* Shaker Community remnants. Furniture and inventions (apple peeler, flat broom, tilter chair, clothes pins).

WAGON TRAILS ANIMAL PARK

Vienna - *907 Youngstown-Kingsville Road (SR 193), 44473. Phone: (330) 539-4494. Hours: Daily, except Tuesday 10:00am-5:00pm (May-October). Admission: $13.00 adult, $10.00 senior (65+), $9.00 child (2-12). Tours: Include wagon ride, bucket of feed and petting zoo. Wagon and zoo are wheelchair and stroller accessible.* From horse-drawn wagons, you'll see and feed animals from the farm to the Outback.

NATIONAL PACKARD MUSEUM

Warren - *1899 Mahoning Avenue NW, 44482. Phone: (330) 394-1899.* ***Web: www.packardmuseum.org***. *Hours: Tuesday - Saturday Noon - 5:00pm, Sunday 1:00-5:00pm. Admission: $5.00 adult, $3.00 senior (65+), $3.00 child (7-12).* Watch a video about Packard's family of vehicles and personal family stories. See memorabilia about the manufacturer's history from 1899 – 1958. Also Packard Electric history display.

TRUMBULL COUNTY HISTORICAL SOCIETY MUSEUM

Warren - *303 Monroe Street, 44483. Phone: (330) 394-4653. Hours: Saturday & Sunday 1:00 – 4:00pm (April –October).* John Stark Edwards/Thomas Denny Webb House, early pioneers of the Western Reserve.

MOST MAGNIFICENT MCDONALD'S IN AMERICA

Warren - *162 North Road SE, 44484. Phone: (330) 856-3611.* A 3-story building (mostly glass) complete with brass and marble fixtures, a glass elevator, an indoor waterfall, and even a baby grand piano! A must see…open daily, except Christmas.

MILL CREEK PARK

(South of Mahoning Avenue off Glenwood Avenue)

Youngstown 44406

- ❑ Phone: (330) 740-7115 (Lanterman's Mill). (330) 740-7107 (Ford Nature Center) or (330) 740-7109 (Winter)
  Web: www.millcreekmetroparks.com
- ❑ Hours: Tuesday - Friday 10:00am - 5:00pm, Saturday and Sunday 11:00am - 6:00pm (Center/Mill).
- ❑ Miscellaneous: Gift Shop. Lanterman's Mill (May - October), small admission.

This park has your basic scenic trails, lakes, falls, gorges, gardens and covered bridges but it also has more. The Ford Nature Center is a stone house with live reptiles and hands-on exhibits about nature. Recorded messages are available for the different stations along the trail beginning outside the Center. Lanterman's Mill is a restored 1845 water- powered gristmill with a 14-foot oak wheel. While in the mill, observe the pioneer ingenuity involved in the early production of meal and flour. Smell the aroma of freshly ground grains. Hear the gentle trickle of water as it flows toward the wheel. Feel the rumblings of the stones as they whirl, grinding the various grains. Later, if you would like, try baking some Johnny Cakes, a staple of an early American diet made with stone-ground corn meal. As you travel through the park, be on the look out for the Silver

Bridge *(reminiscent of Old England and Mary Poppins).* Fellowship Riverside Gardens is a colorful mixture of greens and flowers. The best community park system (and very well kept) you'll find anywhere!

BUTLER INSTITUTE OF AMERICAN ART

Youngstown - *524 Wick Avenue, 44502. Phone: (330) 743-1711.* ***Web: www.butlerart.com****. Hours: Tuesday – Saturday 11:00am - 4:00pm, Sunday Noon - 4:00pm. Open Wednesday evenings until 8:00pm. FREE admission.* Showcases American art from colonial times to the present. Children's Gallery (hands on) and American Sports Art Gallery. FREE Sunday Family Programs and FEE paid "gift art" classes available.

YOUNGSTOWN HISTORICAL CENTER OF INDUSTRY & LABOR

151 West Wood Street (Wood Street is off of Market Street two blocks north of downtown), **Youngstown** 44503

- Phone: (330) 743-5934 or (800) 262-6137
  Web: www.ohiohistory.org /places/youngst/
- Hours: Wednesday – Saturday 9:00am – 5:00pm, Sunday & Holidays Noon – 5:00pm. Closed winter holidays.
- Admission: $6.00 adult, $5.50 senior, $2.00 child (6-12).

If your family has a heritage of steelworkers in the family, then this is the place to explain their hard work. The history of the iron and steel industry in the Mahoning Valley area can be viewed easily looking at the life-sized dioramas titled, "By the Sweat of Their Brow" or from the numerous videos shown throughout the building. Rooms are set up like typical steel mill locker rooms, company houses, and a blooming room. They certainly give you the "feel" of the treacherous work at the mill.

YOUNGSTOWN SYMPHONY

Youngstown - *260 Federal Plaza West, 44503. Phone: (330) 744-4264.* ***Web: www.youngstownsymphony.com***. Performs Pops Concerts with guest artists in Powers Auditorium (tours). Community site Storytyme concerts provide opportunities for the Symphony to engage young people in programs on their common ground. Youngstown Symphony Youth Orchestra and Youngstown Symphony Symphonette programs.

YOUNGSTOWN PLAYHOUSE

Youngstown - *600 Playhouse Lane (near Mill Creek MetroParks' entrance on Glenwood Avenue), 44511. Phone: (330) 782-3402.* Community theatre offers mainstage productions. The season runs from September to June and also has a summer musical running on the weekends in August. Youth Theatre.

GORANT CANDIES

8301 Market Street (State Route 7, Boardman)

Youngstown 44512

- ❑ Phone: (800) 572-4139 Ext.1236
- ❑ Tours: Tuesday-Thursday until 1:30 p.m. (March only). Maximum 50 people. 1st grade and above
- ❑ Miscellaneous: Candy store. Displays of chocolate history. Hair net (provided) must be worn.

Put on your paper hat and watch up to 375,000 pieces of chocolate candy being made each day. See the 2000-pound chocolate melting vats and color-coded rooms. The brown walls are the molding room where chocolate is poured and shook on vibrating tables (takes out the air bubbles). The yellow room is the coating room. A personalized hand dipper (only one) dips 3600 candies a day. Receive a free candy bar at the end of the tour.

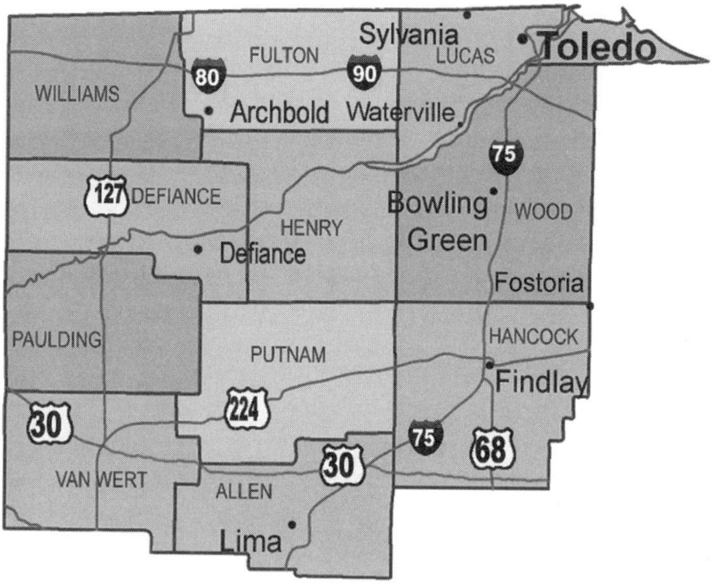

Chapter 6
North West Area

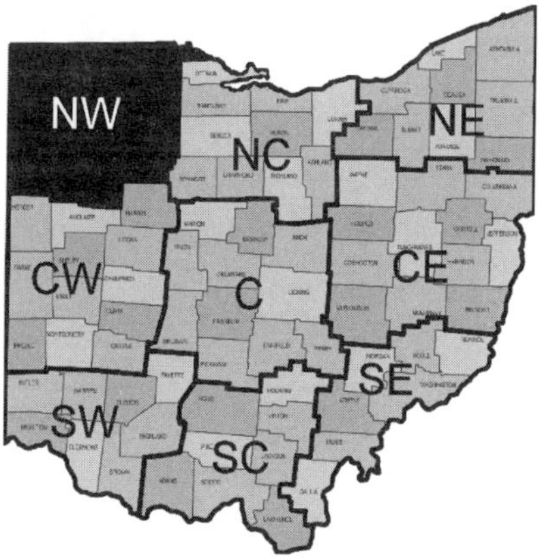

Our Favorites...

COSI Toledo

Fort Meigs

Sauder Farm & Village

SS Willis Boyer

Sauder Homestead

SAUDER VILLAGE

22611 State Route 2 (off SR 66, 2 miles Northeast on State Route 2 or off turnpike exit 25), **Archbold** 43502

- Phone: (419) 446-2541 or (800) 590-9755, **Web: www.saudervillage.com**
- Hours: Monday – Saturday 10:00am – 5:00pm. Sunday 1:00 – 5:00pm (Late-April – October)
- Admission: $11.50 adult, $5.50 child (6-16). $1.00 Carriage, Train, Wagon rides - Group Rates available for 25+.
- Miscellaneous: The Barn Restaurant serves wonderful homestyle food with a children's menu ($3.00-5.00). Meals served buffet or family style. Gift Shop. Bakery. Country Inn.

Learn the history of Sauder Woodworking & Erie Sauder (his teenage woodworking shop is open for touring). He started from using wood scraps. Meet famous & very talented glass, pottery and wood crafters (you'll flip over the beautiful giant marbles!). Maybe get locked in jail, trade furs or take a lick from an old-fashioned ice cream cone. In the Homestead (1910), look for baby animals, an old baby walker, a Mother's Bench Rocker or a baby bottle warmer. Walk along the craft village where you can meet a weaver, broom maker, tinsmith or blacksmith all dressed in early 20th Century clothing. New in 2003 is Natives & Newcomers: Ohio in Transition - a living-history experience telling the story of Northwest Ohio from 1803 to 1839. Covered with swamps and thick forests, this region of the state was one of the last to be settled by Europeans. The settlement will depict the family lives of the many Native American nations who called this area home. Workers here love what they do!

SNOOKS DREAM CARS MUSEUM

Bowling Green - *13920 County Home Road (adjacent to US 6), 43402.* ***Web: www.snooksdreamcars.com****. Phone: (419) 353-8338. Hours: Tuesday-Sunday 11:00am-4:00pm.* Begin in a 1940's era Texaco filling station, featuring "automobilia" - everything from hood ornaments to backseat games to seat covers. Operational mechanics area leads to coin-operated amusement games (even a Model T kiddie ride). Remember pedal cars? The showroom has dream cars showcased in themed rooms from the 30's-60's.

AUGLAIZE VILLAGE FARM MUSEUM

Defiance - *Off US 24 (3 miles SW of Defiance - follow signs), 43512.* ***Web: www.defiance-online.com/auglaise.*** *Phone: (419) 784-0107. Hours: Event Weekends Only 11:00am - 4:00pm (May-October). Small admission.* A recreated late 19th Century village - 17 new, restored or reconstructed buildings that serve as museums. The Red Barn with the Street of Shops and Hall of Appliances is probably the most interesting - especially the old-fashioned appliances and authentic period food they serve. Best to visit during festivals or special events when there is an abundance of costumed guides.

INDEPENDENCE DAM STATE PARK

Defiance - *State Route 424 (4 miles East of Defiance), 43512.* ***Web: www.dnr.state.oh.us/parks/parks/indpndam.htm.*** *Phone: (419) 784-3263.* Independence Dam State Park is situated along the banks of the beautiful Maumee River. The river is ideal for boating, fishing or a scenic canoe trip. The park offers the perfect setting for a picnic or overnight camping experience. 604 acres of camping, hiking trails, boating, fishing, and winter sports.

MUSEUM OF POSTAL HISTORY

Delphos - *131 North Main Street (Lower Level of Post Office), 45833. Phone: (419) 695-2811. Hours: Monday, Wednesday, Friday 1:30 – 3:30pm.* 7000 square feet of displays plus media presentations that show development of American history and the influences of the U.S. Mail. See the progress of mail processing, development of the letter, stamps, postmarks and the idea of a post office. You can actually sit in a 1906 rural mail coach.

HARRISON LAKE STATE PARK

Fayette - *(4 miles South of Fayette off State Route 66), 43521.* ***Web: www.dnr.state.oh.us/parks/parks/harrison.htm.*** *Phone: (419) 237-2593.* A green island of scenic woodlands in a rich agricultural region. Harrison Lake is popular for swimming, fishing, camping and canoeing. 249 acres of camping, hiking trails, boating, fishing, swimming, and winter sports.

DIETSCH BROTHERS

Findlay - *400 W. Main Cross Street (State Route 12), 45839. Phone: (419) 422-4474. Tours: Wednesday & Thursday mornings (1st grade & up). (Fall & Spring). ½ hour long, 20 people maximum. Reservations required.* Three brothers (2nd generation) run an original 1937's candy and ice cream shop. In the summer, see ice cream made with real cream. They make 1500 gallons per week. Fall, heading into the holidays, is the best time to see 500 pounds of chocolate treats made daily.

GHOST TOWN MUSEUM PARK

Findlay - *(US 68 to County Road 40 West), 45840. Phone: (419) 326-5874. Hours: Tuesday - Sunday 9:30am - 6:00pm (Memorial Day Weekend - Mid-September). Admission: $4.00 adult, $2.00 child (under 12).* A ghost town recreation with 28 buildings from the 1880's including a general store and barbershop.

MAZZA COLLECTION / GARDNER FINE ARTS PAVILION

Findlay - *1000 North Main Street (University of Findlay Campus) 45840. Phone: (419) 424-4777 or (800) 472-9502.* ***Web: www.mazzacollection.org****. Hours: Wednesday-Friday Noon – 5:00pm, Sunday 1:00-4:00pm. Closed all holidays. Admission: FREE. Tours: Tuesday-Thursday between 9:00am-2:00pm and Friday 9:00am-Noon.* All the artwork here is based on children's storybooks and the teaching units include such exhibits as printmaking, the Mother Goose Corner, a borders section, the book-making process, an historical art gallery, and an art media exhibit. After a tour, some groups opt to have an art activity where the students get to use the ideas they saw in the galleria to produce their own artwork.

ISAAC LUDWIG MILL

Grand Rapids - *Providence Park (US 24 and State Route 578), 43522. Phone: (419) 535-3050. Hours: Wednesday-Sunday 10:00am-5:00pm (May-October). Admission: FREE demonstrations of mill. 45 minute mule drawn canal boat rides leave every hour until 4:00 p.m. Narrated. $4.00 adult, $3.00* *senior (59+), $2.00 child (3-12).* Another one of the few mills left in Ohio. This 19th century mill sits on the Maumee River and demonstrates how a flour mill, sawmill and electric generator can be powered by water from the old canal below.

MARY JANE THURSTON STATE PARK

Grand Rapids - *State Route 65 (2 miles West of Grand Rapids), 43534.* ***Web: www.dnr.state.oh.us/parks/parks/mjthrstn.htm.*** *Phone: (419) 832-7662.* 555 acres of hiking trails, boating, fishing and winter sports. Boaters have access to the river while history buffs may explore the remnants of the old canal.

CULBERTSON'S MINI ZOO SURVIVAL CENTER

Holland - *6340 Angola Road (State Route 2 to Holland-Sylvania Road, North to Angola West), 43537. Phone: (419) 865-3470. Hours: Monday – Saturday 9:00am – 5:00pm. Small admission.* Specializes in the rescue and refuse of exotic animals like cougars, lions, tigers, baboons, buffaloes, deer, birds, and fish.

ALLEN COUNTY MUSEUM

Lima - *620 West Market Street, 45801. Phone: (419) 222-9426.* ***Web: www.co.allen.oh.us/mus.html.*** *Hours: Tuesday – Sunday 1:00 – 5:00pm. Closed holidays. Miscellaneous: While in town, stop for lunch or dinner at the Old Barn Out Back (3175 W. Elm St - (419) 991-3075) serving country-style food in the "Chicken Coop" or "Pig Pen" - known for their fried chicken and cinnamon rolls.* Indian and pioneer artifacts. Antique automobiles and bicycles. Barber Shop, Doctor's office, country store, log house on grounds. Next door is MacDonell House (wall of purses). Lincoln Park Railroad exhibit locomotive and Shay Locomotive (huge train) is something the kids will love. The most unusual display is a collection of objects that people have swallowed (ex. Bolts, diaper pins).

POPCORN GALLERY

59 Town Square, **Lima** 45801

- Phone: (419) 227-2676, **Web: www.metroevents.com/popcorn**
- Admission: FREE
- Tours: Monday – Friday Mornings. Reservations Required. 45 minute tour and store browsing.

- ❑ Miscellaneous: Nearby old-fashioned fast-food is Kewpee Burgers since 1928 with wrappers that say "Hamburger with pickle on top, makes your heart go flippity flop".

See how 40 flavors of popcorn are made. Begin with an explanation of why corn pops. Then see industrial poppers spill out oodles of popped corn that is then flavored using a slurry that is cooked onto corn. The American Indians had over 700 varieties of popcorn and brought some to the first Thanksgiving.

LIMALAND MOTOR SPEEDWAY

Lima - *1500 Dutch Hollow Road (off State Route 81), 45805. Phone: Rac Headqtrs (419) 998-3199 or Raceday (419) 339-6249.* ***Web: www.limaland.com***. 1/4 mile, high-banked, clay oval track. (April - September)

ARAWANNA II

Maumee - *1321 Chantilly Drive, 43537. Phone: (419) 255-6200. Hours: Weekends. (April – November).* Be a part of Toledo's rich river history by riding aboard the Arawanna II on the Maumee River. Enjoy the breathtaking scenery in Maumee, Perrysburg and Toledo. Public departures from Rossford City Marina.

FORT MEIGS

29100 West River Rd (1 mile SW of SR 25, I-475 to exit 2), **Perrysburg** 43552

- ❑ Phone: (419) 874-4121 or (800) 283-8916, **www.ohiohistory.org/places/ftmeigs**
- ❑ Hours: Wednesday - Saturday 9:30am - 5:00pm. Sunday Noon - 5:00pm (Memorial Day Weekend - Labor Day). Weekends Only (September and October).
- ❑ Admission: $6.00 adult, $2.00 child (6-12)
- ❑ Miscellaneous: Military History Center with Gift Shop at the stone shutterhouse describes role of Ohioans at War.

A War of 1812 era authentic castle-like log and earth fort with seven blockhouses that played an important role in guarding the Western frontier against the British. The walls of the blockhouses are 2 feet thick with 4-inch deep windows and cannon hole ports on the second floor. See actual cannons fired as the air fills with smoke. Notice how much manpower was needed to "run" a fort.

MAUMEE STATE FOREST

Swanton - *3390 County Road D, 43558. Phone: (419) 822-3052.* ***www.dnr.state.oh.us/forestry/Forests/stateforests/maumee.htm.*** 3,068 acres in Fulton, Henry and Lucas counties. Bridle trails (15 miles), All-purpose vehicle area with 5 miles of trails (also snowmobile- weather permitting, Windbreak arboretum area. Open daily 6:00am - 11:00pm.

FRANCISCAN CENTER

Sylvania - *6832 Convent Boulevard, 43560. Phone: (419) 885-1547.* ***Web: www.franciscancenter.org.*** Summer arts camp. Presents season of music, ballet and theatre. (September – May)

WOLCOTT HOUSE MUSEUM COMPLEX

Toledo - *1031 River Road, 43537. Phone: (419) 893-9602.* ***Web: www.maumee.org/wolcott/wolcott.htm.*** *Hours: Wednesday – Sunday 1:00 – 4:00pm (April – December). Admission: $1.50-$3.50.* Life in the mid-1800's in the Maumee Valley. Costumed guides lead you through a building complex of a log home, depot, church and gift shop.

COSI TOLEDO

One Discovery Way (Downtown riverfront, corner of Summit and Adams Streets), **Toledo** 43604

- Phone: (419) 244-COSI, **Web: www.cositoledo.org**
- Hours: Monday - Saturday 10:00am - 5:00pm, Sunday Noon - 5:00pm. Closed Thanksgiving, Christmastime, New Years & Eastertime.
- Admission: $8.00 adult (13-64), $6.50 senior (65+) & child (3-12)
- Miscellaneous: Science 2 Go Gift Shop. Atomic Cafe - restaurant of food, "Science where you're encouraged to play with your food".

Eight learning worlds including Mind Zone (distorted Gravity Room, Animation, T-Rex), Sports (improve your game using science), Life Force (secrets of parts of the body like your skin, brain, and stomach), Water Works (water arcade, water travel, rainstorms), KidSpace, and BabySpace (18 months and under). The older kids will love Whiz-Bang Engineering and Power Force or Pit Stop Challenge (greeted by Ed the animatronic security guard, feel hydraulics with motion simulator, take the Science on the Go Challenge!).

TOLEDO MUD HENS BASEBALL

Toledo - *Fifth Third Field (Warehouse District), 43604. Phone: (419) 725-HENS.* ***Web: www.mudhens.com***. Semi-professional baseball (farm team for the Detroit Tigers) played in a newly built classic ballpark. See "Muddy" the mascot or sit in "The Roost" bleachers. Also, playground and picnic areas. Tickets $6.00-$8.00. (April-September).

TOLEDO SYMPHONY ORCHESTRA

Toledo - *2 Maritime Plaza. 43604. Phone: (800) 348-1253 or (419) 246-8000.* ***Web: www.toledosymphony.com***. Regional symphony performs orchestral masterpieces with guest artists, chamber, contemporary, pops, youth and summer concerts. (September-May)

TOLEDO TROLLEY TOUR

Toledo – *Downtown, 43604. Phone: (419) 245-5225. Tours: Wednesday and Sunday afternoons (June – September). 2 ½ hours long.* Tour downtown Toledo and Maumee on an 1880 streetcar replica.

SS WILLIS B BOYER MARITIME MUSEUM

26 Main Street, International Park (East side of Maumee River – Downtown, **Toledo** 43605

- ❑ Phone: (419) 936-3070, **Web: www.internationalpark.org**
- ❑ Hours: Monday-Saturday 10:00am – 5:00pm, Sunday Noon-5:00pm (May – October). Wednesday – Sunday by appointment (November – April).
- ❑ Admission: $6.00 adult, $4.00 student.
- ❑ Miscellaneous: After seeing the "macho" life of shipsmen, try some fiery or authentic ethnic Hungarian food at Tony Packos Café (1902 Front Street, 419-691-6054 or www.tonypackos.com). Be sure to look for the hundreds of hot dog buns signed by TV stars that have visited the café.

The 617-foot freighter depicts how ships of the Great Lakes worked in the early to mid-1900's. It was the biggest, most modern ship on the Great Lakes (in its day) and as you drive up, it takes up your whole panoramic view. A nautical museum of Lake Erie resides inside with photographs, artifacts and best of all for kids, hands-on exhibits. Have your picture taken "at the wheel". Ask for the "child-oriented" tours.

TOLEDO STORM

Toledo - *Toledo Sports Arena, 1 Main Street, 43605. Phone: (419) 691-0200.* ***Web: www.thestorm.com***. Semi-Professional hockey part of East Coast Hockey League (affiliate for the Detroit Red Wings). Season starts in October.

SANDPIPER CANAL BOAT

Toledo - *2144 Fordway, Riverfront (Jefferson Street Docks), 43606. Phone: (419) 537-1212.* ***Web: www.sandpiperboat.com***. *Admission: Range of $5.00-$15.00.* Replica of a Miami and Erie Canal boat. Educational or historical Cruise up river past riverside estates, downtown or down river. See busy ports, shipyards and dry docks. Public and group tours average 2-4 hours. Mostly weekends (daytime) or Thursdays (at Noon). Some evening cruises. Seasonal Fireworks and Fall Cruises. Bring a picnic. Reservations suggested.

OHIO THEATRE

Toledo - *3114 LaGrange Street, 43608. Phone: (419) 241-6785.* Former vaudeville/movie house presents classical music, live stage, film and children's series.

TOLEDO ZOO

2700 Broadway (I-75 to US 25 - 3 miles South of downtown)

Toledo 43609

- Phone: (419) 385-5721, **Web: www.toledozoo.org**
- Hours: Daily 10:00am - 5:00pm (May - Labor Day). Daily, 10:00 am - 4:00 pm (Rest of the Year)

- Admission: $8.50 adult, $5.50 senior (60+) and child (2-11). Parking fee.
- Miscellaneous: Carnivore Cafe (dine in actual cages once used to house big cats!). Children's Zoo - petting zoo and hands on exhibits (open late spring through Labor Day).

They have areas typical of a zoo but they are known for their Hippoquarium (the world's first underwater viewing of the hippopotamus) along with a well-defined interpretive center and hands- on exhibits. The Kingdom of Apes and African Savanna are other popular exhibits. The renovated Aviary, new Primate Forest and Arctic Encounter (a nose-to-nose view thru a cabin window to observe gray wolves and an underwater view of seals) are hot spots too.

TOLEDO FIREFIGHTERS MUSEUM

Toledo - *918 Sylvania Avenue, 43612. Phone: (419) 478-FIRE. Hours: Saturday Noon – 4:00pm. FREE.* Feel what 150 years of history of fire-fighting must have meant to the fireman. Learn fire safety tips. See actual vintage pumpers, uniforms, and equipment used that trace the growth of the Toledo Fire Department. Located in the former No. 18 Fire Station.

TOLEDO SPEEDWAY

Toledo - *5639 Benore Road, 43612. Phone: (419) 729-1634.* Stock car racing. 1/2 mile, asphalt, high-banked oval. (May – October)

TOLEDO BOTANICAL GARDENS

Toledo - *5403 Elmer Drive (off North Reynolds Road), 43615. Phone: (419) 936-2986.* ***Web: www.toledogarden.org****. Hours: Open dawn to dusk.* Fifty-seven acres of meadows and gardens. Outdoor sculpture and storybook garden appeal to kids. Gallery and gift store. FREE except for special events.

TOLEDO MUSEUM OF ART

Toledo - *2445 Monroe at Scottwood (off I-75), 43620. Phone: (419) 255-8000.* ***Web: www.toledomuseum.org****. Hours: Tuesday-Saturday 10:00am-4:00pm, Sunday 11:00am-5:00pm. Open Friday evening til 10:00pm. Free admission.* Discover treasures from the riches of the medieval, the splendors of a French chateau and the tombs of Egypt. Also glass, sculpture, paintings.

MAUMEE BAY STATE PARK

Toledo (Oregon) - *1400 Park Road #1 (8 miles East of Toledo, then 3 miles North off State Route 2), 43618. Phone: (419) 836-7758 park, 836-1466 Lodge or 836-9117 Nature Center,* ***Web: www.dnr.state.oh.us/parks/parks/maumebay.htm*** *or* ***Web: www.maumeebayresort.com***. 1,845 acres of camping, hiking trails, boating, fishing, swimming and winter sports. Resort cottages and rooms, golf, racquetball, sauna, whirlpool, fitness, tennis, volleyball and basketball are available. The lodge, cottages and golf course are nestled among the scenic meadows, wet woods and lush marshes teeming with wildlife.

VAN BUREN LAKE STATE PARK

Van Buren - *State Route 613 (1 mile East of Van Buren), 45889.* ***Web: www.dnr.state.oh.us/parks/parks/vanburen.htm***. *Phone: (419) 832-7662.* 296 acres of camping, hiking trails, boating, fishing, and winter sports.

BLUEBIRD PASSENGER TRAIN

Waterville - *49 North 6th Street (3rd and Mill Street - Grand Rapids Depot - departures), 43566. Phone: (419) 878-2177.* ***Web: www.tlew.org***. *Hours: Wednesday & Thursday, Saturday, Sunday and Holidays- Afternoon Departures (Summer). Weekends and Holidays Only (May, September, October). Visit website for updated departure/arrival schedule. Admission: $8.00 adult, $7.00 senior (65+), $4.50 child (3-12). Round trip.* Can you guess why they call it "Bluebird"? Answer: The bluebirds come back to Ohio in the spring and leave in the early fall. That's when the train runs. The 45-minute trip (each way) on a 1930's era passenger train includes a spectacular view from a 900-foot long bridge over the Maumee River and Miami & Erie Canal (now the millrace for Isaac Ludwig Mill).

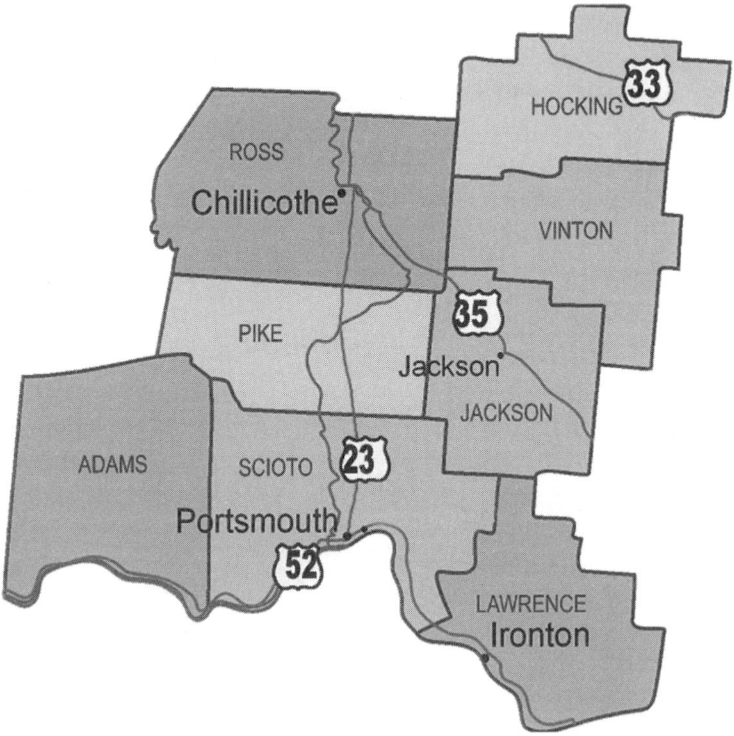

Chapter 7
South Central Area

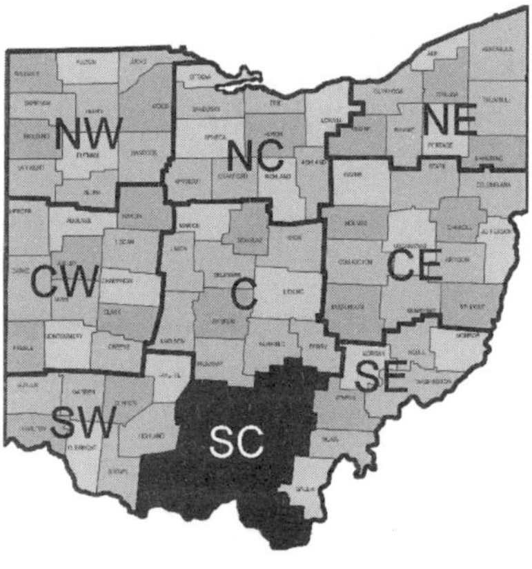

Our Favorites...

Hocking Hills Area

Portsmouth Murals

Ross County Historical Society Museum

Seven Caves

Shawnee State Park

Seven Caves Natural History

7 CAVES

7660 Cave Road (US 50, 4 miles Northwest, follow signs)

Bainbridge 45612

- Phone: (937) 365-1283, **Web: www.7caves.com**
- Hours: Daily 9:00am – 6:00pm.
- Admission: $10.00 adult, $5.00 child (4-14).
- Miscellaneous: Many stairs. Snack bar and shelter house.

Wear layered clothing and comfortable walking shoes because your family is going on an adventure! An absolutely wonderful way to spend almost the entire day in nature as you explore a series of small caves you actually walk into. Self-guided tours allow for the kids to push buttons to light structures as they walk along. Cute, clever names are given to each naturally carved figure – many from Bible stories (Samson) and fairy tales (Goldilocks & the Three Bears). Some areas require following "corkscrew" paths to deep dungeons or grottos (optional, best for the limber and true spelunkers). Three different trails lead to caves with cemented walkways, handrails, and lighting showing specific formations. See cliffs, canyons, and waterfalls. About a hundred kinds of birds inhabit The Seven Caves, the Pileated Woodpecker is the rarest. A hidden treasure here!

MAGIC WATERS AMPHITHEATRE

Bainbridge - *7757 Cave Road, 45612. Phone: (937) 365-1388. **Web: www.highlandcounty.com/magic.htm**. Performances Friday-Saturday 8:00pm, Sunday 7:00pm (mid-June- Labor Day). Pre-show picnics available with reservations. Admission: $6.00 adult, $3.50 senior, $3.00 child.* Live outdoor drama in a rustic amphitheater featuring magic shows and kid's theatre (i.e. The Wizard of Oz).

PAINT CREEK STATE PARK

Bainbridge - *14265 US 50 (17 miles East of Hillsboro on US 50), 45612. **Web: www.dnr.state.oh.us/parks/parks/paintcrk.htm**. Phone: (937) 365-1401.* Located amid the scenery of the Paint Creek Valley, Paint Creek State Park features a large lake with fine fishing, boating and swimming opportunities. A modern campground and meandering hiking trails invite outdoor enthusiasts to explore the rolling hills and streams of this area. Nature programs. On the west side of the lake is Paint Creek Pioneer Farm. The pioneer farm includes a log house, collection of log buildings, livestock, gardens and fields which represent a typical farm of the early 1800's. A walk through Pioneer Farm provides further insight into the settlers' lives. Boating rentals and winter sports. Bicycle rental is available and miniature golf can be enjoyed for a small fee.

PIKE LAKE STATE PARK

Bainbridge - *1847 Pike Lake Road (6 miles Southeast of Bainbridge), 45612. Phone: (740) 493-2212.* ***Web: www.dnr.state.oh.us/parks/parks/pikelake.htm***. The forest is known for its variety of ferns, mosses, lichens and fungi. The wildflowers are diverse, creating spectacular displays--spring through autumn. Nature programs. 613 acres of camping, hiking trails, boating and rentals, fishing, swimming and winter sports. Family cabins.

TAR HOLLOW STATE FOREST

Chillicothe - *(northeast of Chillicothe, south of Adelphi), 43101.* ***www.dnr.state.oh.us/forestry/Forests/stateforests/tarhollow.htm***. *Phone: (740) 663-2523 (Waverly office), Hours: Open daily 6:00am - 11:00pm.* 16,120 acres in Ross, Vinton and Hocking counties. Bridle trails (33 miles), horse campground, hiking trails (22 miles), grouse management area. Tar Hollow State Park is adjacent.

ADENA STATE MEMORIAL

Chillicothe - *(West of State Route 104 off Adena Road), 45601.* ***Web: www.ohiohistory.org/places/adena***. *Phone: (740) 772-1500 or (800) 319-7248. Hours: Wednesday - Saturday 9:30am - 5:00pm, Sundays and Holidays Noon - 5:00pm (Summer). Weekends Only (Rest of year). Admission: $6.00 adult, $2.00 child (6-12).* View the overlook of the hillside that was used to paint the picture for the Ohio State Seal. Looking east from the north lawn, one can see across the Scioto River Valley to the Mount Logan range of hills (the Seal view). Adena is an important site for many reasons. It is the only plantation-type complex of its kind in our state and the 1807 stone mansion built by the 6th Ohio governor, Thomas Worthington, Father of our Statehood. Also visit a tenant house, smoke house, wash house, barn and spring house. Begin at the Visitors Center for an overview.

CHILLICOTHE PAINTS BASEBALL

Chillicothe - *VA Memorial Stadium (Gift shop/tickets at 59 N. Paint St.), 45601.* ***Web: www.chillicothepaints.com****. Phone: (740) 773-TEAM.* Enjoy the Single A Frontier League Team as they continue into a new season of professional baseball in a "Hometown" atmosphere. "Come Have Some FUN!" Tickets $3.00-$6.00. (First week of June - September)

GREAT SEAL STATE PARK

Chillicothe - *Marietta Pike (3 miles Northeast of Chillicothe), 45601.* ***Web: www.dnr.state.oh.us/parks/parks/grtseal.htm****. Phone: (740) 773-2726. Miscellaneous: Cross-country skiing, Bridle trails.1,864 acres of camping, and winter sports.* Great Seal State Park is dedicated to the wilderness spirit of Ohio. The history of the Shawnee nation and Ohio's early statehood is in these hills. Rugged trails take visitors to scenic vistas of distant ridgetops and the Scioto Valley below. These very hills are depicted on the Great Seal of the State of Ohio, from which the park gets its name.

HOPEWELL CULTURE NAT'L HISTORICAL PARK

16062 State Route 104 (two miles north of the intersection of US 35 and SR 104), Chillicothe 45601

- Phone: (740) 774-1126, Web: www.nps.gov/hocu
- Hours: Daily 8:30am - 5:00pm. Extended closing at 6pm in the summer. Closed Thanksgiving, Christmas and New Year's Day, and on Monday/Tuesday during December-February. Grounds open daily dawn til dusk.
- Admission: $3.00 per adult. Maximum charge per vehicle is $5.00.
- Miscellaneous: There is a popular activity booklet for kids that come to the park. Along with this, they also offer Native American games and pottery making for kids.

The 120-acre park with 13-acre earthwall enclosure is home to 23 prehistoric burial and ceremonial mounds of the Hopewell Indians. The center presents the story of the prehistoric Hopewell culture with exhibits, brochures and the 17-minute video "Legacy of the Mound Builders." Question: How did they make so many trinkets from materials like copper, seashells and mica (materials not found in Ohio)? After viewing many effigy (animal-shaped) pipes, maybe purchase a reproduction (inexpensively) as a souvenir.

LUCY HAYES HERITAGE CENTER

Chillicothe - *90 West Sixth Street, 45601. Phone: (740) 775-5829 or 775-1780. Hours: Friday & Saturday 1:00-4:00pm (April-October) and by appointment. Admission: $2.00 general.* They provide guided tours through the former home of Lucy Ware Webb Hayes, the wife and "First Lady" of the 19th President of the United States, Rutherford B. Hayes. They especially welcome students.

PUMP HOUSE CENTER FOR THE ARTS

Chillicothe - *Enderlin Circle, Yoctangee Park, 45601. Phone: (740) 772-5783.* ***Web: www.bright.net/~pumpart.*** *Hours: Tuesday-Friday 11:00am-4:00pm, Saturday-Sunday 1:00-4:00pm. Admission: FREE.* Visit art gallery and cultural center in restored water pumping station. It features regional artists including school children (ie. Trash can art & historical themes).

ROSS COUNTY HISTORICAL SOCIETY MUSEUMS

45 W. Fifth Street (near Paint Street, downtown)

Chillicothe 45601

- Phone: (740) 772-1936, **Web: www.rosscountyhistorical.org**
- Hours: Tuesday-Sunday 1:00-5:00pm (April-August). Weekends only (September-December).
- Admission: $4.00 adult, $2.00 senior & student.

See the table upon which Ohio's Constitution was signed and Thomas Worthington's sea chest! See exhibits on early Chillicothe (diorama of town in 1803) and Ohio, Civil War (Camp Sherman -- "Ohio's World War I Soldier Factory,"), World War I and the Mound Builders. Also the McKell Library, the Knoles Log House Museum (everyday life in early

1800's Chillicothe) and Franklin House Women's Museum. Kids will be intrigued by the stories of olden times like: No garbage pickup? Just throw it in the streets and let roving animals eat the "slop". Or, how did the saying: Peas, Porridge Hot...Peas, Porridge Cold...Nine Days Old" come about (something to do with leftovers!). And, why didn't they use forks? Learn the real "scoop" about Conestoga wagons and how kids used miniature wagons to train their "pets". Look through an authentic old-fashioned ViewMaster (Megalethoscope). Because this complex showcases the first capital of Ohio, it has Bicentennial value hidden in every corner!

SCIOTO TRAIL STATE PARK

Chillicothe - *44 Lake Road (10 miles South of Chillicothe off US 23), 45601. **Web: www.dnr.state.oh.us/parks/parks/sciototr.htm**. Phone: (740) 663-2125.* A small, quiet park nestled in beautiful 9,000-acre Scioto Trail State Forest, this state park is an undisturbed wooded refuge. 248 acres of camping, hiking, boating, fishing and winter sports.

TECUMSEH!

Sugarloaf Mountain Amphitheater (US 23 to Bridge St. exit, left on SR 159, right on Delano Road), **Chillicothe** 45601

- Phone: (740) 775-0700 or (866) 775-0700
  Web: www.tecumsehdrama.com
- Hours: Monday – Saturday, Show time 8:00pm. Show ends around 10:45pm. Reservations please. (Mid-June to Labor Day)
- Admission: $16.00 General (slightly reduced Monday-Thursday), Half Price for children (under 10).
- Tours: Backstage Tours 4:00 or 5:00pm ($2.50-$3.50). - HIGHLY RECOMMENDED for all ages.The stuntmen of TECUMSEH! give a dazzling display of stage-combat and flintlock firing, then pitch headfirst from a twenty-one foot cliff, get up, and explain how they did it. Tours last approximately one hour and also includes make-up demonstrations(including mock "yummy" blood bags & Native "tanning" products) and detailed historical information on the drama and area. A great preparation so kids can better understand the storyline and not be frightened by savage conflicts.

- Miscellaneous: Free Prehistoric Indian Mini-Museum. Gift Shop & Restaurant with buffet served a few hours before the show. Warning: We recommend the Drama for 4th graders and older who have studied Ohio History and understand the savage, violent conflicts that occurred in Revolutionary War times.

This production has received national attention. Witness the epic life story of the legendary Shawnee leader as he struggles to defend his sacred homelands in the Ohio country during the late 1700's (before Ohio was a state). Fast action horses, loud firearms and speeding arrows make the audience part of the action especially when costumed actors enter the scene from right, left and behind. Lots of lessons learned about courage, honor, wisdom and greed...for kids and adults.

TELEPHONE MUSEUM, JAMES M. THOMAS

Chillicothe - *68 East Main Street, 45601. Phone: (740) 772-8200. Hours: Monday – Friday 8:30am – 4:30pm. Closed holidays.* Run by the Chillicothe Telephone Company, it shows the telephone from its invention stages to modern times. The museum features telephone equipment and paraphernalia dating back to 1895. Included are telephone instruments, early local directories, wooden underground conduit and a working section of electro-mechanical "step-by-step" switching equipment. Free tours by appointment. To add to your "telephone" experience, eat a casual lunch or dinner (ordered from table telephones) at Sumburger Restaurant (740-772-1055) at 1487 North Bridge Street on the retail strip.

NOAH'S ARK ANIMAL FARM

Jackson - *1527 McGiffins Road (5 miles East on State Route 32), 45640. Phone: (740)384-3060 or (800)282-2167.* ***Web: www.placesohio.com/noahsark/index.htm****. Hours: Monday – Saturday 10:00am – 6:00pm, Sunday Noon – 7:00pm (April – October). Admission: Avg. $5.00 per person (age 3+). Miscellaneous: A-1 Diner.* You will enjoy miniature golf, playground equipment, and fairy-book characters. They also have a train that travels 3/4th of a mile around the farm. Exotic animals and birds (more than 150). Pay Fishing lake and train ride (additional $1.00). Most love the black bears and their cubs best.

SPLASH DOWN

Jackson - *6173 SR 327, 45640. Phone: (888) SPLASH-1 or (740) 384-5113. Hours: Monday-Saturday 10:00am-7:00pm, Sunday 11:00am-6:00pm (Memorial Day-late August). Weekends only til Labor Day. Admission: $14.95 adult, $9.95 child (4-11).* The water adventure theme park and campgrounds have log cabins, 850 foot Lazy River, 2 Thrill Slides, Kids Water Activity Pools, Putt-Putt, concessions, Paddle Boats/Kayaks, Game Room and Sand Volleyball.

PIKE STATE FOREST

Latham - *334 Lapperrel Road (on SR-124, just west of Latham), 45646.**www.dnr.state.oh.us/forestry/Forests/stateforests/pike.htm**. Phone: (740) 493-2441. Hours: Open daily 6:00am - 11:00pm.* 11,961 acres in Pike and Highland counties. Hiking/Bridle trails (33 miles), APV trails (15 miles), Pike Lake State Park is adjacent.

TAR HOLLOW STATE PARK

Laurelville - *16396 Tar Hollow Road (10 miles South of Adelphi off State Route 540), 43135. Phone: (740) 887-4818. **Web: www.dnr.state.oh.us/parks/parks/tarhollw.htm**.* Dense woodlands of scattered shortleaf and pitch pines growing on the ridges were once a source of pine tar for early settlers, hence the name Tar Hollow. Dogwoods, redbuds and a variety of wildflowers color the hillsides in the springtime. 634 acres of camping, hiking trails, boating, fishing, swimming.

HOCKING HILLS STATE PARK

20160 State Route 664 (Route 33 south to Route 664, follow signs)

Logan 43138

- Phone: (740) 385-6841 or (800) HOCKING
  Web: www.dnr.state.oh.us/parks/parks/hocking.htm
- Hours: 6:00am - Sunset (Summer), 8:00am (Winter)

In the mid 1700's, several Indian tribes traveled through or lived here including the Wyandot, Delaware and Shawnee. Their name for the river, from which the park gets its name, was Hockhocking or "bottle river." Nature trails are found throughout the park, many of them lead to obscure, out-of-the-way natural creations. The park includes: Ash Cave (an 80 acre cave and stream), Cantwell Cliffs, Cedar Falls, Conkle's Hollow, Rock House, and the most popular, Old Man's Cave (a wooded, winding ravine of waterfalls and caves). The recess caves at Ash Cave, Old Man's Cave and Cantwell Cliffs are all carved in the softer middle rock. Weathering and erosion widened cracks found in the middle layer of sandstone at the Rock House to create that unusual formation. Overnight accommodations, bed and breakfasts, camping, cabins with A/C, heat and fireplaces, recreation, picnic grounds, and hiking. Your children's sense of adventure will soar! Concessions available at Old Man's Cave or dining in the Lodge (with outdoor pool). We recommend close supervision on the hiking trails for your child's safety.

LAKE LOGAN STATE PARK

Logan - *(4 miles West of Logan off State Route 664), 43138.* ***Web: www.dnr.state.oh.us/parks/parks/lklogan.htm****. Phone: (740) 385-3444.* One of the best fishing lakes in Ohio, the lake sports northern pike, bass, bluegill, crappie, catfish and saugeye. 717 acres of hiking, boating and rentals, fishing, swimming and winter sports.

LAKE HOPE STATE PARK

McArthur - *27331 SR 278 (12 miles Northeast of McArthur on State Route 278), 45651. Phone: (740) 596-5253.* ***Web: www.dnr.state.oh.us/parks/parks/lakehope.htm****.* Lake Hope State Park lies entirely within the 24,000-acre Zaleski State Forest in the valley of Big Sandy Run. It is a rugged, heavily forested region traversed by steep gorges, narrow ridges, abandoned mines, ancient mounds and beautiful scenery. Nature programs. 3,223 acres of camping, family cabins, hiking, boating and rentals, fishing, swimming.

SMOKE RISE RANCH RESORT

Murray City - *6751 Hunterdon Road (US 33 to SR 78 to CR 92), 45732. Phone: (740) 767-2624 or (800) 292-1732.* ***Web: www.smokeriseranch.com****.* Full service campground or cabins.

Working Cattle Ranch (Ridin' & Ropin'), Riding Arenas, Trail riding. Activities Include: Round Up Rides , Pool and Hot Tub Parties, Hay Rides, BBQ's , Team Ropings and Team Pennings, Music Events and Dances.

JACKSON LAKE STATE PARK

Oak Hill - *(2 miles West of Oak Hill on State Route 279), 45656.* ***Web: www.dnr.state.oh.us/parks/parks/jacksonl.htm****. Phone: (740) 682-6197.* The park's serene lake is a focal point for excellent fishing and provides the ideal setting for a peaceful walks. 335 acres of camping, boating, fishing, swimming and winter sports.

DEAN STATE FOREST

Pedro - *149 Dean Forest Road, Rte. 1, 43558. Phone: (740) 532-7228.* ***www.dnr.state.oh.us/forestry/Forests/stateforests/dean.htm****. Hours: Open daily 6:00am - 11:00pm.* Located in the unglaciated hill country of extreme south central Ohio, the early history of the region centered around Dutch and Irish farmers who emigrated from Pennsylvania. From the early 1800's to about 1900, most of the timber in the area was cut for charcoal to supply blast furnaces for the smelting of locally mined iron ore. Reforestation has created 2,745 acres in Lawrence County of 20 miles of bridle/hiking trails. Wayne National Forest is adjacent.

SERPENT MOUND STATE MEMORIAL

Peebles - *3850 State Route 73 (six miles north of State Route 32), 45660.* ***Web: www.ohiohistory.org/places/serpent****. Phone: (937) 587-2796 or (800)752-2757. Hours: Museum open Daily 10:00am - 5:00pm (April-October). Park open year-round. Admission: $6.00 per vehicle. Miscellaneous: Profile of the "cyptoexplosion" doughnut shape can be seen off State Route 770 - East of Serpent Mound.* The largest earthwork in the United States, it measures 1335 feet from head to tail and is about 15 feet high. The mound appears as a giant serpent uncoiling in seven deep curves. The oval doughnut at one end probably represents the open mouth of the snake as it strikes.

MITCHELLACE SHOESTRING FACTORY

830 Murray Street (Corner of Gallia Street off US-52)

Portsmouth 45662

- Phone: (740) 354-2813 or (800) 848-8696
  Web: www.mitchellace.com *(to see product line)*
- Tours: Groups of 10 (no more than 50). One hour tour. Age 8+
- Miscellaneous: All guests receive a free pair of laces.

The former shoe factory works 2-3 shifts per day to make more than 4,000,000 pairs of shoelaces per week. They are the world's biggest shoelace manufacturers for shoes and skates (especially RollerBlades). Family descendants still run the company started in 1902. Start the tour by watching weaving and braiding machines (over 1300) producing strands of fabric. This process takes up an entire floor and when you step onto the floor, all you see are flashes of color. The tipping department takes long strands and cuts them into different lengths and then they are tipped with aglets of nylon or metal. Automatic machines band, fold, label and seal. Other laces are blister packed (plastic pouch over laces is melted onto backing card). The shortest lace is 10 inches. The longest made is 120 inches (for ice skates).

PORTSMOUTH MURALS

State Route 23 South (Washington Street to Ohio River - follow green mural signs), **Portsmouth** 45662

- **Web: www.portsmouth.org**

Artist Robert Dafford (internationally known muralist) can be seen working on new murals in the months of May – September. Look for the paint dotted scaffold and the artist dressed in paint- dotted white painter's pants and shirt. Our two favorites were Chillicothe Street 1940's (a very colorful, tremendously detailed, cartoon-like mural) and Twilight (a modern day view of the bridge over the river, looks like a photograph).

HOCKING STATE FOREST

Rockbridge - *19275 SR-374 (off SR 374 and 664, northeast of Laurelville), 43149. Phone: (740) 385-4402,* ***Web: www.dnr.state.oh.us/forestry/Forests/stateforests/hocking.htm****. Hours: Open daily, 30 minutes before sunrise - 30 minutes after sunset.* 9,267 acres in Hocking County. Hiking trails (9 miles), Bridle trails (40 miles), horse campground, see a former fire lookout tower, rock climbing a rappelling area, and state nature preserves. Hocking Hills State Park is adjacent.

KC RACEWAY

Waverly - *2535 Blain Hwy, Huntington Twp (12 miles south of town, off US 23, turn right on Blain Hwy), 45690. Phone: (740) 663-4141.* ***Web: www.kc-raceway.com****. Hours: Gates open at 4:30 p.m. Racing begins at 7:30 p.m. (late April-September). Admission.* Experience Saturday night excitement at Ohio's fastest 3/8 mile, high-banked dirt track.

LAKE WHITE STATE PARK

Waverly - *2767 State Route 551 (4 miles Southwest of Waverly on State Route 104), 45690. Phone: (740) 947-4059.* ***Web: www.dnr.state.oh.us/parks/parks/lkwhitew.htm****.* Part of Lake White State Park includes the remains of the old canal channel. 358 acres of camping, boating, fishing, swimming and wintersports.

BUCKEYE FURNACE MUSEUM

123 Buckeye Park Road (two miles south of SR 124 on Buckeye Furnace Road in Jackson County), **Wellston** 45692

- Phone: (740) 384-3537, **Web: www.ohiohistory.org/places/buckeye**
- Hours: Park open daylight hours year-round. Museum open by appointment.
- Admission: Donations.

Visit Ohio's only restored charcoal furnace which remains from the original 80 furnaces in Ohio. In the mid – 1800's, this industry took root as large trees were converted into charcoal to make iron for railroads and ammunition. The self-guided tour of the furnace shows you where raw materials (charcoal, iron ore, etc.) were brought to the top of the hill and poured into the furnace to be heated to 600 degrees F. Impurities (slag) stayed on the top while liquid iron (which is heavier) flowed to the base. The reconstructed company store serves as a visitor orientation area. There are two nature trails.

LAKE ALMA STATE PARK

Wellston - *Rte. 1 (3 miles Northeast of Wellston on SR 349), 45692.* ***Web: www.dnr.state.oh.us/parks/parks/lakealma.htm****. Phone: (740) 384-4474.* A quiet lake and a gentle creek meandering through a wooded valley provide a restful setting for park visitors. 279 acres of camping, hiking, boating, fishing and swimming.

RICHLAND FURNACE STATE FOREST

Wellston - *(off State Route 327, near Byer, NW of Wellston), 45692. Phone: 740-596-5781 (Zaleski office),* ***Web: www.dnr.state.oh.us/forestry/Forests/stateforests/richlandfurnace.htm****. Hours: Open daily 6:00am - 11:00pm.* The stone remnant of the old Richland iron furnace still stands on private property just north of Richland Furnace State Forest and is adjacent to Vinton Township Road 6. These furnaces were operated on the resources from the surrounding area. The required iron ore was mined by oxen from the underlying sandstone and limestone. The trees were cut and burned to produce charcoal to fire the furnace. The old ore pits are still noticeable near the ridges throughout the state forest. With the development of the ore fields in Missouri and the Lake Superior region at the end of the 19th century, the Hanging Rock iron industry quickly faded away. 2,448 acres in Jackson and Vinton counties. APV trails (7 miles).

BRUSH CREEK STATE FOREST

West Portsmouth - *(off State Route 73, about one mile west of the village of Rarden), 45663. Phone: (740) 858-6685.* ***Web: www.dnr.state.oh.us/forestry/Forests/stateforests/brushcreek.htm*** *Hours: Open daily 6:00am - 11:00pm.* The vast majority of these 12,000+ acres is made up of steep hillsides, deep hollows, and narrow ridge tops. Combined with the climate in the region, this land is ideally suited to the growth of deciduous hardwood forests. 12 miles bridle trails, 3 miles hiking trails.

SHAWNEE STATE FOREST

West Portsmouth - *13291 US-52, 45663. Phone: (740) 858-6685.* ***www.dnr.state.oh.us/forestry/Forests/stateforests/shawnee.htm*** *Hours: Open daily 6:00am - 11:00pm.* 62,583 acres in Scioto and Adams counties. Ohio's largest state forest. Backpack trails (60 miles) with 8 walk-in camp areas (self-registration permit - no fee), Bridle trails (75 miles), horse campground (no fee), 5 small forest lakes, 8000 acre wilderness area. Shawnee State Park is adjacent.

SHAWNEE STATE PARK

4404 State Route 125 (8 miles West of Portsmouth on State Route 125), **West Portsmouth** 45663

- Phone: (740) 858-6652, **Web: www.ShawneeLodgeResort.com**
- Miscellaneous: Watch out for thousands of ladybugs visiting each mid-October.

Lodge rooms are furnished with American Indian and Appalachian furnishings and the restaurant serves an extensive children's menu (even steak), plus many good sandwiches and entrees (good food, slower service). Weekends, the restaurant has a guitar player. Many seasonal events include hayrides, hikes, campouts and cookouts (Autumn: Cornbread and Beans Black Pot Supper Days). Their one mile hiking trails are unpaved and just right for families. Nature programs, acres of camping, boating and rentals, fishing, swimming, winter sports and food service. Family cabins, lodge with indoor/outdoor pools, sauna, whirlpool, fitness center, tennis and basketball.

ZALESKI STATE FOREST

Zaleski - *State Route 278 (south of Logan), 45698. Phone: (740) 596-5781. Hours: Open daily 6:00 am -11:00 pm.* ***Web: www.hcs.ohio-state.edu/ODNR/Forests/stateforests/zaleski.htm***. The Zaleski State Forest Sawmill is Ohio's only publicly owned and operated sawmill. It began operation in 1967. The "low-tech" approach taken at Zaleski gives the mill an almost historical significance. It is an efficient functioning mill that turns out specialty orders for many public works projects. Additionally, demonstrations and training activities (for example, grading workshops) are held every year at Zaleski. 26,827 acres in Vinton and Athens counties. Bridle trails (50 miles), Backpack trails (23 miles), 3 walk-in camp areas (self-registration permit - no fee), Forest of Honor, Hunter's campground (in season - no fee), grouse management area, and sawmill. Lake Hope State Park is adjacent.

Chapter 8
South East Area

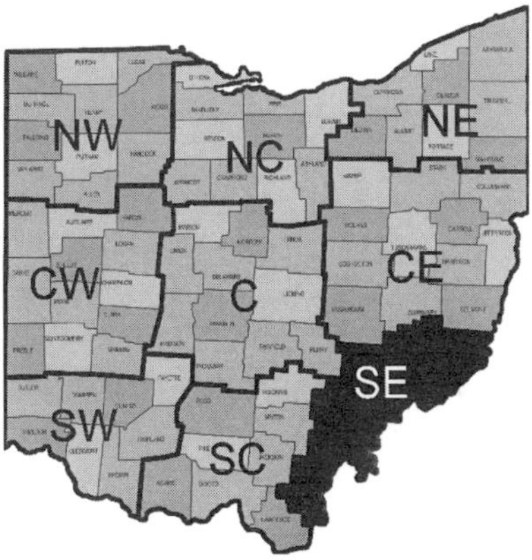

Our Favorites...

Campus Martius Museum

Lee Middleton Doll Factory

Marietta Soda Museum

Rossi Pasta Factory

Sternwheeler Pilothouse

STROUD'S RUN STATE PARK

Athens - *County Road 20 (8 miles Northeast of Athens off US 50A), 45701.* ***Web: www.dnr.state.oh.us/parks/parks/strouds.htm****. Phone: (740) 592-2302.* The first settlers arrived in the Athens County region in 1796. Two townships of land in the area had been apportioned by the Ohio Company in 1795 for the benefit of a university. Settlers were encouraged to settle on these college lands so as to make them attractive, productive and to form a fund for the institution. The park derives its name from the Strouds family who settled in the area in the early 1800s. 2,767 acres of camping, hiking trails, boating and rentals, fishing, swimming and winter sports.

LEE MIDDLETON ORIGINAL DOLL FACTORY

1301 Washington Boulevard (I-77 to SR 50/618)

Belpre 45714

- Phone: (740) 423-1481 or (800) 233-7479
  Web: www.leemiddleton.com
- Tours: Monday – Friday 9:00am – 2:00pm (Hourly) March – December. Approximately 20 minutes. Reservations Suggested. FREE.
- Miscellaneous: Factory Store with bargain buys and Nursery where you can adopt a life-sized Middleton infant baby doll complete with papers, promises and pictures.

Hopefully during your visit you'll get to experience a little girl adopting her first Middleton baby. It's so real, you'll swell with emotion as you see the new "Mom" promise the nursery worker to care for her baby properly. Lee Middleton started making dolls at her kitchen table in 1978 and modeled them after her children and children she knew. On tour a guide shows you techniques critical to the distinctiveness of these high-quality collectable dolls that look and feel almost real. One machine makes feet, hands and heads out of liquid vinyl cured in molds. Watch them put eyes in by blowing up the mold head like a balloon (with an air compressor) and popping in the eyes. Then, they release the air and the eye is set in place (*this is the part the guys like!*). See the artist's hand paint each doll's face using stencils and paint makeup. What a fun "girl's place" to visit. Prepare to fall in love with a doll and want one for your own!

OUR HOUSE MUSEUM

Gallipolis - *434 1st Avenue (off State Route 7), 45631. Phone: (740) 446-0586.* ***Web: www.ohiohistory.org/places/ourhouse****. Hours: Tuesday – Saturday 10:00am – 5:00pm, Sunday 1:00 – 5:00pm (Summer). Weekends only (May, September, October). Small Admission ($.50-$3.00).* A restored river inn with furnishings of early Americana. On 22 May 1825, General Lafayette visited Gallipolis and was entertained at Our House Tavern.

BURR OAK STATE PARK

Glouster - *10220 Burr Oak Lodge Road (6 miles Northeast of Glouster off State Route 13), 45732. Phone: (740) 767-3570 or (740) 767-2112 Lodge.* ***Web: www.burroakresort.com****. or* ***Web: www.dnr.state.oh.us/parks/parks/burroak.htm****.* Located in southeast Ohio, quiet and remote Burr Oak State Park has a rustic country charm in its scenery of wooded hills and valley farms. Nature programs, Bridle trails, Family cabins with A/C, Guest rooms in the Lodge with an indoor pool, tennis and basketball courts are highlights of this park. Also camping, hiking trails, boating and rentals, fishing, swimming, and winter sports.

CAMPUS MARTIUS: MUSEUM OF NORTHWEST TERRITORY

601 2nd Street (2nd and Washington Street, Downtown), **Marietta** 45750

- Phone: (740) 373-3750 or (800) 860-0145
  Web: www.ohiohistory.org/places/campus
- Hours: Wednesday - Saturday 9:30am - 5:00pm and Sundays and Holidays, Noon - 5:00 pm (Summer, October & November). Weekends only. (March & April).
- Admission: $6.00 adult, $2.00 child (6-12)

Campus recreates early development of Marietta as the first settlement in the Northwest Territory. The Putnam House is the oldest residence in

Ohio. The home and land office display replicas of the hardships of early pioneer life including old surgical and musical instruments. An exhibit titled "Paradise Found and Lost: Migration in the Ohio Valley" highlights migration from farms to cities and from Appalachia to industry. See the stage jacket worn by Appalachian born Country Singer, Dwight Yoakum. Videos and interactive computer games on migration. You can actually create a feeling of being taken back in time by walking through the train passenger car and listening to actual stories of passengers taking a trip to the "big city" for business or jobs (Stories are told on telephone handsets). See actual huge photographs of downtown Columbus and Marietta in the early 1900's that take up an entire wall - you'll feel as if you're walking into them!

MARIETTA SODA MUSEUM

109-111 Maple Street, Harmar Village

Marietta 45750

- Phone: (740) 376-COKE
  Web: www.harmarvillage.com/harmarcoke
- Hours: Thursday – Saturday 11:00am – 3:00pm, Sunday Noon - 5:00pm (Spring – Fall). Friday and Saturday 10:00am – 4:30pm (Winter).
- Admission: FREE
- Miscellaneous: Down the street is the Children's Toy & Doll Museum open Saturday afternoons (740-373-0799).

Memorabilia from 1900 to the present traces the history of this beverage and its marketing. Buy a bottle of COKE or Sarsaparilla (vanilla Root Beer) and sip it while you browse. Although it's rusted, you can still see the COCA-COLA logo on the front of many old dispensers and metal signs. The soda fountain features 10 cent cokes and serves lunch items. The building has hundreds of soda collectibles (both on display and for sale).

MARIETTA TROLLEY TOURS

Marietta - *127 Ohio Street (Levee House Café), 45750.* ***Web: www.mariettaonline.com/thingstodo/attractions/tours.php****. Phone: (740) 374-2233. Hours: Afternoon 12:30 and 2:30 pm (April – November). Schedule can vary. Call or visit website for details. Admission: $5.00-$8.00 (ages 5+).* Narrated one-hour tours describing and viewing historic architecture, shops along Front Street, Marietta College and more.

OHIO RIVER MUSEUM

601 Second Street (St. Clair & Front Street, Downtown)

Marietta 45750

- Phone: (740) 373-3717 or (800) 860-0145
  Web: www.ohiohistory.org/places/ohriver
- Hours: Weekends only (March-April). Wednesday-Saturday 9:30am – 5:00pm. Sunday Noon – 5:00pm (May-November).
- Admission: $6.00 adult, $2.00 child (6-12).

The WP Snyder, Jr. moored along the museum is the last surviving stern-wheeled towboat in America. Also, see a model of a flat boat and other scale models of many riverboats. A video titled, "Fire on the Water" describes dangerous early times when boilers might explode, killing many. Diorama (full scale) of wildlife along the Ohio River.

ROSSI PASTA

114 Greene Street (Downtown)

Marietta 45750

- Phone: (740) 376-2065 or (800) 227-6774
  Web: www.rossipasta.com
- Hours: Monday - Friday 9:00 am - 6:00pm, Saturday 9:00am-5:00pm, Sunday Noon - 5:00pm. Pasta making times vary, best weekdays before 3:00 pm. Call ahead for best times to tour.
- Miscellaneous: Upscale gourmet pasta with unusual twists of flavors like Artichoke, Wild Mushroom, Calamari, Linguini. Free sample bag of pasta to first time visitors.

They hand roll dough adding fresh flavor ingredients as they "turn" the dough. Their secret is using spring wheat flour instead of highly manufactured semoline flour. A machine cuts the pasta into very long and wide strips (linguini) or thin soup noodles. Teardrop shapes are stamped out. Next, the cut pasta goes into one of two large drying chambers which are precisely regulated to insure even temperatures. Finally, the pasta is packaged in clear Rossi-labeled bags. Be sure you invite your favorite gourmet cook along for this tour - it's a new level of pasta to experience!

SHOWBOAT BECKY THATCHER

Marietta - *237 Front Street on the River, 45750. Phone: (877) SHO-BOAT.* ***Web: www.marietta-ohio.com/beckythatcher****.* Vintage early 1900's sternwheeler that has a theater that was once a boiler room. Talented performers create a "Mark Twain" mood with melodramas like "Little Mary Sunshine" and favorites of composer Stephen Foster ("Oh Susanna" and "Camptown Races"). Funny signs appear during the performance instructing you when to "boo" or "cheer". The restaurant on board serves basic American food and Riverboat Pie (secret recipe) for dessert! Closed Sunday and Monday (March-December). Matinee and Evening shows. See schedule on website for details.

THE CASTLE

Marietta - *418 Fourth Street, 45750. Phone: (740) 373-4180.* ***Web: www.mariettacastle.org****. Hours: Monday - Sunday (Summer), Thursday – Monday (April, May, September - December). Weekdays 10:00am – 4:00pm, Weekends 1:00 – 4:00pm. Admission: $2.50-$4.00 (age 6+).* Historic area furnishings. Impressive parlor and chandelier. Video.

VALLEY GEM STERNWHEELER

Marietta - *601 Front Street (State Route 60 and State Route 7) (Docks next to the Ohio River Museum under the Washington Street Bridge), 45750. Phone: (740) 373-7862.* ***Web: www.valleygemsternwheeler.com****. Hours: Tuesday – Sunday. Departs every hour from 1:00 – 4:00pm (Summer). Rest of Year and Holidays, call for schedule. Admission: $3.00-$5.50 (ages 2+). Saturday dinner cruises $13.00-$27.00 (2 hours). Fall*

Foliage 3-4 hour tours $9.00-$15.00. Miscellaneous: Gift and snack area on board. Fall foliage cruises very popular in October. Heated or A/C main cabin. Take the 300 passenger, 60 minute cruise on the Valley Gem where the captain points out historic interests. See who can find the large stone blocks spelling "Marietta" on the landing welcoming steamboats. Why was the boat named after a piano company?

HOCKING VALLEY SCENIC RAILWAY

Nelsonville - *33 Canal Street (Off US 33), 45764. Phone: (740) 470-1300 or (800) HOCKING. (513) 753-9531 (Saturday and Sunday).* ***Web: www.hvsr.com****. Hours: Weekends Noon and 2:30 pm, (June – October). Special Holiday Schedule. Admission: $8.00-$11.00 adult, $5.00-$7.00 child (2-11).* Ride through the hills of scenic Hocking Valley on an authentic 1916 steam locomotive or a 1950 diesel locomotive (trips are 14 & 22 miles roundtrip). Both rides include a 30-minute stop over at Robbins Crossing Visitor's Center (small 1850's settler village). Enjoy the blooming dogwood trees in the spring, summertime fun, nature's spectacular fall foliage or a special winter ride with Santa (heated cars). No A/C or restrooms on train.

FORKED RUN STATE PARK

Reedsville - *(3 miles Southwest of Reedsville off State Route 124), 45772.* ***Web: www.dnr.state.oh.us/parks/parks/forkedrn.htm****. Phone: (740) 378-6206.* Located in the heart of Appalachia, colorful history, riverboats, scenic vistas and abundant wildlife give the park its rural charm. 817 acres of camping, hiking, boating and rentals, fishing, swimming, winter sports and food service. Shade River State Forest (hiking trails) is adjacent (740-554-3177).

BOB EVAN'S FARM

Rio Grande - *State Route 588 (off US 35 to State Route 325 South), 45674.* ***Web: www.bobevans.com****. Phone: (800) 944-FARM. Hours: Daily 9:00am - 5:00pm (Summer). Weekends in September. Admission: FREE for tour - Activities additional.* Begin or end your visit at the restaurant, once named "The Sausage Shop"-Bob's first restaurant. Then, wander round to visit the Farm

Museum (implements of yesteryear farms and a pictorial history of the company). See a log cabin village with a one-room school house, small animal barn yard, hay rides, horseback riding, canoe trips, craft barn and demonstrations, plus the Homestead (an old stagecoach stop and former home of Bob and Jewel Evans). Nearby in Bedwell (State Route 50/35) is Jewel Evan's Mill where you can view millstones grinding flour. Also in the area are good horseback riding stables and canoe liveries.

THE BARN

Stockport - *State Route 78, 43787. Phone: (740) 962-4284.* ***Web: www.chuckglass.com***. 1904 stained glass studio used by nationally known artist, Chuck Borsari. Sunday-Thursday 1:00-5:00pm.

PARRY MUSEUM

Woodsfield - *217 Eastern Avenue, 43793. Phone: (740) 472-1933.* ***Web: www.monroehistoricalsociety.com***. *Hours: Monday-Friday 10:00am-2:00pm, Sunday 2:00-5:00pm (June-October).* 1800's and early 1900's displays in home. Dairy Barn visit is where cheese and butter were made (late 1800's). Unusual, dog-powered cheese and butter churn and molds and tools used. One room schoolhouse classroom made of stone block, too.

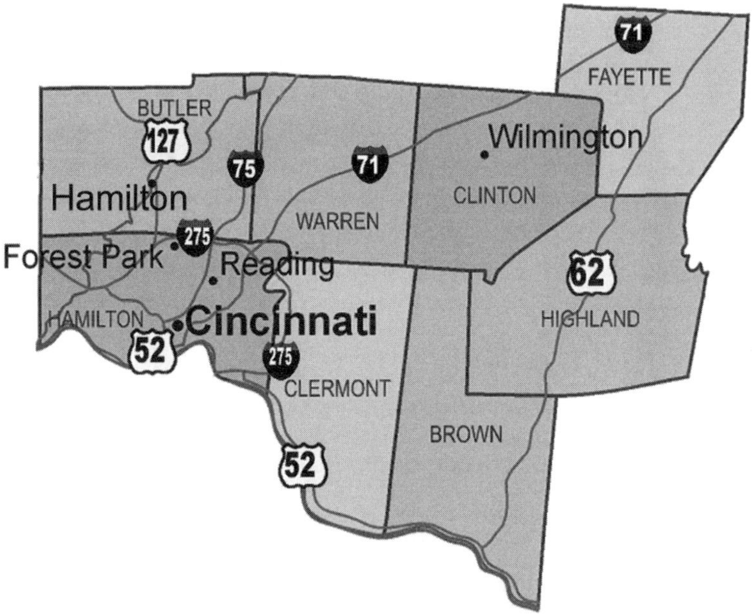

Chapter 9
South West Area

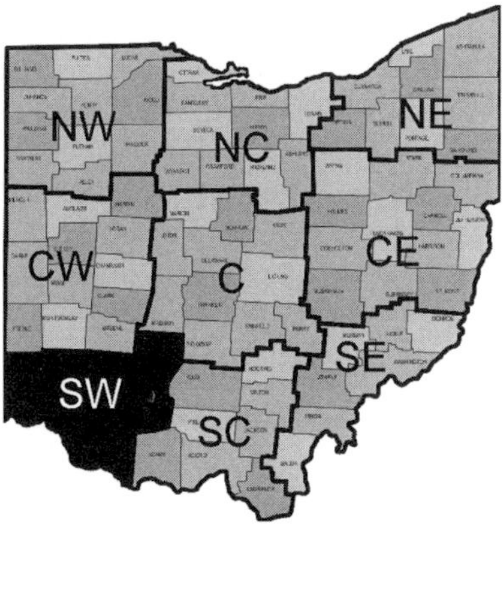

Our Favorites...

Cincinnati Fire Museum

Cincinnati History Museum

Cincinnati Museum of Natural History & Science

Cinergy Children's Museum

Heritage Village

Hueston Woods State Park

Loveland Castle

United Dairy Farmer's Factory

Historic Fire Wagon

EAST FORK STATE PARK

Amelia - *(4 miles Southeast of Amelia off SR 125, I-275 exit 63 or 65), 45106.* ***Web: www.dnr.state.oh.us/parks/parks/eastfork.htm****. Phone: (513) 734-4323.* East Fork offers a great diversity of recreational opportunities and natural history only 25 miles from Cincinnati. The park's terrain includes both rugged hills and open meadows. Bridle trails. 10,580 acres of camping, hiking, boating, fishing, swimming and winter sports.

CAREW TOWER

Cincinnati - *441 Vine Street (5th and Vine), Downtown, 45202. Phone: (513) 241-3888. Hours: Monday - Friday 9:30am - 5:30pm, Saturday 10:00am - 9:00pm, Sunday 11:00am - 4:45pm.* A 1930's Art Deco building that is the tallest building downtown. Observation deck with panoramic view. Small admission fee per person.

CINCINNATI ART MUSEUM

Cincinnati - *953 Eden Park Drive, 45202. Phone: (513) 721-ARTS.* ***Web: www.cincinnatiartmuseum.org****. Hours: Tuesday-Saturday 11:00am-5:00pm, Sunday Noon-6:00pm. Extended Wednesday evening hours. Closed Thanksgiving and Christmas. Admission: (Effective May 17, 2003 FREE admission daily except during special exhibits).* Art collection presents 5000 years of visual arts. Favorites include the Syrian Damascus Room, Blue glass chandelier, old musical instruments, Andy Warhol's Pete Rose and the futuristic robot (good size Contemporary Art Section). Family Fun Tour: Saturday, 1:00pm. Summer ArtVentures. Museum shop and café.

CINCINNATI BALLET

Cincinnati - *Aronoff Center, 650 Walnut Street, 45202. Phone: (513) 621-5219.* ***Web: www.cincinnatiballet.com****.* Classically based professional ballet company performs classic and contemporary works. The Nutcracker is performed each holiday season at Music Hall. Often limited backstage tours can be arranged. (September – May)

CINCINNATI BENGALS

Cincinnati - *Paul Brown Stadium (downtown, riverfront), 45202. Phone: (513) 621-3550.* ***Web: www.bengals.com***. Professional football. Join the Bengals Kids Club for great novelty items. Average ticket price $35.00-$50.00 (August – December).

CINCINNATI CYCLONES

Cincinnati - *Firstar Center, 45202. Phone: (513) 421-PUCK.* ***Web: www.cycloneshockey.com***. Part of the East Coast Hockey League. Tickets range from $5.00-$17.00. Kids Club. (October-March)

CINCINNATI FIRE MUSEUM

315 West Court Street, Downtown

Cincinnati 45202

- Phone: (513) 621-5553, **Web: www.cincyfiremuseum.com**
- Hours: Tuesday – Friday 10:00am – 4:00pm, Weekends Noon – 4:00pm. Closed holidays.
- Admission: $5.00 adult, $4.00 senior (55+), $3.00 child (2-12).

From the minute you walk in the restored fire station, the kids will be intrigued by the nation's first professional fire department exhibits. Displays chronicle fire fighting history from antique equipment to the cab of a newer fire truck where you can actually pull levers, push buttons, ring bells, operate the siren and flash emergency lights. The museum has an emphasis on fire safety with "Safe House" models (touch and demo area)and a video about fire fighting dangers. Before you leave be sure you slide down the 5-foot fire pole or push the hand pump engine. This is the most kid-friendly fire museum we know!

CINCINNATI PLAYHOUSE IN THE PARK

Cincinnati - *962 Mt. Adams Circle, Marx Theatre (I-75 to US 50 exit), 45202. Phone: (513) 421-3888.* ***Web: www.cincyplay.com***. *Prices begin at $13.00. Same day half-price discounts and coupons. Performances daily except Monday. Matinees on Saturday, Sunday, & Wednesday (September-June)* Professional resident theatre offers dramas, comedies and musicals (Abracadabra, A Christmas Carol).

CINCINNATI REDS

Cincinnati - *Great American Ballpark (downtown, riverfront), 45202. Phone: (513) 421-REDS or (877) 647-REDS.* ***Web: www.cincinnatireds.com*** Professional Major League baseball. First professional baseball team. Several family-friendly ticket days and fun promotions for kids on game days. ($5.00 - $25.00+) (April – September)

KROHN CONSERVATORY

Cincinnati - *950 Eden Park Drive, 45202. Phone: (513) 421-4086.* ***Web: www.cinci-parks.org****.* A rainforest full of 5000 varieties of exotic desert and tropical plants. One of the nation's largest - check out their seasonal displays. Small admission for special exhibits.

SHOWBOAT MAJESTIC

Cincinnati - *Moored at Broadway Street Landing, 45202. Phone: (513) 241-6550.* ***Web: www.cypt.org****. Hours: Wednesday-Saturday 8:00pm, Sunday 2:00pm & 7:00pm (mid-April-mid-October). Weekends (November, December seasonal shows). Admission: Must purchase 6 ticket subscription during regular season. Seasonal holiday performances are separate tickets.* Live riverfront shows like musicals, comedies and dramas performed by the Cincinnati Young Peoples Theatre. The original owner, actor Thomas Jefferson Reynolds, raised eleven kids on board while moving from rivertown to town entertaining folks in the early 1900's.

TAFT MUSEUM OF ART

Cincinnati - *316 Pike Street (Broadway to Fifth to Pike Sts), 45202. Phone: (513) 241-0343.* ***Web: www.taftmuseum.org****.* See works of European and American painters, Chinese porcelains, Limoges enamels displayed in a federal period mansion. Select Saturdays "Families Create!" programs.

ATI HISTORY MUSEUM

nati Museum Center (I-71 south to I-275 west to I-
-75 north exit 1), **Cincinnati** 45203

- 00 or (800) 733-2077, **Web: www.cincymuseum.org**
- onday - Saturday (& Holidays) 10:00am - 5:00pm, Sunday 11:00am - 6:00pm. Closed Thanksgiving and Christmas.
- Admission: $5.00-$7.00 per person. Toddler (age 1-2) rates are slightly lower. Combo prices with other museums in the Center. Parking fee.
- Miscellaneous: Gift Shops - Worth a good look!

As you enter the museum, your eyes will race around the Cincinnati in Motion model of the city (from 1900-1940) with interactive computer booths and most of the transportation moving (planes, trains, cars, etc). Such an easy and fun way to learn about historical buildings in town or, just reminisce or admire the fascinating layout. Next, you'll visit with The Flynns (ring the doorbell first) talking about life at home during World War II. Hop on board a streetcar with the conductor telling news of the war. Moms and grandmothers will have to check out the "Leg Makeup Bar" (clue: there was a stocking shortage during the war). Now, walk through a life-like forest with shadows and birds wrestling and singing. Then, walk through re-created streets of Cincinnati. Visit the Fifth Street Market and Millcreek Millery - try on hats of the early 1900's and then shop next door at the pretend open air market. The kids can play in a miniature cabin and flat boat, then actually board a steamboat and pretend you're the captain. Very authentically presented, clever displays throughout the whole museum. Cincinnati folks should be proud.

CINCINNATI MUSEUM OF NATURAL HISTORY AND SCIENCE

1301 Western Avenue, Cincinnati Museum Center (I-71 south to I-275 west to I-75 south exit 2A; I-75 north exit 1), **Cincinnati** 45203

- Phone: (513) 287-7000 or (800) 733-2077. **Web: www.cincymuseum.org**
- Hours: Monday - Saturday (& Holidays) 10:00am - 5:00pm, Sunday 11:00am - 6:00pm. Closed Thanksgiving and Christmas.
- Admission: $5.00-$7.00 per person. Toddler (age 1-2) rates are slightly lower. Combo prices with other museums in the Center. Parking fee.

- Miscellaneous: Gift shops. All are worth a visit
  to do at home.

Want to know a lot about the Ohio Valley's N
history? The Glacier and Cavern simulated areas are
walk-thru reproductions that are so real, it's almost spooky.
Ice Age of fossils and re-created walk-through glaciers. Maybe
solve the Ice Age mystery or change the landscape of glaciers. The Paleo Lab (within the Ice Cave) is the place to watch actual scientists at work on lots of fossils. On to the simulated Limestone Cavern with underground waterfalls and a live bat colony (behind glass!). (There are two routes - one that is challenging and involves much climbing and navigating, and the other that is wheelchair or stroller accessible). Look for lots of dino skeletons in Dinosaur Hall. In the recycling center, take a look at the garbage used by an average family and ways to reduce it. When you see a pile of garbage bags stacked on end and towering to the ceiling, your family will want to consider ways to sort recyclables and reduce unnecessary waste. Find out "All About You" as you explore inside, outside and beneath your great body. Brush a huge tooth, see under the skin of your hand, pretend in the office of doctors and dentists, or maybe play pinball as your "food ball" goes through the digestive system. Plan a few hours at this extremely well done museum - we promise it will engage you and you'll learn many new things...easily!

CINERGY CHILDREN'S MUSEUM

Cincinnati Museum Center, 1301 Western Avenue (I-71 south to I-275 west to I-75 south exit 2A; I-75 north exit 1), **Cincinnati** 45203

- Phone: (800) 733-2077 or (513) 287-7000
  Web: www.cincymuseum.org
- Hours: Monday - Saturday (& Holidays) 10:00am - 5:00pm, Sunday 11:00am - 6:00pm. Closed Thanksgiving and Christmas.
- Admission: $5.00-$7.00 per person. Toddler (age 1-2) rates are slightly lower. Combo prices with other museums in the Center. Parking fee.
- Miscellaneous: Museum stores (great kids gift ideas). Snack Bar.

Start in the Woods, kiddies. The dim lighting adds mystery to the slides, tunnels, rope climbing mazes and walls, and treehouses. The Energy Zone has kids move plastic balls along a conveyor to a gantic dump bucket. It's actually a gigantic physics experiment n this Zone - lots of machines and tubes to move balls. Kids At Work lets them make real-life and pretend structures from blocks, pebbles and Legos. They can even use a 12 foot crane to move and lift blocks. Other highlights are the Little Sprouts Farm (age 4 and under), Water Works, Kids Town (pretend town), or Animal Spot (lots of unusual skeletons). Each area is so interactive and so different from the other. Each exhibit had activities for toddlers up to pre-teens. We liked how most areas required friend's/parent's participation to complete a task. Make a new friend each visit!

OMNIMAX THEATER

Cincinnati - *Cincinnati Museum Center, 1301 Western Avenue (I-71 south to I-275 west to I-75 south exit 2A; I-75 north exit 1), 45203. Phone: (513) 287-7000 or (800) 733-2077.* ***Web: www.cincymuseum.org****. Hours: Sunday 11:00am-6:00pm, Monday-Friday beginning at 1:00pm for several shows, Saturday 11:00am-9:00pm, hourly. Extended holiday hours. Admission: $5.00-$7.00 per person. Toddler (age 1-2) rates are slightly lower. Combo prices with other museums in the Center. Parking fee.* Shows viewed on a 5 story, 72-foot wide domed screen. Unique themes change each season.

FRISCH'S COMMISSARY

Cincinnati - *3011 Stanton Avenue (I-71 to Taft Road West Exit), 45206. Phone: (513) 559-5288. Tours: Wednesday 9:00am. Reservations suggested. Ages 8 and above. Maximum 15 people. One hour. Reservations required.* This commissary supplies 85 Big Boy Restaurants in Ohio, Indiana, and Kentucky (and they're still family owned). They prepare cooked soups, salad dressings, raw meats, vegetables, and baked goods. Children will marvel at large-scale production, especially when the tour guide describes the quantities of ingredients used for each product. For example, two people peel 600 pounds of carrots by hand each day. The bakery ovens can hold 24 pies at one time. They save the restaurants time by pre-slicing or shredding vegetables and bagging them. We understand they use an air compressor to blow the skins off onions!

CINCINNATI SYMPHONY ORCHE

Cincinnati - *1241 Elm Street, 45210. Phone:* (
Web: www.cincinnatisymphony.org. The CSO presen pops concerts and an artist series in Music Hall. CSO RiverB Music Center hosts Symphony/Pops Orchestra, plus contemporary artists (May-September). Parties of 1/2 Note are parties designed especially for children ages 3–14. The purpose of these fun theme parties is to create awareness of, and cultivate future audiences for, the Cincinnati Symphony Orchestra.

ENSEMBLE THEATRE OF CINCINNATI

Cincinnati - *1127 Vine Street (Over-the-Rhine), 45210. Phone: (513) 421-3555.* ***Web: www.cincyetc.com***. Professional resident theatre develops and produces new works with an emphasis on Ohio and Cincinnati artists (ex. Pinocchio) (September – June).

CINCINNATI MIGHTY DUCKS

Cincinnati - *2250 Seymour Avenue, 45212. Phone: (513) 351-3999.* ***Web: www.cincinnatimightyducks.com***. Semi-Professional hockey. Home games at Cincinnati Gardens. ($5.00 - $15.00 range) (October – March). Look for the mascot, Buster.

UNITED DAIRY FARMERS

3955 Montgomery Road

Cincinnati 45212

- Phone: (513) 396-8700 - Ask for Consumer Relations
- Admission: FREE
- Tours: Mondays and Fridays, 9:30 a.m. - 1 ½ hours, Ages 6+. Maximum 25 persons.

As a group, weigh yourselves on their giant truck scale! See milk being filled in containers (and the large vats where they store raw and treated milk). The plastic bottles are also made on the premises from tiny pellets of plastic melted, blown up and compressed (see it up close). Stop in and visit with the Food Scientists in the Flavor Lab (maybe help pick a new flavor). Best of all, watch ice cream packed and frozen (you even get to step inside the deep-freeze room). Get a free ice cream sundae (flavor of the day - right off the production line!) as a souvenir. We have found this to be one of the best organized, interesting and fun factory tours around!

HARRIET BEECHER STOWE HOUSE

Cincinnati - *2950 Gilbert Avenue (SR 3 and US 22), 45214. Phone: (513) 632-5120. **Web: www.ohiohistory.org/places/stowe**. Hours: Tuesday - Thursday 10:00am - 4:00pm. Admission: Donations. Miscellaneous: Look for the National Underground Railroad Museum open in 2004.* The home of the author of "Uncle Tom's Cabin" novel that brought attention to the evils of slavery. Displays describe the Beecher family, the abolitionist movement and the history of African-Americans. Request the video about the story of the book. Mrs. Stowe's journal is available for viewing, as are photo quilts of slave faces. This museum is best visited after some study of the anti-slavery roots along the Ohio River. The videos are long, but helpful.

TAFT, WILLIAM HOWARD NATIONAL HISTORIC SITE

2038 Auburn Avenue (I-71 north to exit 2, Mt. Auburn)

Cincinnati 45219

- Phone: (513) 684-3262, **Web: www.nps.gov/wiho**
- Hours: Daily 8:00am – 4:00pm. Closed Thanksgiving, Christmas and New Year's.
- Admission: Donations
- Miscellaneous: Check out the orientation video first in the Education Center adjacent.

Visit the birthplace and boyhood home of a US President and Chief Justice. Four of the rooms are furnished to reflect Taft's family life 1857-77. Other exhibits depict his public service career. The signature exhibit of the center is an animatronic figure of the President's Son, Charlie Taft. Charlie tells stories about different family members. Children's group tours give kids the opportunity to dress up from a trunk of period hats and over-garments and play with old fashioned toys. This really helps the children understand life for a young person in the mid-1800's.

CINCINNATI ZOO & BOTANICAL GARDENS

3400 Vine Street (I-75 to exit 6, Mitchell Ave)

Cincinnati 45220

- Phone: (513) 281-4700 (800) 94-HIPPO, **www.cincyzoo.org**
- Hours: Daily 9:00am – 5:00pm (Summer); 9:00am - 4:00pm (Winter), 9:00am – 6:00pm (Summer Weekends), Children's Zoo – 10:00am 4:00pm.
- Admission: $11.50 adult, $9.00 senior, $6.00 child (2-12). Children's Zoo and rides are $1-2 additional. Parking Fee.
- Miscellaneous: Safari Restaurant. Concessions. Tram and train rides. Children's Zoo & Animal Nursery. Wildlife Theatre. Stroller rentals. We recommend lodging at Homewood Suites by Hilton – 2670 E. Kemper Road (I-275 exit 44, Mosteller Rd.). Cincinnati-North (866) 613-9330. Full breakfast, all suites (w/kitchenette), pool, whirlpool, sport courts, and Family Fun Packages.

Ranked one of the top 5 zoos in the United States, its highlight is the successes in breeding white Bengal tigers and other rare wild animals (ie. the first zoo in over 100 years to announce the birth of a healthy sumatran rhinocerous). Kemodo dragons (10 feet long and 300 lbs!) and endangered Florida Manatees are some of the large, unusual animals there. The Lords of the Artic area features polar bears on land and nose-to-nose through underwater glass panels. Dramatic waterfalls and a polar bear cave, with educational interactives complement the exhibit. Their landscaped gardens duplicate the animals' world and the Jungle Trails exhibit even has a tropical rainforest. The first Insectarium (you guessed it!) in the nation is also here.

CONEY ISLAND

Cincinnati - *6201 Kellogg Avenue (Off I-275 East), 45228. Phone: (513) 232-8230.* ***Web: www.coneyislandpark.com****. Hours: Daily: Pool 10:00am – 8:00pm, Rides 11:00am – 9:00pm (Memorial Weekend – Labor Day). Admission: Average $11.00-$12.00 for pool. $8.00 day pass or $1-2.00 each for rides. Discount combo park passes. Ages 4+. Half price after 4:00pm. Parking $5.00.*

Sunlite, the world's largest re-circulating pool (200' x 401' and holding more than three million gallons of water!) with a huge slide and 6 diving boards, is one of the many fun attractions. Also, Zoom Flume water toboggan, Pipeline Plunge tube water slide, Giant Slide, kiddie rides, miniature golf, bumper boats, pedal boats and picnic areas.

PARKY'S FARM

Cincinnati - *1515 West Sharon Road (Winton Woods Park) (Winton Road & Lake Forest Drive), 45240. Phone: (513) 521-PARK. Free.* The park has a 3-mile paved hike-bike trail (bike rental is available), bridle trail and riding center on the south side of Winton Lake. The park also has picnic areas, a 1-mile fitness trail, a boathouse, nine shelters and an 18-hole Frisbee golf course and a regular golf course. At Parky's Farm explore orchards and crops plus farm animals. Pony rides and PlayBarn (farm theme play pits with plastic apples and eggs to jump in). Some parts of farm open only in the summer.

HERITAGE VILLAGE MUSEUM

11450 Lebanon Pike, Sharon Woods Park (US 42, 1 mile south of I-275 exit 46),
Cincinnati (Sharonville) 45241

- Phone: (513) 563-9484, **Web: www.heritagevillagecincinnati.org**
- Hours: Wednesday-Saturday Noon-4:00pm, Sunday 1:00-5:00pm. (May – October). Weekends (April, November, & December)
- Admission: $6.00 adult, $5.00 senior (62+), $4.00 child (5-11)
- Miscellaneous: Dressed interpreters. Bicycle rental, hiking trails. $1.00 entry into Sharon Woods park (per vehicle). Many picnic and shelter areas, mostly wooded for shade. General Store with many pioneer hand-make items and lots of American Girl clothes and books for sale.

See 18th Century Ohio. Nine actual buildings from Southwest Ohio including: The Elk Lick House - "fancy house", learn about the gothic Ohio clock and why the "mouse ran up the clock"; the Train Station - with its treasure trunk hands-on pieces to play with; Kemper Log House - look for Isabella's sampler (Little House on the Prairie theme here) and the "Y" staircase; the kitchen and smokehouse - during festivals they cook here; and the medical office - see Civil War medical and pharmaceutical equipment- amputation city! Their Kids History Camps are wonderfully organized and a great way to "participate" in history.

BB RIVERBOATS

Cincinnati Area (Covington, KY) - *Covington Crossing, just over the blue suspension bridge, 45202. Phone: (800) 261-8586.* ***Web: www.bbriverboats.com****. Admission: $10.00 and up. Children half price. Tours: 1 1/2 hour sightseeing cruises on the Ohio River. Several times daily (best to call for schedule). Reservations Required (May-October).* Docked at the foot of Madison Street see the Modern "Funliner", "Mark Twain" sternwheeler or steamboat "Becky Thatcher". Also theme cruises like mini-vacation, holiday or "Skyline Chili". Many cruises offer additional lunch, brunch and dinner cruise options.

LITTLE MIAMI STATE PARK

Corwin - *(North of Corwin), 45068. Phone: (513) 897-3055.* ***Web: www.dnr.state.oh.us/parks/parks/lilmiami.htm****.* As the river twists and bends, visitors will discover many natural wonders such as steep rocky cliffs, towering sycamores and elegant great blue herons on the wing. Bridle trails. 452 acres of hiking, fishing, and winter sports.

STONELICK STATE PARK

Edenton - *2895 Lake Drive (1 mile South of Edenton off State Route 727), 45162. Phone: (513) 625-7544.* ***Web: www.dnr.state.oh.us/parks/parks/stonelck.htm****.* An interesting feature of the Stonelick landscape is the significance of sweet gum trees. Normally, sweet gum is a subordinate tree but co-dominates the woodlands of Stonelick with beech and maple. Also, colonies of dense flying star, purple fringeless orchid and Virginia mountain mint - all uncommon wildflowers in Ohio - can be found in the park. 1,258 acres of camping, hiking trails, boating, fishing, swimming and winter sports.

JUNGLE JIM'S INT'L FARMERS MARKET

5440 Dixie Highway

Fairfield 45014

- Phone: (513) 674-6000, **Web: www.junglejims.com**
- Hours: Open daily 8:00am-10:00pm.

A grocery store is an adventure? This store, selling exotic and even normal foods, is! Ohio's Famous Playground for Food Lovers. Customers shop in four acres of food from all around the world all under one roof. Plastic animals and giant fruits greet you. Once inside, the store is divided into theme areas. Visit Amish Country, The Ocean, Europe, South America, India and the Middle East. Try some new food like *medallions of alligator!*

GRANT SCHOOLHOUSE & BOYHOOD HOME

Georgetown - *Water Street (one block west of SR 125), 45121. Phone: (937) 378-4222.* ***Web: www.ohiohistory.org/places/grantsh.*** *Hours: By Appointment only, Boyhood Home: Monday-Saturday 9:30am-5:00pm. Schoolhouse: Wednesday-Sunday Noon-5:00pm. Small admission.* Ulysses worked in his father's tannery and, from the ages of about six to thirteen, he attended classes in the little schoolhouse on Water Street. He lived nearby on 219 East Grant Avenue.

THE GLASS REFACTORY

Georgetown - *9262 Mt. Orab Pike, 45121. Phone: (888) 291-5690.* ***www.glassrefactory.com****. Admission: FREE. Tours: By appointment, Tuesday-Friday 9:00am-5:00pm. Minimum group size is 8, maximum is 75. Must be at least 6 years old.* Recycling with a twist…recycling bottles into pieces of art. First collect used glass, melt it and form it into suncatchers. Custom designed molds and some whimsical. Plan to bring $6.00-$10.00 to purchase one.

PYRAMID HILL SCULPTURE PARK

Hamilton - *1763 Hamilton-Cleves Road (I-275 to SR 27 to SR 128), 45011. Phone: (513) 868-8336.* ***Web: www.pyramidhill.org****. Hours: Tuesday-Sunday 10:00am-6:00pm (April-October). Weekends only (winter). Tea Room open for lunchtime Tuesday-Friday. Admission: $1.50-$4.00 (age 5+).* Pyramid Hill is an outdoor museum focusing on monumental pieces of sculpture in an environment of meadows, forests, and various gardens. Their mission includes the eventual establishment of a collection which will demonstrate the complete history of sculpture, making Pyramid Hill the only art park in the world working on the accomplishment. This park currently has over 10 titled sculptures. Especially noticeable is "Abracadabra" by internationally famous sculptor, Alexander Liberman. Many passengers flying into Cincinnati can see the 2 ½ story high, bright red contemporary walk-thru sculpture from above. The Baroque Trajectory arrived the summer of 2002. This piece survived the September 11 attack - it stood just 3 blocks away in New York City!

FORT HILL STATE MEMORIAL

Hillsboro - *13614 Fort Hill Road (Rte. 23 south to Rte. 50 west to Rte. 41 south), 45133.* ***Web: http://www.ohiohistory.org/places/fthill.*** *Phone: (937) 588-3221 or (800) 283-8905. Hours: Wednesday - Saturday 9:30am-5:00pm, Sunday and holidays Noon-5:00pm (Memorial Day-Labor Day). Weekends only Noon-5:00pm (day after Labor Day-October). Admission: $3.00 adults, $2.00 students (6-12).* Atop one of the only flat hills in the area, the Hopewell Indians built a walled structure that enclosed almost 50 acres. Inside, they built two large covered structures. The original mound (obscured by trees) still stands at 40 feet wide and up to 15 feet tall. There is an educational museum, two 2-4 mile trails, a picnic area and restrooms on the premises.

ROCKY FORK STATE PARK

Hillsboro - *9800 North Shore Drive (6 miles Southeast of Hillsboro off State Route 124), 45133. Phone: (937) 393-4284.* ***Web: www.dnr.state.oh.us/parks/parks/rockyfrk.htm.*** Unlimited horsepower boating allows for excellent skiing on the lake which also provides catches of bass, muskellunge and walleye. A scenic gorge, dolomite caves and natural wetlands add to the popularity of this recreation area. 3,464 acres of camping, hiking, boating rentals, and swimming.

PARAMOUNT'S KINGS ISLAND

I-71 to Exit 25A or 24 (24 miles North of Cincinnati)

Kings Mills 45034

- Phone: (513) 754-5700 or (800) 288-0808, **Web: www.pki.com**
- Hours: Daily 9:00am – Dark (Memorial Day – Late August), Weekends Only (April, May, September, October).
- Admission: ~$43.00 general, ~$25.00 child (3-6) and senior (60+). Discounts available at area hotels, online and at local stores. Check local tourism site. Parking Fee $9.00.
- Miscellaneous: Three restaurants plus 60 fast food areas.

Some of the featured attractions at King's Island are: Several Shows & 80 Different Family Rides Plus:

- WATERWORKS – heated wave pool, children's play area, lazy river, plus 16 water slides and rides.
- ACTION ZONE – The Beast (longest wooden coaster), The Outer Limits (1st indoor coaster to catapult in the dark at high velocity), Days of Thunder (racing car simulator of high speed stock car racing).
- TOMB RAIDER: THE RIDE - journey into ancient temples, proceed thru chambers and strap into a vehicle to make a daring escape.
- DROP ZONE - pulse pounding height.
- FACE OFF - 5 G's inverted face to face coaster.
- HANNA BARBERA LAND – Scooby Doo's Magic-To-Do, Cartoon characters.
- NICKELODEON CENTRAL – Slime Time Live Show and Slime Zone Area (water spray, pipe work maze, Mess-A-Mania). Most popular with school age kids. Favorite Nick Jr. Characters might visit (ie. Dora or Jimmy Neutron)

TURTLE CREEK VALLEY RAILWAY

Lebanon - *198 South Broadway (US 42), 45036. Phone: (513) 398-8584 or (513) 933-8022 info line.* ***Web: www.ci.lebanon.oh.us/external/railway/index.htm****. Departures: Late Morning, Noon, Early Afternoon. Wednesday, Friday, Saturday, Sunday (June-August). Saturday, Sunday (May,*

September, December). Admission: $10.00 adult, $9.00 $7.00 child (3-12). Special rates for theme Miscellaneous: Station Depot with Gift Shop. The passenger cars do not have restrooms and are not heated or air-conditioned. A one-hour ride in a refurbished 1930's train car reminiscent of yesteryear in the old Indiana and Ohio Railroad through rural countryside (fields and farmlands). The popular open air gondola car on the rear of the train allows you to enjoy a panoramic view of the countryside. A concession stand is onboard the train. Turtle Creek was named for the famous Indian Chief "Little Turtle".

WARREN COUNTY HISTORICAL SOCIETY MUSEUM & AREA

Lebanon - *105 South Broadway, 45036. Phone: (937) 932-1817. Hours: Tuesday-Saturday 9:00am-4:00pm, Sunday Noon-4:00pm.* Village Green with shops and collection of Shaker furniture. The Golden Lamb (Ohio's oldest inn) is open for lunch/dinner. Many Presidents have spent the night here. Historical rooms.

"LOVELAND CASTLE", CHATEAU LAROCHE

12025 Shore Drive (2 miles South of Kings Island)

Loveland 45140

- Phone: (513) 683-4686, **Web: www.lovelandcastle.com**
- Hours: Daily 11:00am – 5:00pm (April – September). Weekends 11:00am – 5:00pm (October – March)
- Admission: $3.00 adult, $2.00 child (under 12). Self-guided tour.
- Miscellaneous: Only authentically built medieval castle in the United States. Started as a shelter house for scouts. Call for directions, or for a map that you can print, visit our website: **www.kidslovepublications.com/Lovelandcastlemapscan.jpg**

This is a real hidden castle and a huge family favorite! Chateau LaRoche was the vision of Harry D. Andrews and construction spanned some 50 years beginning in 1929. He actually did 99% of the work himself! The castle is authentic in its rugged structure with battlement towers, a princess chamber, a dungeon, narrow passageways, tower staircases, a "king's" dining room, and tower bedrooms. Over 32,000 hand-made (cast in milk cartons donated by neighbors) bricks were used to build the structure. Learn a lot about castle building and why the front door has over 2500 nails in it. A real Knight of the Golden Trail will greet you and answer any questions throughout your visit. Don't miss this real adventure that your children and you will love (maybe even play pretend - bring along dress up clothes)!

THE BEACH

2590 Waterpark Drive (I-71 Exit 25B - 20 miles North of Cincinnati)

Mason 45040

- Phone: (513) 398-SWIM or (800) 886-SWIM
  Web: www.thebeachwaterpark.com
- Hours: Daily opens 10:00am- Closing varies(usually at dark). (Memorial Weekend to Mid-September).
- Admission: ~$10.00-$25.00 Children – Senior – Adult. Discounts after 4:00pm. Parking fee.
- Miscellaneous: Food Service. No outside food or drink allowed into the park. Bags are checked.

Over 40,000 square feet of beach and two million gallons of water and waves await you! Favorites include the Pearl leisure heated tropical spa pool, Aztec Adventure watercoaster, Thunder Beach Wave Pool and the Lazy Miami River inner tube ride. The young children's water area has Splash Mountain with warm water and Jolly Mon non-water areas!

LESOURDSVILLE LAKE, THE GREAT AMERICAN AMUSEMENT PARK

5757 Middletown-Hamilton Road (I-75 south, exit Rte.63 west to Rte. 4). **Middletown** 45044

- Phone: (513) 539-2193, **Web: www.lesourdsvillelake.com**
- Hours: Thursday Noon - 9:00pm, Friday-Saturday Noon-10:00pm, Sunday Noon-9:00pm.(June-October).
- Admission: $3.00 per person (5-64). Rides & games - most $1.00 each. Passes $10.00-$16.00. Parking $4.00. Thursday is Dollar Day…$1.00 for parking, for entrance and for all rides. After Labor Day, ride passes are ~$10.00.

Known for 20 years as "*Americana*", this new/old amusement park is from another era. The Screechin' Eagle roller coaster is nearly eighty years old and names like the Scrambler and the Whip are familiar to all. They have the classic fun house, merry-go-round, sky ride and swinging ship rides too. 40 rides in all and a swimming pool. Usually there are shorter lines and fireworks on Friday nights.

CINCINNATI NATURE CENTER

Milford - *4949 Tealtown Road, 45150. Phone: (513) 831-1711. Hours: Open all year, dawn to dusk. Admission: FREE.* Hike a trail through pristine natural habitat at Rowe Woods, Milford or Long Branch in Goshen. Or, explore the children's garden and farmyard at Gorman Heritage Farm, Evendale.

GOVERNOR BEBB PRESERVE

Morgan Township - *1979 Bebb Park Lane (follow SR 129 (Hamilton-Scipio Road) about 8 miles. Turn left on California Road then right on Cincinnati-Brookville Road), Phone: (513) 867-5835 or (877) PARK-FUN. Hours: Saturday and Sunday 1:00 - 5:00pm (May-September). $2.00 per vehicle fee.* Visit the small 1812 village with the restored log cabin (birthplace of William Bebb - born in 1802). He was the governor of Ohio from 1846 - 48 and a trial lawyer noted for his emotional zeal. There is an 1850's covered bridge, picnic sites, a group picnic shelter, playgrounds, nature trails, restrooms and an on-site park ranger. Rustic family campsites, youth group campsites and a reservable cabin are also available. Good to visit during special events.

THE DUDE RANCH

Morrow - *3205 Waynesville Road (I-71 to exit 32, SR 123 southeast), 45152.* ***Web: www.theduderanch.com****. Phone: (513) 956-8099. Hours: Open year round. Daytime and evening programs. Admission: $20.00-$35.00 per person. Miscellaneous: Just 10 minutes from Kings Island. Camps and birthday programs. Paddleboats and petting zoo, too.* Horseback riding thru woods and meadows, authentic cattle drives, hayrides, pony rides and party/picnic facilities. Learn to rope like a real cowboy or cowgirl or fish awhile. Ask about Dinner Rides (eat out on the trail around a campfire), Western Family Fun Night or the Campfire Hayride (marshmallow roasts, wiener roasts).

FORT ANCIENT STATE MEMORIAL

6123 State Route 350 and Middleboro Road (I-71 to Rt. 123 to State Route 350), **Oregonia** 45054

- Phone: (513) 932-4421or (800) 283-8904
  Web: www.ohiohistory.org/places/ftancien
- Hours: Daily & Holidays 10:00am-5:00pm (May-September). Wednesday-Sunday 10:00am-5:00pm (March, April, October, November).
- Admission: $6.00 adults, $2.00 child(6-12).

Ohio's entire Indian heritage is displayed from prehistoric to modern times. The 100 acre field is where graves and artifacts were found and is also home to the second largest earthwork in the nation (constructed by Hopewell Indians between 300 BC - 600 AD). Best to visit during Indian Celebration weekends, Children's Day (games and chores) or Night Hiker evenings. Hiking trails.

MCGUFFEY MUSEUM, MIAMI UNIVERSITY WALKING TOUR

Spring and Oak Streets (Miami University campus area)

Oxford 45056

- Phone: (513) 529-2232 or (513) 529-1809 campus tours, **Web: www.miami.muohio.edu/about_miami/Virtual_Tour/campus map/sw/mcguffey_museum.cfm**
- Hours: Weekends 2:00 - 4:00pm (Except August and Holidays). Campus tours are at your leisure during University hours of operation.
- Admission: FREE
- Miscellaneous: Points of interest around campus are: Gardens, Anthropology & Zoology Museums (Upham Hall), Geology Museum (Shideler Hall on Patterson), the Library & the Chapel.

See an original collection of McGuffey Readers (lesson books on the three R's and morality, i.e. brotherly love, honesty and hard work). The First Eclectic Readers, published in 1836, started the series of books that was to educate five generations of Americans by 1920. They are still in print and still used today. The home, (built in the early 1830's) is where William Holmes McGuffey wrote his readers while preparing classwork for children. On display is Professor McGuffey's lectern and traveling 3-part secretary/bookcase. Check out his eight-sided desk!

HUESTON WOODS STATE PARK

6201 Park Office Road (5 miles North of Oxford off State Route 732), **Oxford (College Corner)** 45003

- Phone: (513) 523-6381or (800) 282-7275 reservations

  Web: www.huestonwoodsresort.com

A big feature of this park is the Nature Center with programs including their nature crafts, movies, fossils, and fabulous animals (like bobcat, cougar, bunny, snakes, turtles). The Raptor Rehab Center is where they care for injured animals, nursing them back to health (hawks, owls, etc). At the park is also a Rent-a-Camp, biking and rentals, camping, hiking/bridle trails and rentals, boating and rentals, fishing, swimming and winter sports. Kids/Family activities include swimming pool games, candy crafts, guided hikes (fossil hunts) and the ever popular, Bingo games. Evening hikes and bonfire/marshmallow roasts, too. There are cute, cozy, newly remodeled family cottages and a lodge with overnight rooms, indoor / outdoor pools, sauna and fitness areas.

GRANT BIRTHPLACE MUSEUM

Point Pleasant - *219 East Grant Avenue (off US 52), 45157. **Web: www.ohiohistory.org/places/grantbir.** Phone: (513) 553-4911 or (800) 283-8932. Tours: Wednesday – Saturday 9:30am – 5:00pm, Sunday Noon-5pm (April-October). 5th grade and above. Very small admission fee.* Civil War General and 18th President's birthplace cottage with period furniture. The small white home has no heat and is sparsely lit – daytime in comfortable weather is best.

RANKIN HOUSE STATE MEMORIAL

Ripley - *6152 Rankin Road, Rankin Hill (Northeast off US 52, Race Street or Rankin Road), 45167. Phone: (937) 392-1627 or (800) 752-2705. **Web: www.ohiohistory.org/places/rankin.** Hours: Wednesday –*

Saturday 10:00am – 5:00pm, Sunday Noon-5:00pm (Summer). Weekends Only (September and October). Admission: $2.00 adult, $0.50 child (6-12). This restored home of Reverend John Rankin (early Ohio abolitionist) was part of the Underground Railroad and home to Eliza, a character in "Uncle Tom's Cabin", who found refuge off the Ohio River. They sheltered (along with neighbors) more than 2,000 slaves escaping to freedom. In this modest home, there were as many as 12 escapees hidden. Winding roads lead to the remote cabin hidden in a clearing in the woods.

FAYETTE COUNTY HISTORICAL MUSEUM

Washington Court House - *517 Columbus Avenue (eastern junction of U.S. Routes 62 and 22), 43160. Phone: (740) 335-2953.* 14 rooms that contain fine pieces depicting the County's history. See a Wonder Stove (made in The City of Washington in 1906). It sold for $37.50 and operated on artificial gas, a collection of unusual tools, an 1850's piano forte and an 1870 pump organ. A trip to the museum's tower, offers an interesting panorama of the city. At the courthouse look for the "Spirit" murals painted by famous Archibold Willard (Spirit of 76). Around town are brightly colored murals on buildings.

CAESAR CREEK STATE PARK

Waynesville - *8570 East State Route 73 (State Route 73, 6 miles West of I-71, near Waynesville), 45068. Phone: (513) 897-3055.* ***Web: www.dnr.state.oh.us/parks/parks/caesarck.htm***. Bridle trails. 10,771 acres of camping, hiking trails, boating, fishing, swimming & beach, and winter sports. Pioneer Village is open seasonally. The park area sits astride the crest of the Cincinnati Arch, a convex tilting of bedrock layers caused by an ancient upheaval and where some of the oldest rocks in Ohio are exposed. The park's excellent fossil finds give testimony to the life of this long vanished body of water. The Caesar Creek area was named for a black slave captured by the Shawnee on a raid along the Ohio River. The Shawnee adopted Caesar and gave him this valley as his hunting ground. Caesar lived in this area during the time Blue Jacket was war chief and was said to have gone on many raids with him.

COWAN LAKE STATE PARK

Wilmington - *729 Beechwood Road (5 miles South of Wilmington off US 68), 45177. Phone: (937) 289-2105.* ***Web: www.dnr.state.oh.us/parks/parks/cowanlk.htm***. The limestone near Cowan and other parts of the exposed arch are some of the most famous fossil hunting fields in the world. (Collection of fossils requires a permit from the Chief). American Lotus, a brilliant water lily, is abundant in the lake's shallow areas. It is unusual to find such a large colony of lotus on an inland lake. The plant's leaves grow up to two feet in diameter supporting large yellow flowers. Nature programs. Bike Rental. 1,775 acres of camping, hiking trails, boating and rentals, swimming, winter sports and family cabins.

Seasonal & Special Events

(Listings sorted by Area and City within each month)

JANUARY

WINTERFEST

CE – Zanesville, Secrest Auditorium. (740) 454-6851. Chili cook-off, prayer breakfast, floral contest, ice carving competition and parade tribute to Dr. King. (Saturday before Martin Luther King Day-January)

MARTIN LUTHER KING PROGRAM

NE – Cleveland. (216) 231-1111. Museums FREE throughout the city plus Orchestra Concert. (Martin Luther King Day-January)

WINTERFEST

NE – Chesterland, Alpine Valley Skiing, 10620 Mayfield Rd.. **www.alpinevalleyohio.com**. Enjoy volleyball in the snow, snowshoe obstacle race course, bikini slalom, and a children's obstacle slalom. Lift ticket fee. (Saturday before Martin Luther King Day-January)

FEBRUARY

BLACK HISTORY MONTH

CW – Wilberforce, National Afro-American Museum. (937) 376-4944. Events/exhibits month-long.

ICE FESTIVAL

NE – Medina, Uptown Square. (330) 723-8773. Cash prizes and medals for an ice carving competition. Sculpting demos and a "parade" of ice sculptures in front of uptown merchants' businesses. FREE. (mid-February long weekend)

MARCH

BUZZARD DAY

NE – Hinckley, Cleveland Metroparks Reservation. (440) 351-6300. Annual migration of the buzzard with breakfast watch. Admission. (March)

MAPLE SYRUP FESTIVALS

Syrup making demos. Pancake dinners/breakfasts. Sugarbush tours by foot or by wagon or by train.

- C - *Camp Lazarus*, **Delaware**. (740) 548-5502.
- C - *Dawes Arboretum*, **Newark**. (740) 323-2355 or (800) 44-DAWES.
- CW - *Bellbrook Park*, **Bellbrook**. (937) 848-7050.
- CW – *Aullwood Audubon Center/Farm*, **Dayton**. (937) 890-7360
- NC - *Malabar Farm*, **Mansfield**. (419) 892-2784
- NE - *Holden Arboretum*. **Kirtland**. (440) 946-4400. Daily except Monday. Admission.
- NE – *Cuyahoga Valley National Park/ Hale Farm & Scenic RR.* **Peninsula - www.cvsr.com**
- SC - *Mapleberry Farms*. **Waverly**. (740) 947-2331

ST. PATRICK'S DAY PARADES & CELEBRATIONS

Cincinnati, Cleveland, Dublin (Columbus), and Toledo - Downtown.

LIVING HISTORY WEEKEND

CE – **Frazeysburg**. Longaberger Homestead. (740) 322-5588. **www.longaberger.com**. Special American history displays and re-enactors bring history to life. FREE. (March weekend)

APRIL

EASTER EGG HUNTS

Easter Bunny appearance, treat stations, egg hunts, and kids' entertainment and crafts. Usually held the Saturday before Easter.

- C - *Slate Run Farm*, **Ashville**. Egg decorating & egg rolling contests. Admission.
- C - ***Columbus** Recreation & Parks*, (614) 645-3300.
- C - *Great Eggspectation*. ***Columbus** Zoo*, (614) 645-3550, ages 2-12. Admission.
- C – *Buckeye Central Scenic Railroad*. **Hebron**. (800) 579-7521. **www.buckeyecentralrailroad.org**. Train ride with the Easter Bunny.
- CE – *Elderberry Line Railroad*. **Carrollton**. **www.elderberryline.com**. Train ride.
- CE – *Longaberger Homestead*. **Frazeysburg**. (740) 322-5588.

APRIL - *Easter Egg Hunts (cont.)*

- ❑ **CW** - *Zane Shawnee Caverns*. **Bellefontaine**. (937) 592-9592
- ❑ **CW** – *Young's Dairy*, **Yellow Springs**, Over 4000 colored Easter eggs. Free. (937) 325-0629
- ❑ **NE** – *Nautica Queen boat ride*. **Cleveland. www.nauticaqueen.com**
- ❑ **NE** - *Easter Bunny Express*, Cuyahoga Valley Railroad, **Peninsula**. (800) 468-2000 or **www.cvsr.com**.
- ❑ **SE** – *Lunch with Easter Bunny*. Bob Evans Farms, **Rio Grande**. (800) 994-FARM or **www.bobevans.com**. Small animal barnyard.
- ❑ **SW** - *Great Easter Egg Scramble*, **Cincinnati** Zoo, (513) 281-4700.
- ❑ **SW** - *Easter Eggstravaganza*, **Hamilton** County Park, (513) 521-PARK.

GEAUGA COUNTY MAPLE FESTIVAL

NE - **Chardon** Square. (440) 286-3007. Sap Run contest, midway, parades, bathtub races and maple syrup production and sales. (Sundays in April, plus long third weekend)

I-X CENTER INDOOR AMUSEMENT PARK

NE – Cleveland (Brookpark) - 6200 Riverside Drive, next to airport. (800) 897-3942 or **www.ixamusementpark.com**. Hours vary daily (Call for details). *Admission:* $13.00-$16.00 (age 3+), Seniors (60+) FREE. Food service. After riding the World's Tallest Indoor Ferris Wheel (10 stories high) you can SCREAM through 150 rides! Also features a video arcade, miniature golf, laser kareoke, Kidzville, and live entertainment. (month-long in April)

MAY

MOTHERS DAY

Mother's Day Free Admission to MOMS!

- ❑ **NE** – *Cuyahoga Valley Scenic Railroad*, **Cleveland (Peninsula)**
- ❑ **SW** – *Heritage Village Museum*, **Cincinnati (Sharonville)**

ASIAN FESTIVAL

C – **Columbus**, Franklin Park. (614) 292-0613 or **www.asian-festival.org**. Entertainment, children's activities, cultural demos, food demos. FREE. (Memorial Day weekend)

ICE CREAM FESTIVAL

C – **Utica**, Ye Olde Mill. (800) 589-5000. **www.velvet-icecream.com.** Velvet Ice Cream hosts a tribute to our national dessert, ice cream, with family entertainment and lots of food made from ice cream. Kids can watch sheep herding with border collies, catch the kiddie tractor pull and wheelbarrow races, or watch the parade or magic circus. Admission. (Memorial Day Weekend)

RAILROAD FESTIVAL

CE – **Dennison.** (877) 278-8020. Enjoy the heritage and history of the famous World War II Dennison Depot with food, games, contests, rides and parade. Train rides. (week in the middle of May)

STRAWBERRY FEST

NC – **Norwalk**, Huron County Fairgrounds. (419) 663-4062. A Strawberry theme street fair with crafts and foods. Bake-off, pie eating contest, parade. Free. (Memorial Day Weekend)

CIVIL WAR RE-ENACTMENT

NE – **Burton**, Century Village. (440) 834-1492. Annual Civil War Encampment. The Civil War years come to life as Union and Confederate soldiers and civilians demonstrate camp life and stage battle maneuvers. (last weekend in May)

DAY OUT WITH THOMAS THE TANK ENGINE

NE – **Cleveland (Peninsula),** Cuyahoga Valley Railroad, Boston Mills Ski Resort, 7100 Riverview Road. (800) 468-4070 or **www.cvsr.com**. Four day event offering 20 minute rides onboard coaches pulled by a real-live 55 ton steam engine Thomas. Play games, watch Thomas videos, interact with exhibits, clowns, magic shows, food and Sir Topham Hatt. Admission, reservations suggested. (long Memorial Day Weekend)

FEAST OF THE FLOWERING MOON

SC – **Chillicothe**, Yoctangee City Park. (800) 413-4118. This three-day themed event features Native-American dancing, crafts and village as well as a mountain-man encampment depicting pioneer life in the early 1800's. Extensive quality arts and crafts displays, food, entertainment, and a variety of activities to see and do. Free. (Memorial Day Weekend – Friday thru Sunday)

JUNE

FATHER'S DAY

All Dad's receive Free Admission Today:

- ❑ NE – *Father's Day Express*, Cuyahoga Valley Scenic RR, **www.cvsr.com**, **Independence**.

CRANBERRY BOG ANNUAL OPEN HOUSE

C - **Buckeye Lake**, Cranberry Bog State Nature Preserve. (800) 589-8224. Take a tour of the island's rare and fascinating plants by pontoon boat. Admission. (last Saturday in June)

FESTIVAL LATINO

C – **Columbus,** Downtown Riverfront. (614) 645-7995. **www.musicintheair.org**. Celebrate Latin culture, food (contemporary and traditional) and music (Mambo, Salsa, Conjunto, Flamenco). Children's workshops. FREE (third weekend in June)

BALLOON FESTIVAL

C – **Grove City**, Beulah Park. (877) 9-FUNFEST or **www.balloonfestival.com**. One of the largest in North America with close to 70 balloons, top name entertainment, food, evening glows. Admission. (third full weekend in June)

OLDE CANAL DAYS FESTIVAL

CE – **Canal Fulton**, Clays Park. **www.oldecanaldays.com**. (last weekend in June)

ITALIAN AMERICAN FESTIVAL

CE – Canton, Stark County Fairgrounds, 305 Wertz Avenue. (330) 494-0886. Italy in Ohio with entertainment, foods, dancing, exhibits, rides and a bocci tournament. Thursday - Sunday. Admission. (last weekend in June)

HOT AIR BALLOON FESTIVAL

CE – Coshocton, County Fairgrounds, 707 Kenilworth Avenue,. (740) 622-5411. Balloon launches at dawn and dusk, Nightglow (Saturday), entertainment and rides. FREE. (second weekend in June)

TRI-STATE POTTERY FESTIVAL

CE - East Liverpool, 43920. (330) 385-0845. Celebration of pottery heritage featuring pottery olympics, industry displays, potters at work, ceramic museum, international doorknob tossing championships, factory tours (local companies like Hall China or Pioneer Pottery), art show, rose show, window displays, amusement rides and daily entertainment. (June)

ORRVILLE DEPOT DAYS

CE - **Orrville**. Orrville Depot Museum. 145 South Depot Street. (330) 683-2426 or **www.orrvillerailroad.com**. Mostly railroad-related festival, with both model trains and real trains. Tour Orrville Museums and take rides on trains and track cars. Most activities by donations. (early June weekend)

FORT STEUBEN FESTIVAL

CE – **Steubenville**, Old Fort Steuben Site. (740) 283-4935 or **www.oldfortsteuben.com**. This first American Regiment was built to protect government surveyors from hostile Indians. Next to the fort site is the first Federal Land Office built in the U.S. in 1801. Watch mountain men reenactment groups, storytellers and craftspeople. Admission. (second weekend in June)

JUNE *(cont.)*

CITYFOLK FESTIVAL

CW – **Dayton**, Downtown. (937) 223-3655. Hundreds of the country's best folk performers and artists entertain you with shows, activities, games, crafts and food. (June)

KIDS FEST

CW – **Kettering**, Lincoln Park Commons, 675 Lincoln Park Blvd. (937) 296-2587. Designed for young children and their parents to participate in activities ranging from hands-on crafts to face painting. FREE. (third Saturday in June)

STRAWBERRY FESTIVAL

CW - **Troy**, the Strawberry Capital of the Midwest. (937) 339-7714. The first full weekend in June the fountain on Town Square runs pink water! Loads of fresh-picked berries and strawberry foods (donuts, pizza, fudge) are sold. Parade, entertainment and hot-air balloons. Free. (first weekend in June)

KEEPING THE TRADITIONS NATIVE AMERICAN POWWOW

CW – **Xenia**, Blue Jacket grounds.. (937) 275-8599 or **www.tmvcna.org**. Native American dancing, singing, foods. One of the largest powwows in Ohio. Admission (age 13+). (last weekend in June)

PRAIRIE PEDDLER

NC – **Butler**, Bunker Hill Woods, State Route 97. (419) 663-1818. **www.prairietown.com**. Almost 200 costumed craftspeople offer their items made with frontier style tools, foods cooked over open fires and bluegrass music. Stop by the Medicine Show and buy a bottle of elixir. Admission. (last 2 weekends of June & first two weekends of October)

MEDIEVAL FANTASY FAIRE

NC – **Fremont**, 1313 Tiffin Street (off US 6). (419) 333-2450 or **www.medievalfantasy.net**. Full-armor jousts, feast food, man-powered rides for kids, fire-eating, juggling. Admission. (last weekend in June to last weekend in July)

INTERNATIONAL FESTIVAL

NC – **Lorain**, Downtown Veterans Park. Dance, music and authentically prepared foods from many different countries throughout the world. **www.loraininternational.com**. FREE. (last full weekend in June)

FESTIVAL OF FISH

NC – **Vermilion**, Victory Park. (440) 967-4477. Walleye and perch sandwiches, "crazy" craft race, entertainment, crafts and a lighted boat parade. FREE. (June)

GRAND PRIX OF CLEVELAND

NE – **Cleveland**, Burke Lakefront Airport, Downtown. (800) 498-RACE. The world's top Indy Car drivers compete on the 213 miles of racing. Also a Grand Prix Parade on Friday. Admission. (last weekend in June)

POWWOW

NE – **Cleveland**, American Indian Education Center. (216) 281-8480. Annual competition with traditional dance, song, crafts, storytelling & Native American food. (mid-June weekend).

OHIO IRISH FESTIVAL

NE - **Olmsted Falls**, West Side Irish-American Club, 8559 Jennings Road. (440) 779-6065 or (440) 235-5868. Celebrating the best of Ireland with lively Irish dance reels and lots of Irish food like tasty scones. Admission. (last weekend in June)

TRAINS, PLANES & AUTOMOBILES FEST

NW – **Bluffton**, Airport, 1080 Navajo Drive. (419) 358-5675. Airplane rides, tandem skydiving, antique cars and model trains. FREE. Saturday only. Fees for air rides. (June)

PORK RIND HERITAGE FESTIVAL

NW - **Harrod**. (419) 648-3427. Fresh popped pork rinds (manufactured by Randolph Foods in town), hog roast, parade, crafts and live entertainment. FREE. (June)

JUNE *(cont.)*

LATINOFEST

NW – Toledo, Promenade Park. **www.voceslatinas.com**. Folkloric dancing, ethnic foods, mariachi bands, arts and crafts and gifts . Admission. (second weekend in June)

NATIONAL THRESHERS ANNUAL REUNION

NW – Wauseon, Fulton County Fairgrounds, State Route 108. (419) 335-6006. Working gas tractors and over 30 operating steam engines on the sawmill, threshing wheat and plowing machines. Admission. (June)

KIDS FEST

SW – Cincinnati, Sawyer Point. (513) 621-9326. Three stages of entertainment, boat rides and 130+ activities: Frisbee dog shows, roving entertainers, inflatable interactive games and yard games. FREE. (first weekend in June)

BANANA SPLIT FESTIVAL

SW- Wilmington, Memorial Park. (877) 428-4748. Celebrate the birthplace of the banana split (first made at Hazzard's Drug Store in 1907). Also tribute to Elvis era. (second weekend in June)

JULY

JULY 4TH CELEBRATIONS

All cities listed (by area, alphabetically) include a full day of parades, rides, entertainment and fireworks.

- ❑ **C – *Ashville*.** (740) 983-8122.
- ❑ **C - *Columbus*** (614) 421-BOOM or **www.redwhiteandboom.org**. Red, White & Boom! July 3rd. Largest fireworks display synchronized to music and lights in the Midwest.
- ❑ **C - *Dublin*** (614) 761-6500
- ❑ **CE – *Carrollton***, Atwood Lake. (800) 362-6406.
- ❑ **CE - *Massillon*** Picnic in the Park, Stadium Park.
- ❑ **CE – *Orrville*** (330) 684-5051.
- ❑ **CE - *Zanesville*** (740) 743-2303. Stars & Stripes on the River.

- ❑ **CW** – ***Dayton,*** US Air Force Museum. (937) 255-0776. Balloon Festival.
- ❑ **CW** - ***Lakeview***, Indian Lake. (937) 843-5392. Decorated boat parade.
- ❑ **NC** - ***Mansfield*** (419) 756-6839 Freedom Festival. Airport air show.
- ❑ **NC** - ***Put-in-Bay*** (419) 285-2804 Perry's Victory Mem'l. 3 days.
- ❑ **NE** - ***Cleveland*** (216) 664-2484. Festival of Freedom, Edgewater Park.
- ❑ **SE** -***Marietta*** (800) 331-9336. Red, White & Blues.
- ❑ **SW** - ***Cincinnati*** (513) 621-9326. All American Birthday Party.
- ❑ **SW** - ***Jeffersonville*** (740) 426-6331. Community Days.

FRANKLIN COUNTY FAIR

C – Columbus (Hilliard), County Fairgrounds. Open during the fair is Northwest Village including the church, 1850's log cabin, outhouse, caboose, train station, granary, barn and museum with vintage household equipment. (mid-July for 7 days)

FOLKLIFE CELEBRATION

C - Columbus, (Worthington). Village Green, (614) 431-0329. A celebration of living traditions in crafts, performances and foods. Includes the cultures of Africa, Asia, Germany, India, Europe and Appalachia. (last Saturday in July)

MARION COUNTY FAIR

C – Marion, County Fairgrounds. (740) 382-2558. Huber Machinery Museum open (steam & gas tractors, threshers and road-building equipment, plus Marion steam shovel 6). (first week of July)

KNOX COUNTY FAIR

C – Mt. Vernon, Fairgrounds (SR 3). (740) 397-0484 or **www.visitknoxohio.org**. Check out the traditional favorites plus rodeo, bull-riding, tractor pulls, and Safety Day. The Agricultural Museum that houses hundreds of old-fashioned pieces of equipment and tools is open. (last week of July)

JULY *(cont.)*

CIVIL WAR RE-ENACTMENT

CE – **Coshocton**, Roscoe Village. (800) 877-1830 or **www.roscoevillage.com**. The village transforms into a battlefield. Stroll thru camps, talk with living historians, listen to music of the era, share a campfire and watch a soldier prepare for battle. Children's activities. Admission. (third weekend in July)

U. S. AIR & TRADE SHOW

CW – **Dayton (Vandalia)**, Dayton International Airport. (937) 898-5901. **www.airshowdayton.com**. This is the leading event of its kind highlighted by the outstanding civilian and military air show performances. The event includes ground flight simulators, aerobatics, barnstormers, air races, pyrotechnics and sky divers. Admission. (third weekend in July)

ASHLAND BALLOONFEST

NC - **Ashland,** Main Street. (877) 581-2345 or Hot air balloon races and twilight balloon glow. **www.ashlandoh.com/cvb**. Ashland is a top balloon manufacturer – factory tours available. (long weekend after 4th of July)

EASTERN WOODLANDS GATHERING

NC – **Lexington**, SR 42. (419)362-1600. A Native American gathering of all nations. Friendly Voices will be the host drum and there will be a guest drum. Plus dancers, Native vendors, food, auction, children's candy dance. FREE. (last weekend in July)

GREAT MOHICAN INDIAN POW-WOW

NC – **Loudonville**, Mohican Reservation Campgrounds & Canoeing. (800) 766-CAMP. **www.mohicanpowwow.com**. Nine different tribes gather to a pow-wow featuring foods, music, crafts, hoop dancers and storytellers. Learn the proper throwing of a tomahawk or a new Native American custom. Admission. (second weekend in July and third weekend in September)

ALL AMERICAN SOAP BOX DERBY

NE – **Akron,** Derby Downs, 1-77 & State Route 244 East. (330) 733-8723. The annual gravity "grand prix" of soap box derby racing is still run the same way since 1934. Youths from over 100 local competitions participate and learn workmanship, completing a project and competing. Parade at 10:00am. Admission. (last weekend in July or first weekend in August)

IRISH FESTIVAL

NE – **Berea**, Cuyahoga County Fairgrounds, 164 Eastland Blvd. (440) 251-0711. Irish culture at its best with dancing , music, arts & crafts, storytelling and workshops. Admission. (third weekend in July)

KIDSFEST

NE – **Cleveland,** Nautica Entertainment Complex. (216) 247-2722. Playground World Pavilion, Treasure Island, sand castle building, Edible Art, Thomas the Train and great kids' entertainment. Admission. (second or third weekend in July)

GREAT LAKES MEDIEVAL FAIRE

NE – **Geneva**, 3033 State Route 534. (888) 633-4382 or **www.medievalfaire.com**. The recreation of a 13th century English village with jugglers, jesters, musicians, crafts, full-armored knights and sumptuous foods. Admission. (weekends July to mid-August)

GLASS & HERITAGE FESTIVAL

NW – **Fostoria**, Main Street. (419) 435-1995 or **www.fosterglass.com**. Celebrating glass manufacturing heritage with entertainment, food and glass-making demos. (second weekend in July)

LAGRANGE STREET POLISH FESTIVAL

NW – **Toledo**, Lagrange Street between Central & Mettler Sts. (419) 255-8406. All kinds of Polish foods, polish bands, dancers, a polka contest, rides and craft area. Free. (first full weekend in July, after the 4th)

AUGUST

OHIO'S AGRICULTURAL FAIRS

(614) 728-6200. Schedules available through the Ohio Department of Agriculture.

OHIO STATE FAIR

C – Columbus, Ohio Expo Center, I-71 & 17th Avenue. (614) 644-4000. **www.ohiostatefair.com**. Includes the largest junior fair in the nation, puppet shows, laser light shows, petting zoo, rodeo, tractor pulls, horse shows, fishing and lumberjack shows, exhibitors from agriculture to the arts, rides and big name entertainment. Favorite family areas include: the Natural Resources area (live wildlife, log cabin, butterfly house); the Nursery; and the Butter Cow sculpture and ice cream. Admission. Family Value Days on Mondays. (17 days beginning the end of the first week of August)

IRISH FESTIVAL

C – Dublin, Coffman Park, 6665 Coffman Road. (614) 410-4545 or (877) 67-GREEN or **www.dublinirishfestival.org**. A weekend of all things Irish, from entertainment, dance competitions and sports demos to the very best in Irish foods. Admission. (first weekend each August)

ZUCCHINI FESTIVAL

C – Obetz, Lancaster Park. (614) 497-2518. Try some yummy zucchini fudge or burgers while seeing a parade, riding amusement rides, listening to music or looking over crafts. FREE. (weekend prior to Labor Day in August)

OLDE CANAL DAYS

CE – **Canal Fulton**. (330) 854-6295 or **www.oldecanaldays.com**. Along the Ohio/Erie canal see a water float parade, fireworks, music contests, saw carving and concerts. (last weekend in August)

PROFESSIONAL FOOTBALL HALL OF FAME FESTIVAL

CE - Canton. (800) 533-4302. Check out the 9 days of celebrating football greats including a parade, hot air balloon show, enshrinement ceremony and a televised professional game. Some fees. (first week of August)

CANAL FESTIVAL

CE - **Coshocton**. Historic Roscoe Village. (800) 877-1830 or **www.roscoevillage.com**. Canal boat rides highlight the celebration of the canal boat era. Parade and crafts show, entertainment, kiddie tractor pull, and fiddle contests. Admission. (third weekend in August)

PIONEER DAYS

CE – **Gnadenhutten**, Historical Park & Museum, 352 Cherry Street,. (330) 254-4143. An 1840's pioneer encampment, entertainment, parade, arts and crafts. FREE. (first weekend in August)

TUSCARAWAS COUNTY ITALIAN-AMERICAN FESTIVAL

CE– New Philadelphia, downtown. (330) 339-6405. Italian foods, pizza eating contests, bocci and morri tournaments, music and dance. FREE. (second weekend in August)

INDIAN FESTIVAL

CE – **Powhatan Point**. (740) 795-4440. An authentic Native American event including crafts, dancing, an historic reenactment, storytelling, archery and more. FREE. (last weekend in August)

HOLES CREEK GATHERING

CW – **Centerville**, Washington Twp. Rec Center. (937) 433-0130 or **www.holescreek.org**. A hands-on games and activities oriented celebration of American History. Colonial, Native American and Pioneer (1765-1865) re-enactments, crafts, tools, fashion (try on clothes), chores (washing day), carriage & canoe rides. Small Admission. (first weekend in August)

AUGUST *(cont.)*

SWEET CORN FESTIVAL

CW – Community Park East, Dayton-Yellow Springs Road, **Fairborn**. (937) 879-3238. Steamed corn-on-the-cob, crafts, entertainment, and a corn eating contest. Free. (August)

ANNIE OAKLEY DAYS

CW – **Greenville**, Darke County Fairgrounds, 752 Sweitzer Road. (800) 504-2995. Annie Oakley's hometown celebrates with a parade, live entertainment, a sharpshooter's contest and a contest to name Miss Annie Oakley. (first weekend in August)

BUCYRUS BRATWURST FESTIVAL

NC – **Bucyrus**, Sandusky Avenue. (419) 562-2728 or **www.bratfest.org**. "Ohio's eatingest festival". German foods, live entertainment, rides, kids' activities during the day. (mid-August weekend)

GREAT LAKES WOODEN SAILBOAT REGATTA

NC – **Sandusky**, Battery Park Marina. (440) 871-8174. Wooden sailboats large and small are raced for special awards in many categories. Free. (August)

LORAIN COUNTY FAIR & SCENIC RAILWAY

NC – **Wellington**, County Fairgrounds. (440) 647-2781 or **www.loraincountyfair.com**. Rides, livestock, horse races, big name entertainment and Lakeshore Railroad rides. (August)

ASHTABULA COUNTY FAIR

NE – **Jefferson**, Corner of Poplar & Walnut Sts. (440) 576-0755 or **www.ashtabulafair.com**. The first fair in Ohio features an octagon barn, log cabin home to Camp Gidding (Civil War encampment). Family rides, entertainment, livestock shows and harness racing. (first week of August)

TWINS DAYS FESTIVAL

NE – **Twinsburg,** I-80/90 to SR-91, follow signs. (330) 425-7161. The largest gathering of twins in the world (*usually over 2500*) includes twins contests, entertainment, fireworks and the nationally televised "Double Take" parade. Small fee for non-twins. Twinsburg was originally named by the Wilcox twins in the early 1800s. (first weekend in August)

FULTON COUNTY FAIR

NW – **Wauseon**, County Fairgrounds, SR 108 at OH Turnpike exit 34/3. (419) 335-SHOW or **www.fultoncountyfair.com**. Top name entertainment, motorcycle stunt spectacular, harness racing, tractor & truck pull, demolition derbies, rough truck challenge, midway rides, fair food and all the traditional agricultural displays/exhibits. Admission. (week up to Labor Day)

ALL ABOUT KIDS EXPO

SW – **Cincinnati**, Convention Center, 525 Elm Street. (513) 684-0501 or **www.aak.com**. Event for kids ages 2 to 12 including interactive play, games, animals, nature, and entertainment. Admission. (third weekend in August)

OHIO RENAISSANCE FESTIVAL

SW – **Harveysburg,** 5 miles East of Waynesville on SR-73. (513) 897-7000 or **www.renfestival.com**. The recreation of a 16th century English Village complete with costumed performers, strolling minstrels, may pole dances, full-armored jousting, sword play or feast on giant turkey legs and hearty bread bowls. Two Student Days (Wednesdays) are open special each year. This is the recommended time to attend with families: Interview Sessions with Queen Elizabeth, Puppet Theatre, Experiment with Historical Games & Rides, Pirate Invasions on the 65-foot Pirate Ship, Combat Demonstrations, Knighthood & Chivalry Discussions, Scottish Dance & Bagpipe Demonstrations, Music Workshops. Admission avg. $8-15.00 (age 5+). (weekends beginning end of August through mid-October)

SEPTEMBER

OHIO STATEHOUSE CIVIL WAR ENCAMPMENT

C – **Columbus**, Ohio Statehouse,. (614) 752-9777. Living history demos, artillery & infantry drills, medical talks and civilian activities. Free. (fourth weekend in September)

GREEK FESTIVAL

C – **Columbus**, Greek Orthodox Cathedral, Short North Area. (614) 224-9020 or **www.greekcathedral.com**. Gyros, baklava, music, dance, tours of the church, cooking demos and videos about Greece. Admission. (Labor Day Weekend)

FAMILY FUNFEST

C – **Columbus**, Downtown Riverfront. (614) 645-3335. Cruise the River, roving performers, games & prizes, hands-on crafts, rides, obstacle course, rock climbing and a fish pond. FREE. (weekend after Labor Day)

LITTLE BROWN JUG

C – **Delaware**, County Fairgrounds, 236 Pennsylvania Avenue,. (800) 335-3247. The most coveted horse race for three-year old pacers held on the fastest half-mile track in the world. Kick off parade with the largest all-horse, mule and donkey parade east of the Mississippi. Admission. (mid-September - Saturday only)

NATIVE AMERICAN POWWOW

C – **Grove City,** Helmat Haus, 4555 Jackson Pike,. (614) 443-6120. Authentic Native American dancing, arts, crafts and singing. (Labor Day weekend)

POPCORN FESTIVAL

C – **Marion**. (740) 387-FEST or **www.popcornfestival.com**. Highlights include a parade, tours of the Popcorn Museum, popcorn sculptures and nationally known entertainment nightly. Free. (weekend after Labor Day)

TOMATO SHOW

C – **Mt. Vernon**, off SR 13. (800) 837-5282. Bathtub Race (maneuverable bathtub on wheels is pushed and driven thru obstacle course –bathtub full of water, tomatoes and tomato juice). **www.visitknoxohio.org**. Baking contest, pedal tractor pulls, food. (four days after Labor Day)

BUCKEYE FLINT FESTIVAL

C – **Newark**, Courthouse Square,. (740) 345-1282. Ohio's gemstone is flint rock and you'll learn everything you could want to know about flint through displays, entertainment, crafts and food preparation. FREE. (last weekend in September)

TOMATO FESTIVAL

C – **Reynoldsburg**, Civic Park, 6800 Daugherty Drive. (614) 866-2861. Ohio's tomato harvest is celebrated with things like free tomato juice, fried green tomatoes, tomato pies, tomato fudge, tomato cakes & cookies, Tiny Tim Tomatoland, crafts, parade and The Largest Tomato Contest ($100 per pound). Fee for parking. (September - Wednesday through Sunday)

BUCKEYE TREE FESTIVAL

C – **Utica**, Ye Olde Mill, 11324 SR-13. (740) 892-3921 or (800)589-5000. Celebrate Ohio's heritage and state tree. Step from a time machine into the 1800s to see Ohio artisans and craftsmen dressed in the clothing of the era to demonstrate life on the Ohio frontier. Historical tall tales of the Buckeye Tree in Ohio. Children can enjoy crafts, pony rides, zoo animals, and horse-drawn wagons. Or, dance to authentic Indian dances. Free. (second Sunday in September)

OHIO PUMPKIN FESTIVAL

CE – **Barnesville**. **www.ohiopumpkinfestival.8k.com**. or (740) 695-4359. All kinds of pumpkin contests (largest pumpkin, pumpkin rolling and pie eating), parade, foods, fiddle contest, rides, crafts and entertainment. Free. (Thursday – Sunday - last full weekend of September)

SEPTEMBER *(cont.)*

OHIO SWISS FESTIVAL

CE – Sugarcreek. (330) 852-4113 or (888) 609-7592. Experience the best of Switzerland from Polka bands, dancing, tons of Swiss cheese, Steinstossen (stone throwing) and Schwingfest (Swiss wrestling). FREE (last Friday & Saturday of September)

POPCORN FESTIVAL

CW – Beavercreek. (937) 426-5486. A balloon rally, live entertainment and most of all, "popcorn showers". FREE. (September)

KITE FESTIVAL

CW – Dayton, U.S. Air Force Museum, Wright-Patterson AFB. (937) 255-0776. Kite making, safety and flying workshops. Fee for workshops. Free. (late September)

OHIO FISH AND SHRIMP FESTIVAL

CW – Urbana, downtown. (937) 652-1161. Food, music, kids games (old time crawfish races, trout grabs, frog-jumping contest, water battles, sand castle building, and radio-controlled boat races). (second Saturday in September)

RASPBERRY FESTIVAL

CW – Urbana, Rothschild Berry Farm, 3143 East SR-36. (800) 356-8933. Celebrate the raspberry harvest with entertainment, foods and children's activities. (September)

MELON FESTIVAL

NC – Milan, SR 113. (419) 499-2766. **www.accnorwalk.com**. Melons in baskets, by the slice, muskmelon ice cream and watermelon sherbet. Melon eating contests. Parade, rides, crafts and a kiddie pedal tractor pull. Free. (Labor Day Weekend)

HISTORICAL WEEKEND

NC - **Put-In-Bay**. Perry's Monument. **www.lake-erie.com.** or (800) 441-1271. Military living history camps with displays of Indian wars to the present. Boy Scout camporee. Parade, live entertainment. (second long weekend in September).

TIFFIN-SENECA HERITAGE FESTIVAL

NC – **Tiffin**, Hedges Boyer Park. (888) SENECA1. Living history village and entertainment, food, fireworks. Tours of area glass factory (888-298-7236). (third weekend in September)

INDIAN VILLAGE

NC – **Upper Sandusky**. Harrison-Smith Park, US 30. (419) 294-3349. The site of the last Wyandot Council House in Ohio re-enacts history. Activities: Indian crafts, lacrosse, blanket & moccasin games, historic face painting, food, a working village, native music and lantern tours. Admission per car. (third weekend in September)

CANFIELD FAIR

NE - Canfield Fairgrounds. **www.canfieldfair.com** or (330) 533-4107. Grandstand headliners, the World's Largest Demolition Derby, Truck and Tractor Pull, agricultural displays, milk a cow, pet pigs, Elephant Encounter. Admission. (Wednesday thru Sunday-Labor Day week)

CLEVELAND NATIONAL AIR SHOW

NE – **Cleveland**, Burke Lakefront Airport, downtown. (216) 781-7747. **www.clevelandairshow.com**. One of the nation's top air shows featuring the best in military jet demonstrations and civilian aerobatics performers. Thunderbirds and Blue Angels Flybys. Tour the International Women's Air & Space Museum on premises. Admission. (Labor Day weekend)

SEPTEMBER *(cont.)*

GRAPE JAMBOREE

NE – **Geneva**, downtown. (440)466-1317. The local grape harvest is celebrated with parades, fresh-picked grapes, grape stomping contests, grape products, ethnic foods, rides and entertainment. FREE. (last weekend in September)

MAHONING RIVER FEST

NE – **Warren**, riverfront. (800) 672-9555. Celebrate the river history with canoe rides, activities, storytelling, music and bike tours. (September)

RIVERFEST

NW – **Toledo**, Promenade Park, downtown. (419) 243-8024. Festival and parade. Free. (Labor Day Weekend)

RIVER DAYS

SC – **Portsmouth**. (740) 354-6419. Parade, rides, crafts, entertainment and children's events. Free. (Labor Day Weekend)

OHIO RIVER STERNWHEEL FESTIVAL

SE – **Marietta**, Ohio River Levee. (800) 288-2577. Thirty plus sternwheelers dock for the weekend, some for commercial and some for residential use. Continuous musical entertainment, fireworks and grand finale sternwheeler races. FREE. (weekend after Labor Day)

OKTOBERFEST-ZINZINNATI

SW – **Cincinnati**. Fifth Street, downtown (513) 579-3191 or **www.oktoberfest-zinzinnati.com**. The nation's largest authentic Oktoberfest featuring seven areas of live entertainment, food and a children's area. FREE. (third weekend in September)

THUNDER IN THE HILLS HYDROPLANE RACE

SW - **Hillsboro** - Rocky Fork Lake State Park. (937) 393-4284. Hydroplane boat racing, 2nd largest race in the country. FREE. (September)

OHIO HONEY FESTIVAL

SW – Oxford, Courthouse Square. **www.ohiohoneyfest.org** or (888) 53-HONEY. Celebrate the "Ohio Bee & Honey Week" by enjoying honey in jars, ice cream, candy and other desserts. Parades, entertainment and the world famous "Living Bee Beard". Free. (September)

SCARECROW FESTIVAL

SW – Washington Court House. (740) 636-2340. A street fair, parade, live entertainment and a living scarecrow contest. FREE. (mid-September long weekend)

SEPTEMBER / OCTOBER

APPLE FESTIVALS

Apples & cider. Apple pie eating contests. Apple peeling contests. Apple butter. Candy apples. Wagon/hayrides. Apple Dumplings, Fritters, Donuts, etc. Parades. Pioneer crafts. Petting Zoo. For contact info, see listings.

Participating Areas:

- ❑ **C – Marion**, Lawrence Orchards, 2634 Smeltzer Rd. (740) 389-3019. (last Saturday in September)
- ❑ **CE – Big Prairie**, Whispering Hills Campground (8248 State Route 514). (330) 567-2137 or **www.whisperinghillsrvpark.com**. (first weekend in October)
- ❑ **CE – Coshocton**, Roscoe Village. **www.roscoevillage.com**. Apple Butter Stirrin' living history tours. (third weekend in October)
- ❑ **CE - Gnadenhutten** Village (second weekend in October)
- ❑ **CE – Millersburg**, Yoders Amish Home. (last 2 Saturdays in September & first 3 Saturdays in October)
- ❑ **CE – Wellsburg**. (304) 737-2787.
- ❑ **CE - Zoar** Village (first weekend in October)
- ❑ **CW – Dayton**, Aullwood Audubon Farm (end of September)
- ❑ **NC – Logan** County, Fairgrounds. (888) 599-2016. (mid-September weekend)

Apple Festivals (cont.)

- ❑ **NC – Mansfield**, Apple Hill Orchards, 1175 Lexington-Ontario Rd. (419) 884-1500. (Saturdays in October)
- ❑ **NC – Rittman**, Bauman Orchards. **www.baumanorchards.com** (first Saturday in October)
- ❑ **NE – Brunswick**, Mapleside Farms, 294 Pearl Road, US 42. (330) 225-5577 or **www.mapleside.com**
- ❑ **NE – Burton**, Century Village. (440) 834-1492. (second weekend in October)
- ❑ **NE – Hinckley**, Hillside Orchard, 2397 Center Road. (330) 225-4748.
- ❑ **NE - Lodi**, The Apple Cabin . (330) 948-1476. (weekends in October)
- ❑ **NW – Archbold**, Sauder Farm Village. **www.saudervillage.com**.
- ❑ **NW – Holland**, MacQueen Orchard. (419) 865-2916. (first weekend in October)
- ❑ **NW – Lima**, 1582 Slabtown Road. (419) 221-1232 or **www.jampd.com** (first weekend in October)
- ❑ **SC - Jackson** (740) 286-1339.
- ❑ **SE – Belpre**, Washington Blvd. (740) 423-5233. (first weekend in October)
- ❑ **SE – Vincent**, Sweetapple Farm, CR805. (740) 678-7447 or **www.sweetapplefarm.com**
- ❑ **SW – Lebanon**, Hidden Valley Fruit Farm, 5474 N SR 48. (513) 932-1869.
- ❑ **SW - Lebanon**, Irons Fruit Farm, 1650 Stubbs Mills Road. (513) 932-2853.

PIONEER / PEDDLER FESTIVALS

Early 1800's frontier life & Indian village. Re-enactors, craft demonstrations, authentic open fire, wood cooked food and folk entertainment.

- ❑ CE – **Columbiana**, Shaker Woods (Rte. 11). (800) 447-8201 or **www.shakerwoods.com**. (3 weekends in August)
- ❑ CW – **Piqua** Historical Area.

- ❑ CW – **Springfield**, George Rogers Clark Park. (937) 882-9216 or **www.grcha.org**. Area where Gen. Clark defeated Shawnee to open NW Territory. Admission. (Labor Day Weekend)
- ❑ NC – **Bellevue**, Historic Lyme Village. (419) 483-6052. (mid-September weekend)
- ❑ NE – **Cleveland** Metroparks, Rocky River Nature Center and Frostville Museum. (440) 734-6660.
- ❑ NE – **Cleveland** Metroparks, Brecksville Reservation. 440-526-1012. (last Sunday in September)
- ❑ NE – **Jefferson**, Buccaneer Lake, Rte. 307, I-90 exit 223. (440) 466-8414 or **www.yankeepeddlerfestival.com**. Admission. (first & second weekend in September)
- ❑ NE – **Medina** , Buckeye Woods Park, (Part of the Medina County Fall Foliage Tour). 330-722-9364. (second weekend in October)
- ❑ NW – **Attica**, Oak Ridge Festival. (419) 426-2715 or **www.oakridgefestival.com**. (mid-October weekend)
- ❑ SW – **Morgan Township**, Governor Bebb Preserve.

HARVEST FESTIVALS

Press cider. Apple butter making. Veggie harvest. Living history demos. Lumberjacks. Butter churning. Grainthreshing. *Participating Areas:*

- ❑ C – **Centerburg**, Memorial Park, US 36/SR 3. Old Time Farming Festival. (second weekend in September)
- ❑ C – **Utica**, Ye Olde Mill. (800) 589-5000. (Sundays in October)
- ❑ CE – **Carrollton**, Algonquin Mill, SR 332. (330) 627-2946
- ❑ CE – **Mineral City**, Atwood Lake. (877) 727-0103. (first weekend in October)
- ❑ NC – **Mansfield**, Malabar Farm. (419) 892-2784 or **www.malabarfarm.org**. (last Saturday in September)
- ❑ NC – **Marblehead**, Lighthouse. (419) 797-4530. (second Saturday in October)
- ❑ NC – **West Portsmouth**. Sorghum Makin Festival, Pond Creek (off Rte. 73). (740) 259-6337.
- ❑ NE – **Bath**, Hale Farm and Village. 330-666-3711. Admission. (first weekend in October)
- ❑ NE – **Kirtland**, Lake Farmpark **www.lakemetroparks.com**. or (440) 256-2122. Includes corn maze, pumpkin patch & pony rides. Admission. (begins third weekend in Sept. – mid-October weekends)

HARVEST FESTIVALS *(Cont.)*

- ❑ **NW** - Sauder Village, St. Rt. 2, **Archbold. 800-590-9755** or **www.saudervillage.org**. Admission. (second Saturday in October)
- ❑ **SE – Marr**, Bethel Community (SR 537). (877) 456-2787. (first full weekend in October)
- ❑ **SE – Monroe County**. (877) 456-2737. Admission. (second weekend in October)

OCTOBER

OKTOBERFEST

German music, dancing, food (potato salad, brats), crafts, games and rides. Kinderplatz area for kids. *Participating Areas*:

- ❑ **C – Columbus**, German Village (614) 221-8888. (first full weekend)
- ❑ **CE - Cambridge**
- ❑ **CW – Urbana**, (937) 653-6721.
- ❑ **NC – Put-in-Bay**, downtown.
- ❑ **NE - Cuyahoga Falls**. Riverfront Center, 330-923-4924. (first weekend in October)
- ❑ **SW – Wilmington**, Main Street (937) 382-2737. (last Saturday in September)

PUMPKIN PATCHES/ HAYRIDES/ CORN MAZES/ FALL PLAYLANDS

All sites charge admission (avg. $5.00). Plan on at least two hours playtime. all are open weekends, some open weekdays (by appointment) and weeknights (late September - late October).

- ❑ **C** – *Miller Country Gardens*. **Delaware**, SR 37. (740) 363-5021.
- ❑ **C** – *Freeman's Farm*. **Galena**. (740) 548-7866.
- ❑ **C** - *Circle S Farms*. **Grove City**. 2 mazes, entertainment on weekends, snack bar & autumn treats. (614) 878-7980.
- ❑ **C** – *Leeds Farm*. **Marysville**, Rte. 36. (740) 666-2020.
- ❑ **C** – *The Maize at Little Darby Creek*, **Milford Center**, 8657 Axe Handle Rd. (937) 349-4781 or **www.cornfieldmaze.com**.
- ❑ **C** – *Pigeon Roost Farm*, **Newark** (I-70 exit 122 to Rte. 40). (740) 928-4925.

- ❑ C - _Lynd Fruit Farm_. **Pataskala** (I-270 exit Morse Rd. east). (740) 927-7013 or **www.lyndfruitfarm.com**. Flashlight nights.
- ❑ **CE** - _Catalpa Grove Farm_. **Columbiana**. (330) 482-4064.
- ❑ **CE** - _Detwiler Farm_. **Columbiana**. (330) 482-2276.
- ❑ **CE** - _Less & Less Farm_. **Salem**. (330) 533-6387.
- ❑ **CW** – _Brumbaughs Fruit Farm_, **Arcanum**. (800) 504-2995.
- ❑ **CW** – _Bonneybrook Farms_. **Centerville** (9400 Clyo Road). **www.bonneybrookfarms.com**
- ❑ **CW** - _Fulton Farms_. **Troy**. (937) 335-6983.
- ❑ **CW** - _Young's Jersey Dairy_. **Yellow Springs**. (937) 325-0629.
- ❑ **NC** – _Family Corn Maze_, **Ashland**. 1327 CR 1475. (877) 581-2345.
- ❑ **NC** - _Rockin'-R-Ranch_, 19066 E. River Road, 252 **Columbia Station** (2 miles south of Rt. 82). 440-236-5454.
- ❑ **NC** – _Klickman's Farms_. **Elmore**. (800) 441-1271
- ❑ **NE** - _Mapleside Farms_. **Brunswick**. (330) 225-5576.
- ❑ **NE** - _Lanterman's Corn Maize_, **Canfield** (8807 Akron Canfield Rd). 330-533-7189.
- ❑ **NE** - _Patterson Farms_. **Chesterland**. (440) 729-9809.
- ❑ **NE** – _Lake Farmpark_. **Kirtland**. **www.lakemetroparks.com**
- ❑ **NE** - _Countryside Farm_. **Lowellville**. (330) 536-2178.
- ❑ **NE** - _Richardson Farms_. **Medina**. 330-722-4029, 877-398-9068.
- ❑ **NE** – _Ridgeview Farm_ (SR 87, west of SR 45), **Middlefield**. (440) 693-4000.
- ❑ **NE** – _Snodes Country Barn_, **Minerva**. 6052 Arrow Rd. (330) 895-4996.
- ❑ **NW** – _Leaders Family Farms_, **Napoleon** (O-064 County Road 16). (419) 599-1570.
- ❑ **SW** - _Turpin Farms_, **Cincinnati** (3295 Turpin Lane). 513-561-2621 or **www.turpinfarms.com**.
- ❑ **SW** – _Schappacher Farms_. **Lebanon**. (513) 398-0904.
- ❑ **SW** - _Shaw Farm_. **Milford**. (513) 575-2022.
- ❑ **SW** – _Barn N Bunk Farm Market_, **Trenton**. State Rt. 73 & Wayne-Madison Road. **www.barnnbunk.com**.

OCTOBER *(cont.)*

PUMPKIN FESTIVAL

C – Circleville. (740) 474-7000 or **www.pumpkinshow.com**. Ohio's largest and oldest harvest celebration has seven parades, lots of pumpkin, squash and gourds, pumpkin foods (cotton candy, burgers, chips and ice cream), rides and entertainment. See some of the largest pumpkins and the world's largest pumpkin pie (approx. 350 lbs. and 5 feet in diameter). Contests galore like hog calling, egg toss, pie eating and carved pumpkins. FREE. (October - Wednesday thru Saturday)

ALL AMERICAN QUARTER HORSE CONGRESS

C – Columbus, Ohio Expo Center, I-71 & 17th Avenue. (614) 943-2346 before October, (614) 294-7469 (during show). The world's largest single breed horse show with seven acres of commercial exhibits and demos. Fee per vehicle. (two weeks long during mid-to-late October)

WORLD'S LARGEST GOURD SHOW

C – Mount Gilead, Morrow County Fairgrounds, U.S. 42 & State Route 61 South. (419) 946-2821. Gourd crafts, fresh gourds, gourd cleaning and carving demos, and the gourd show parade. Even make music from a gourd! Admission. (first full weekend – Friday thru Sunday in October)

WOOLLYBEAR FESTIVAL

NC – Vermilion. (440) 967-4477. An annual tribute to the weather "forecasting" woollybear caterpillar with a huge parade, caterpillar races, woollybear contests for kids, crafts and entertainment. FREE. (first Sunday in October)

ASHTABULA COUNTY COVERED BRIDGE FESTIVAL

NE – Jefferson, Ashtabula County Fairgrounds. (440) 576-3769 or **www.coveredbridgefestival.org**. Ashtabula is known as the working covered bridge capital of the Western Reserve. Enjoy a tour of 15 covered bridges during the beautiful fall season, plus entertainment, crafts, and draft horse contests. Admission. (second weekend in October)

JOHNNY APPLESEED FESTIVAL

NW – **Defiance,** AuGlaize Village, off US-24, west of town. (419) 784-0107. The historic village is busy with crafts, apple butter, cider and molasses making, and harvest demonstrations. Admission. (October)

HOCKING FALL COLOR TOUR

SC – **Rockbridge**, Hocking State Forest. (740) 385-4402. Enjoy a guided tour at Cedar Falls and a hayride through the fall colors, along with a bean dinner. FREE. (October)

PAUL BUNYAN SHOW

SE – **Nelsonville**, Hocking College Campus. (740) 753-3591. Ohio's largest forestry exposition features lumberjack competitions, forestry displays, guitar pickers championship and chainsaw sculpting. Admission. (first weekend in October)

FARM FESTIVAL

SE – **Rio Grande**, Bob Evans Farm, State Route 588. (800) 994-3276 or **www.bobevans.com**. Down on the farm feeling with over 100 craftspeople, country music, square dancers, homestyle foods and contests such as apple peeling, cornshelling, cow chip throwing and hog calling. Admission. (mid-October)

PUMPKIN PATCH EXPRESS

SW – **Lebanon**, Turtle Creek & Lebanon Railroad. (513) 398-8584. (October weekends)

MIDDFEST INTERNATIONAL

SW – **Middletown**, Donham Plaza. (513) 425-7707. Exhibits, music, authentic ethnic dances & menus from many countries. Youth Park. International sports and games, ethnic craft demos, food prep and customs. (October weekend)

OHIO SAUERKRAUT FESTIVAL

SW – **Waynesville**. (937) 897-8855. All kinds of sauerkraut foods like cabbage rolls, sauerkraut candy, pizza, and desserts, fair food, crafts and live entertainment. Fee for parking. (second weekend in October)

NOVEMBER

COLUMBUS INTERNATIONAL FESTIVAL

C – Columbus, Veterans Memorial, 300 West Broad Street. (614) 228-4010. More than 60 nationalities and cultures will participate in a mix of dance, music, foods and crafts. Educational interactive activities for kids. Admission. (first weekend in November)

OHIO VILLAGE JUNIOR ACADEMY EARLY THANKSGIVING

C – **Columbus**, Ohio Village (I-71 exit 17th St). (800) 646-5184 or (614) 297-2666. Talk turkey...then, participate in the creation of an original "Turkey Play" starring this majestic bird, as well as in games and a special craft project. Admission. (Saturday before Thanksgiving)

CLEVELAND CHRISTMAS CONNECTION

NE – Cleveland (Brookpark), I X Center, near Hopkins Airport. (216) 676-6000. Gifts, arts and crafts, regional entertainment, Santa, train rides, ferris wheel rides, nice free gift craft area for kids, variety of ethnic food. Admission. (long weekend after Thanksgiving weekend)

THANKSGIVING WEEKEND PARADES

Downtown Cleveland, Columbus, Cincinnati, Dayton, Gahanna (www.gahanna.gov), Hamilton, Piqua (937-773-9355), Waverly (740) 947-9650 and downtown Toledo (**www.citifest.org**).

DECEMBER

CHRISTMAS DECORATIONS/OPEN HOUSES

Buildings decorated for holidays, Santa visit, entertainment. Great way to expose younger ones to historical homes that might be boring otherwise. Admission. (mostly first weekend of December)

- ❑ C - *Ohio Village*. **www.ohiohistory.org/places/ohvillage/**. **Columbus**. Celebrate a traditional 19th century holiday. Admission. (Wednesday-Sunday beginning first weekend in December)
- ❑ C - *Orange Johnson House*, **Columbus (Worthington)**. (weekends in December)

- ❑ CE – *McCook House*, **Carrollton**. (800) 600-7172. (Thanksgiving weekend)
- ❑ CE – *J.E Reeves Victorian Home*, **Dover**. (800) 815-2794 or **www.doverhistory.org**. (begins Thanksgiving weekend for one month)
- ❑ CE – *Longaberger Homestead*, (**Frazeysburg**). (740) 322-5588 or **www.longaberger.com**. (first three weekends in December)
- ❑ CE – *The Mansion*, **Millersburg**. **www.victorianhouse.org**.
- ❑ CE – ***Zoar***
- ❑ CW – *Logan County Historical*, **Logan**. (937) 593-7557.
- ❑ CW – *Luellen House*, **New Bremen**. (419) 394-1294.
- ❑ CW – *Mac-O-Cheek Castle*, **West Liberty**.
- ❑ NC – *Lyme Village*, **Bellevue**. (419) 483-4949. (1st or 2nd weekend)
- ❑ NC – *Hayes Presidential Center*, **Fremont**. (800) 998-7737 or Special hands-on mini-train display and carriage rides. **www.rbhayes.org**.
- ❑ NC – *Our House*, **Gallipolis**.
- ❑ NC – *Malabar Farm*, **Lucas**.
- ❑ NC – *Kingwood Center & Greenhouses*, **Mansfield**.
- ❑ NC – *Oak Hill Cottage*, **Mansfield**. (800) 642-8282.
- ❑ NC – *Jewett House*, **Oberlin**. (440) 774-1700. Gingerbread house contest display.
- ❑ NE – *Stan Hywet Hall & Gardens*, **Akron**. **www.stanhywet.org**.
- ❑ NE – *Mapleside Farms Santa Fest* **Brunswick**. **www.mapleside.com**. (breakfast, crafts, face painting & sleigh/wagon rides)
- ❑ NE – *Lawnfield*, **Mentor**. (440) 255-8722. (during Winter Break at 2:00pm)
- ❑ NE – *Lanterman's Mill*, Mill Creek Park, **Youngstown**.
- ❑ NW – *Sauder Village*, **Archbold**. (419) 446-2541 or **www.saudervillage.org**.
- ❑ NW – *Wolcott Museum Complex*, **Maumee**. (419) 893-9602.
- ❑ SE – *The Castle*, **Marietta**. (740) 374-4461.
- ❑ SW – *Krohn Conservatory*, **Cincinnati**. (513) 421-4086.
- ❑ SW – *Glendower State Memorial*, **Lebanon**. (513) 932-1100.
- ❑ SW – *Alverta Green Museum*, **Mason**. (513) 398-6750.
- ❑ SW – *Heritage Village Holly Days*, Sharon Woods Park, **Sharonville**. **www.heritagevillagecincinnati.org**.

DECEMBER *(cont.)*

FESTIVALS OF LIGHTS

All include hundreds of thousands of lights and holiday / storybook characters. Daily, evenings (unless noted). Admission. (Thanksgiving - January 1)

- ❑ **C** – *Wildlight Wonderland*. **Columbus** Zoo. (614) 645-3550. Ice skating, carolers, delicious treats and wagon/train rides. Begins Thanksgiving weekend.
- ❑ **C** - *Alum Creek Holiday Fantasy of Lights*. **Delaware**. (740) 548-4068. Entrance is on Hollenback Road, near Alum Creek Lake.
- ❑ **C** – *Christmas by Candlelight.* **Marion** County Fairgrounds. (740) 382-2558. Drive thru.
- ❑ **CE** – *Holiday Lights*. **Carrollton**, County Fairgrounds, SR 9. (877) 727-0103. (Thursday-Sunday)
- ❑ **CE** – *Christian Indian Christmas*. **Gnadenhutten** Historical Park. (740) 254-4143. Drive through display depicting Christian Indians celebrating Christmas.
- ❑ **CW** – *Clifton Mill Legendary Light Display*. **Clifton**. (937) 767-5501. Miniature village, Santa' s workshop and 1802 log cabin. 3.2 million lights. Promptly lit at 6:00pm.
- ❑ **CW** – *The Lights at Ludlow Falls*. **Ludlow Falls**. SR 48. (937) 698-3318. (during Winter Break)
- ❑ **CW** - *A Country Christmas* - **Zanesfield**. Marmon Valley Farm. (937) 593-8000. Costumed characters, carolers, live animals in a presentation of the nativity story. Hayride wagons take guests to different scenes around the barns and fields. Hot chocolate, goodies, singing, Christmas crafts. By reservation. (First two weekends in December).
- ❑ **NC** - *Firelands Festival of Lights*. The Lodge at Sawmill Creek. **Huron/Sandusky**. (419) 433-3800 or **www.sawmillcreek.com**. By car or carriage.
- ❑ **NC** – *Christmas Wunderland*. **Mansfield**. (419) 747-3717 or **www.richlandcountyfair.com**.
- ❑ **NE** – *Holiday of Lights*. **Canfield** Fairgrounds. (330) 392-6527.

- ❑ **NE** – *Zoolights*, **Cleveland** Metroparks Zoo. Walk into the Welcome Plaza (weekend Ice Carving or model railroad display), fun activities / entertainment, seasonal greenhouse, Pachyderm Bldg. w/ Santa, and ride the complimentary Sleighbell Express past the monkeys and polar bear with a stop at the Wolf Cabin (can you spot the wolf in the woods?). Top the visit off with a warm hot chocolate and snack. Admission (ages 2+), FREE for zoo members. **www.clemetzoo.com**. (December, last three weeks).
- ❑ **NE** - *Country Lights* Lake Farmpark, **Kirtland**. **www.lakemetroparks.com**. Horse-drawn sleighbell rides through the light show; live entertainment; baby calves, chicks and pigs; miniature railroad displays; delightful holiday horse shows; and, best of all, the life-like Toy Workshop where elves help kids make an old-fashioned wooden toy to take home. Your kids hammer, drill and paint their own creations. Holiday food served at the Visitor's Center, too. By reservation only! $1.00 extra admission over normal prices.
- ❑ **NE** – *Festival of Lights*. Yellow Duck Park. **Youngstown**. (330) 533-3773. Ohio's largest display.
- ❑ **NW** – *Bluffton Blaze of Lights*. **Bluffton**. (419) 358-5675 or **www.blufftonohio.org**. Wagon rides.
- ❑ **NW** – *Lights Before Christmas*. **Toledo** Zoo. (419) 385-5721 or **www.toledozoo.org**. (begins second weekend of November)
- ❑ **SW** – *Cincinnati Zoo*. (513) 281-4700 or Ice skating, decorated villages, and Santa. **www.cincinnatizoo.org**.
- ❑ **SW** - *Holiday Lights on the Hill*. Pyramid Hill Sculpture Park. **Hamilton**. (513) 868-8336.
- ❑ **SW** – *Holiday in Lights*. Sharon Woods, **Sharonville**. (513) 381-2397.

TRAIN RIDES WITH SANTA

Train trip in decorated coaches with Santa. Songs and treats along the way. Dress warmly. Weekends only.

- ❑ **C** – *Buckeye Central Scenic Railroad*. **Hebron**. (740) 366-2029.
- ❑ **CE** – *Elderberry Line Railroad*. **Carrollton**. **www.elderberryline.com**.
- ❑ **CE** – *Ohio Central Railroad*. **www.amishsteamtrain.com** (866) 850-4676. Dennison (Polar Express) or Sugarcreek (Bethlehem).

Train Rides With Santa (cont.)

- ❑ **CE** – Orrville Railroad. (330) 683-2426 or Christmas in the Depot. **www.orrvillerailroad.com**. (last Nov. weekend only)
- ❑ **NE** – Lolly the Trolley. **Cleveland. http://www.lollytrolley.com/**
- ❑ **NE** – AC & J Railroad. **Jefferson**. (440) 576-6346 or **www.acjrailroad.com.**
- ❑ **NE** –Cuyahoga Valley Scenic Railroad. **Peninsula**. (800) 468-4070 or **www.cvsr.com**. Christmas Tree Adventure (pick own tree) or Polar Express (ride in pajamas). (Some weekdays, too)
- ❑ **SE** - Hocking Valley Scenic Railroad. **Nelsonville**. (800) HOCKING
- ❑ **SW** – Turtle Creek Valley Railway. **Lebanon**. (513) 933-8012.

LIVING CHRISTMAS TREE CONCERTS

C – Columbus (Worthington/Westerville), Grace Brethren Church, 8225 Worthington-Galena Road. (614) 431-8223. 150-voice choir fills the branches of two large trees as they sing along with a themed story and live animals. Admission. (December weekends)

CHRISTMAS CANDLELIGHTINGS

CE – Coshocton, Historic Roscoe Village, State Route 16/83. (800) 877-1830 or **www.roscoevillage.com**. Shop all day for holiday gifts in a 19th century holiday setting and then stay for the candlelighting ceremony each night at 6:00 pm. Strolling carolers, visits with Santa, live arctic reindeer, chestnuts roasting over open fire, free hot-mulled cider & cookies, and carriage rides. Also see display of decorated trees and gingerbread houses on Main Street, downtown. Fee for parking. (first three Saturdays in December)

BETHLEHEM EXPERIENCE

CW – Eaton, Preble County Fairgrounds, SR 122 south (Franklin St.). (937) 456-5507 or **www.bethlehemexperience.org**. Follow the Star to the Bethlehem Experience. You will enter the crowded streets of the small town of Bethlehem as it might have been the night Jesus Christ was born. Wander the streets of Bethlehem at your own pace; visit the shops and talk with the local craftsmen. They will direct you to the live nativity. FREE. Heated building. (first long weekend in December)

BLACK NATIVITY

NE – Cleveland, Karamu House. (216) 795-7070. (December)

UNIVERSITY CIRCLEFEST

NE – Cleveland, University Circle area. (216) 791-3900. FREE admission to University Circle museums plus holiday carolers and Santa. FREE. (first Sunday in December)

CHILDREN'S WONDERLAND

NW – Maumee, 2901 Key Street. (419) 213-2200. Children's Wonderland has received national recognition as the only display of its kind in the nation. The entire 22,000 square feet is turned into a fantasyland filled with animated displays, colorful lighting, and holiday music. Children can ride the North Pole train, visit with Talking Tree, and see over 40 holiday displays. Small Admission. (entire month of December)

HOLIDAY JUNCTION

SW – Cincinnati, Museum Center at Union Terminal, 1301 Western Avenue. **www.cincy.museum.org.** (513) 287-7000 or Annual celebration of model trains. Enjoy the four-level, multi-train layout highlighted by theatrical backgrounds. See vintage trains traveling through one-of-a-kind towns, through hills and mountains, and across bridges. Children will enjoy special activities designed just for them, including a journey by train through a winter wonderland and crafts in the Kids Corner. Museum Admission. (Thanksgiving weekend - New Years Day)

CHRISTMAS DISPLAY

SW – Hamilton, Gregory Creek Inn, 4972 LeSourdsville West Chester Rd. (513) 887-0725. Christmas Display entitled "A Walk Thru the Bible". It is a walking tour around an eleven acre field with thousands of lights illuminating the path as you travel through the Bible. Christmas music is heard through fifty speakers around the field. FREE. (begins Thanksgiving weekend through December 30th)

DECEMBER *(cont.)*

CHRISTMAS FESTIVAL

SW – Lebanon. (513) 932-1100. Holiday characters, musicians strolling the streets, a candlelit parade of sixty horse-drawn carriages, a train display and warm food. Free. (first Sunday of December)

HOLIDAY FEST

SW – Mason, The Beach Waterpark. (513) 398-7946 (800) 886-7946 or **www.thebeachwaterpark.com**. A festive holiday paradise featuring the largest outdoor ice skating rink under the stars, old fashion carriage rides, the area's largest outdoor miniature train display, and twinkling holiday lights. The little ones will have lots to see and do with the North Pole Petting Corral, Santa Stable pony rides, and the Candy Cane Maze. This holiday display is complete with a live Nativity and the chance to visit with Santa. Admission. (Thanksgiving weekend thru New Years Eve)

CHRISTMAS IN THE VILLAGE

SW – Waynesville. **www.waynesvilleohio.com** or (513) 897-8855. Carriage rides, Victorian street strollers, 1300 luminaries, carolers and a live nativity depict a traditional Dickens holiday. FREE. (Two long weekends in early December)

NEW YEARS EVE CELEBRATIONS

A family oriented non-alcoholic event with indoor and outdoor activities such as kid's/parent's food, entertainment and crafts, and a countdown to midnight. Admission.

- ❑ **C** – *First Night Columbus*, Ohio Statehouse Square, downtown **Columbus**. (614) 481-0020. **www.firstnightcols.com**.
- ❑ **NE** - *First Night*, Downtown **Akron**. (330) 762-8555
- ❑ **NE** – *First Night Youngstown*. (330) 742-0445
- ❑ **NW** – *First Night Lima*, Downtown. (419) 222-1096
- ❑ **NW** – *First Night*, Downtown **Toledo**. (419) 241-3777

Master
Index

Activity Index

AMUSEMENTS

ANIMALS & FARMS

MUSEUMS

Museums (cont.)

OHIO HISTORY

Ohio History (cont.)

Outdoors (cont.)

SPORTS

THE ARTS

The Arts (cont.)

TOURS

Tours (cont.)

Unique Recommended Resorts

Travel Journal & Notes:

Travel Journal & Notes:

Travel Journal & Notes:

Travel Journal & Notes:

GROUP DISCOUNTS & FUNDRAISING OPPORTUNITIES!

We're excited to introduce our books to your group! These guides for parents, grandparents, teachers and visitors are great tools to help you discover hundreds of fun places to visit. Our titles are great resources for all the wonderful places to travel either locally or across the region.

We are two parents who have researched, written and published these books. We have spent thousands of hours collecting information and *personally traveled over 20,000 miles* visiting all of the most unique places listed in our guides. The books are kid-tested and the descriptions include great hints on what kids like best!

Please consider the following Group Purchase options: *For the latest information, visit our website:* **www.kidslovepublications.com**

- ❑ **Group Discount/Fundraising** – Purchase books at the discount price of $2.95 off the suggested retail price for members/friends. Minimum order is ten books. You may mix titles to reach the minimum order. Greater discounts (~35%) are available for fundraisers. Minimum order is thirty books. Call for details.

- ❑ **Available for Interview/Speaking** – The authors have a treasure bag full of souvenirs from favorite places. We'd love to share ideas on planning fun trips to take children while exploring your home state. The authors are available, by appointment, *(based on availability)* at (614) 792-6451. A modest honorarium or minimum group sale purchase will apply. Call or visit our website for details.

Call us soon at (614) 792-6451 to make arrangements!

Happy Exploring!

YOUR FAMILY MEMORIES!

Now that you've created memories with your family,

it's time to keepsake them by scrapbooking

in this unique, family-friendly way!

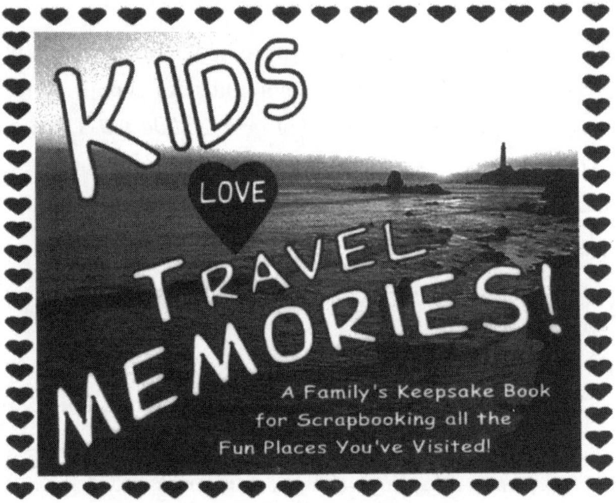
KIDS
LOVE
TRAVEL
MEMORIES!
A Family's Keepsake Book
for Scrapbooking all the
Fun Places You've Visited!

Check Out These Unique Features:

* **The Book That Shrinks As It Grows!** - Specially designed pages can be removed as you add pictures to your book. This keeps your unique travel journal from becoming too thick to use.
* **Write Your Own Book** - The travel journal is designed to get you started and help you remember those great family fun times!
* **Design Your Own Book** - Most illustrations and picture frames are designed to encourage kids to color them.
* **Unique Chapter Names** - help you <u>simply</u> categorize your family travel memories.
* **Acid Free Paper** - was used to print your book to keep your photos safe for a lifetime!

Writing Your Own Family Travel Book is This Easy...

Step 1 - Select, Cut and Paste
Your Favorite Travel Photos

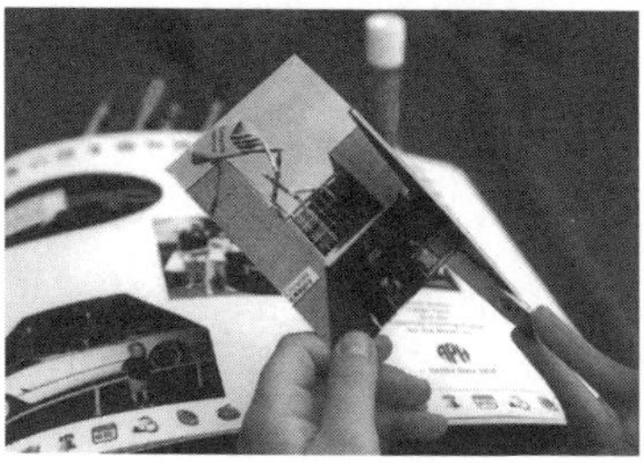

Step 2 - Color the Fun
Theme Picture Frames

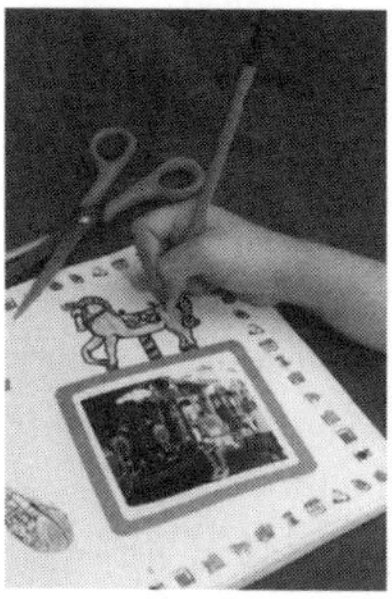

Step 3 - Write about Your
Travel Stories in the Journal
(We get you started...)

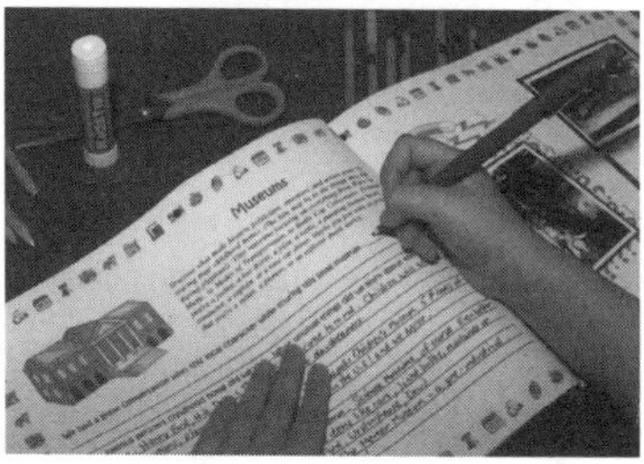

Step 4 - Specially Designed
Pages are removed to reduce
thickness as you add photos

Create Your Family Travel Book Today!

Visit your local retailer,

use the order form in the back of this book,

or our website: www.kidslovepublications.com

Attention Parents:

All titles are "Kid Tested". *The authors and kids personally visited all of the most unique places* and wrote the books with warmth and excitement from a parent's perspective. Find tried and true places that children will enjoy. No more boring trips! Listings provide: Names, addresses, telephone numbers, websites, directions, and descriptions. All books include a bonus chapter listing state-wide kid-friendly Seasonal & Special Events!

- ❑ **KIDS LOVE INDIANA** - Discover places where you can "co-star" in a cartoon or climb a giant sand dune. Over 500 listings in one book about Indiana travel. 8 geographical zones, 213 pages.

- ❑ **KIDS LOVE KENTUCKY** - Discover places from Boone to Burgoo, from Caves to Corvettes, and from Lincoln to the Lands of Horses. Over 500 listings in one book about Kentucky travel. 6 geographic zones. 224 pages.

- ❑ **KIDS LOVE MICHIGAN** - Discover places where you can "race" over giant sand dunes, climb aboard a lighthouse "ship", eat at the world's largest breakfast table, or watch yummy foods being made. Almost 600 listings in one book about Michigan travel. 8 geographical zones, 229 pages.

- ❑ **KIDS LOVE OHIO** - Discover places like hidden castles and whistle factories. Over 800 listings in one book about Ohio travel. 9 geographical zones, 260 pages.

- ❑ **KIDS LOVE PENNSYLVANIA** - Explore places where you can "discover" oil and coal, meet Ben Franklin, or watch your favorite toys and delicious, fresh snacks being made. Over 900 listings in one book about Pennsylvania travel. 9 geographical zones, 268 pages.

- ❑ **KIDS LOVE THE VIRGINIAS** – Discover where ponies swim and dolphins dance, dig into archaeology and living history, or be dazzled by record-breaking and natural bridges. Over 900 listings in one book about Virginia & West Virginia travel. 8 geographical zones, 262 pages.

- ❑ **KIDS LOVE TRAVEL MEMORIES!** – The Perfect Travel Journal & Scrapbook Companion. – See display page (or our website) to learn more about the features of this unique book.